AF811136

Treating Depression in Primary Care

A Manual for Primary Care and Mental Health Providers

Treating Depression in Primary Care

A Manual for Primary Care and Mental Health Providers

by

Patricia Robinson, Ph.D.

Charles Wischman, M.D.

Alison Del Vento, R.N.C.

CONTEXT PRESS
Reno, Nevada

Treating Depression In Primary Care: A Manual For Primary Care And Mental Health Providers
Paperback. 281 pp.
Distributed by New Harbinger Publications, Inc.

Treating depression in primary care : a manual for primary care and mental health providers / by Patricia Robinson, Charles Wischman, Alison Del Vento.
p. cm.
ISBN-13: 978-1-878978-26-4 (pbk.)
ISBN-10: 1-878978-26-8 (pbk.)

©1996 CONTEXT PRESS
933 Gear Street, Reno, NV 89503-2729

All rights reserved.

The publisher allows the purchaser of this book to reproduce materials from this book for use in diagnosing and treating patients for whom he or she is directly responsible. Mass reproductions are prohibited without written permission from the publisher.

for

practitioners whose joy is
bringing *life* back to the living

Table of Contents

About the Authors

Patricia Robinson, Ph.D., is a psychologist who specializes in primary care clinical services and research. She started her practice 16 years ago. During the past eleven years, she has explored potential roles for psychologists in health maintenance organizations. Dr. Robinson's research on depression started over a decade ago. Recent research investigations include evaluation of treatment innovation packages for depressed primary care patients. She and her colleagues conducted several large randomized clinical trials concerning these models in the early 1990's.

Charles Wischman, M.D., is a general internist who has practiced primary care medicine for over 30 years. Dr. Wischman has developed expertise in treatment of depressed primary care patients. He has been a mentor for numerous primary care providers. During the past 15 years, he has become a leader in administration of medical programs. Dr. Wischman serves on many committees that debate and plan for change in the new health care era. He has worked with Alison Del Vento and Patricia Robinson in an urban primary care clinic for many years. His practice has been identified as a "best practice" model in primary care.

Alison Del Vento, R.N.C., is a nurse with over 20 years of experience. She has cared for depressed patients in hospital, hospice and primary care settings. She is a geriatric nurse specialist. Ms. Del Vento pursues both clinical and research activities concerning care of older primary care patients. She is respected by her colleagues as a clinician and teacher. She has served as a nurse leader in numerous primary care research projects. Recently, she received research funding to explore delivery of phone-based medical interventions to older primary care patients. Her work has received "best practice" recognition in the primary care setting.

Acknowledgments

There are many people who helped write this book. The first two worthy of our mention are Kirk Strosahl, Ph.D., and David Brubakken, Ph.D. Both Kirk and David saw a "future" for projects that integrated mental health and primary care over a decade ago. They have supported our work on an on-going basis. Further, Kirk was a gentle and supportive critic at key moments during the writing process. Thank you, Kirk. We also want to acknowledge James Coyne, Ph.D., as he was the first to suggest that we write a book. Judie Wischman, Don McDonald, and John Del Vento provided on-going support and encouragement. Terry Bush, Ph.D., was a source of delight and inspiration throughout the years of experimentation. Regan and Joanna Robinson and Frances Strosahl dreamed great dreams for us. Evette Ludman, Ph.D., contributed her creativity to our efforts "in the field." Judith Lull Strosahl and Christi Landrum-Ricchi provided excellent editorial assistance. Merl Bonnie, Ph.D., E. Robert Sinnett, Ph.D., and Carl Marrs, Ph.D., are very worthy of our acknowledgment. Wayne Katon, M.D., Michael Von Korff, Sci.D., Greg Simon, M.D., Elizabeth Lin, M.D., Ed Walker, M.D., Stephanie Hague, M.S., and the National Institute of Mental Health also helped to inspire this book. Finally, Steve Hayes, Ph.D., helped us "get the book out" and two children, Charlie Hayes and Joanna May Robinson, helped with the cover design. Many others have supported our work. We thank you all.

Preface

Depression is the most common mental health problem in the world. Many people who suffer from depression do not seek help. Of those who do reach out, more are likely to go to see their doctor than a mental health therapist. The prevalence of major depression in primary care clinics is between 5% and 8%. If you include minor depression, prevalence rates move to double digits. In select primary care settings, such as women's health clinics, and, with selected populations such as women aged 18 to 45, almost 1 in 4 patients suffer from depression.

Most health care providers are all too familiar with the costs of depression. Depressed patients miss more work, experience more pain and illness, utilize more medical services, and have significant family and marital relationship problems. Repeat episodes of depression are the rule rather than the exception with depression. Almost three-quarters of primary care patients diagnosed with depression report previous episodes of moderate to severe depression. In addition, depressed patients are more likely to present with high-risk lifestyles and unhealthy habits. Furthermore, suicidal behavior is not unusual among depressed patients.

Primary care providers do a good job of recognizing depression and responding to it with the materials and methods presently available for use in the primary care setting. Primary care providers work in 15-minute units. They have prescription pads readily available. They have pamphlets that describe the syndrome of depression. They have a group of mental health providers in the community to whom they can refer. Primary care providers also have skills. They are skillful diagnosticians, patient listeners, and supportive advisors. Even with these strengths, treatment outcomes are less than good. Many patients fail to adhere to prescriptions or follow good advice. Primary care providers want better outcomes and, as a group, they welcome better materials, additional training in efficacious methods, *and* availability of on-site mental health services in primary care.

The purpose of this book is to provide a model for effective treatment of depression designed for the primary care clinic setting. We refer to our model as the *Integrated Care Program (ICP) for the Treatment of Depression*. We have developed the ICP through years of experience in working together and through development and evaluation of a similar model in a recent series of large clinical trials. The ICP defines (1) new methods for assessment and clinical management by primary care providers and (2) brief, on-site assessment and treatment by mental health providers. The ICP addresses treatment needs for all patients, ranging from minor, transitory depression to severe, longer-term depression. All providers work collaboratively and give theoretically consistent information to patients. The ICP subscribes to a biopsychosocial theory of depression that justifies either a pharmacological or psychotherapeutic treatment or both. Assessment approaches are thorough, yet brief and linked to treatment goals.

We are practicing clinicians, and we know how pressured providers are in today's health care world. We introduce chapters with "Instructions for Speed Readers" and conclude with a "Summary and Helpful Hints." Chapter 1 provides an overview. We discuss obstacles to recognition and diagnosis of depression and current treatment approaches in both primary care and mental health settings. We suggest areas to target in efforts to improve care. Chapter 2 provides several methods for screening in primary care. Additionally, we suggest specific assessment targets and measurement approaches. Chapter 3 introduces the ICP assessment protocol. This two-tier approach is time-effective and comprehensive. All readers need to read chapters 1, 2, and 3.

Primary care providers need to read Chapters 4 and 5. Chapter 4 introduces the "Effective Triad" of primary care clinical management. We suggest strategies to help providers apply sound principles of education, collaborative planning, and monitoring to behavioral and pharmacological treatment efforts. Additionally, we suggest techniques to help providers change levels of care, including what to say to patients who are tapering from antidepressant therapy and how to make written relapse prevention plans. Chapter 5 introduces the ICP Clinical Management Protocol. An educational booklet and patient planning format support implementation of the protocol. We include practical tips for managing time and conveying critical concepts to patients.

Mental health providers need to read Chapters 6 and 7. Chapter 6 helps mental health providers plan programmatic behavioral health services for the primary care setting. We present basic concepts and suggest adaptations for the 30-minute hour. We present guidelines for developing a general consultation model and an example to illustrate the model. We also provide information to help mental health providers develop educational presentations concerning behavioral health that are likely to be well-received by primary care colleagues. Chapter 7 presents the ICP behavioral health protocols. The "Brief Protocol" involves one to three contacts with patients, while the "Behavioral Protocol" involves four to seven contacts with the patient. Educational booklets and a self-help book are available to support patients working with Behavioral Health Consultants in these two protocols of treatment. The self-help book *Living Life Well: New Strategies for Hard Times* is brief and practical. Dr. Robinson wrote this book for depressed patients presenting to primary care because they *differ* from patients presenting to mental health settings. In Chapter 7, we also recommend strategies for working with medication issues and writing relapse prevention plans for the primary care team to support. Chapter 8 is a short chapter that provides guidelines for adding group services to ICP clinics.

Chapter 9 expands the context of caring for depressed patients to include the current environment of health care reform. We review important changes in the last twenty-five years and suggest ways to address current challenges. The ICP Managed Care Package provides you with forms to efficiently address the nine accountability issues most commonly required by review staff. Finally, chapter 10 presents detailed information on the studies that most influenced the development of the ICP. Information in this chapter may be useful in training programs conducted for primary care and mental health providers.

It is our hope that you will be able to see the need for more effective models and understand how to use the ICP in your setting after you read this book. Unfortunately, you probably face hurdles beyond your own beliefs and skills in starting a model like the ICP in your clinic. Starting something new is always difficult. To help you just a little more, we include copies of all ICP materials in the Appendices. Materials include assessment and treatment planning forms, educational booklets for patients, protocol implementation forms, and even forms for creating provider report cards.

We are a primary care physician, nurse, and psychologist team. We have worked together for the past seven years. Our differences have enriched our perspectives and strengthened our ability to respond to depressed patients. In this book, we suggest protocols that help health care professionals develop collaborative and complementary working relationships. We try to balance presentation of practical strategies with research evidence supporting these strategies. For those of you who want more practical details, please read *Living Life Well: New Strategies for Hard Times.* For those of you who want more research information, we include an extensive reference list.

Many of our patients are suffering. They seek our help and often do not understand the source of their pain. When we respond with unnecessary tests, procedures, and prescriptions, we fail to help them and drive up the costs of health care needlessly. Sadness and discouragement limit our patients' relationships with loved ones, their efforts to cope effectively with physical disease, their ability to meet job responsibilities, and, indeed, even their will to live. Let's roll up our sleeves and *start working together.*

Patti Robinson   Chuck Wischman   Alison Del Vento

Chapter 1

An Introduction to Depression in Primary Care

This chapter provides an overview of the types of depression experienced by primary care patients, the prevalence of different forms of depression in primary care settings, and the responsiveness of different types of depression to treatment. Additionally, this chapter presents a summary of the current treatments provided for depressed patients by primary care and mental health providers. The chapter concludes with a discussion of new integrated models designed to improve treatment outcomes. In this chapter, you will learn the following.

- the prevalence of different types of depression in the primary care setting
- current treatments practiced by primary care and mental health providers
- potential target areas for improving treatment outcomes
- key characteristics of integrated primary care and behavioral health care models

---

Instructions for Speed Readers: Allow 15 minutes to read and review information in this chapter. Read information in bold print in the first three sections "Overview," "Current Treatments by Primary Care Providers," and "Current Treatments by Mental Health Providers." Read the last section "New Integrated Approaches to Treatment" more carefully and take a moment to reflect on your particular practice environment and the opportunities therein.

Overview

Primary care physicians are generalists who practice medicine with a wide range of patients and provide medical care for many types of health problems. In the United States, primary care physicians include family practice physicians, pediatricians, general internists, obstetricians-gynecologists, and general practitioners. The generalist nature of the primary care setting requires providers to play multiple roles in the health care system. These roles include the following.

- direct providers of treatment for the majority of public health problems
- case managers regarding chronic medical health conditions
- gatekeepers who determine patient referral for specialty services

Primary care physicians and other primary care providers, including physician assistants, nurses, and pharmacists, provide a great deal of mental and behavioral health services in this country (Shapiro, 1984). Howard and colleagues (1992) estimated that **primary care physicians spend 12.1 hours per week (23.1% of a 52.8-hour work week) providing direct treatment for psychiatric conditions.** According to Magil and Garret (1988), 60% of all health care visits involving mental health issues occur in the general practitioner's office. Knesper and Pagnucco (1987) estimated that **primary care physicians provide 53% of the mental health services in America.** Many patients see the primary care setting as the preferred setting for treatment of mental as well as physical problems. This comfort may derive from the fact that primary care providers often have a relationship with a patient that precedes the development of mental problems. Indeed, primary care providers often play the role of family caregiver and have considerable status derived from years of "being there" during critical life events. Further, many patients may feel less stigmatized in seeking care from a physician as opposed to a provider who specializes in mental disorders.

The primary care provider plays a central role in recognition and diagnosis of depression and in determining its severity. Indeed, Regier (1978) describes the primary care system as the "de facto mental health system" in America. At least half of the depressed people in America who receive mental health care do so through their primary care provider (Narrow, Reiger, Rae, et al., 1993). Further, the trend in managed health care toward "gatekeeper" roles will result in even more depressed patients seeking treatment from providers working in the primary care setting (Hoy, Curtis & Rice, 1991).

Obstacles to Recognition and Diagnosis

Unfortunately, **recognizing depression in the primary care patient may be more challenging than recognizing depression in a patient presenting to a mental health setting.** Patients suffering from depression in the primary care setting may be less willing to admit to feeling sad, blue or depressed. Older patients may be more concerned about the stigma of "being crazy." Further, the context of care may encourage depressed patients to focus on more vague, general physical symptoms, such as muscular pain, fatigue, insomnia, or headaches.

Other obstacles to recognition and diagnosis of depression reside within the provider. **Wise (1995) suggests three reasons why primary care physicians tend to under-diagnose depression. These include (1) less comfort in discussing psychological problems, (2) lack of knowledge of formal diagnostic criteria, and (3) time constraints.** Some primary care providers may still feel that mental illness is not a serious problem or that problems such as depression are "disorders of will." Also, providers may simply be less comfortable discussing mental illness with patients. Primary care providers are trained to ask about physical symptoms of depression because physical symptoms are extremely important to the diagnosis and treatment of primary care patients. Patients may present with physical symptoms of depression that are actually due to a general medical condition (e.g., hypothyroidism). However, **when a patient has only a few physical symptoms of depression and a general medical problem is ruled out, the primary care provider needs to assess for the presence of psychological symptoms of depression.**

Manuals for classification systems used in the mental health setting may not be "user friendly" for primary care providers. The Diagnostic and Statistical Manual of Mental Disorders, 4th Edition (DSM-IV, 1994) is a rather large and complex volume. It is not adapted to the needs of busy primary care practitioners and is hard to use as a reference in daily practice. The average primary care encounter is completed in less than 15 minutes. Asking open-ended questions about life problems is time-consuming. Strategies for improving recognition in primary care are useful to the extent that they can work within the time constraints of primary care.

Types of Depression

Accurate diagnosis promotes accurate treatment. Table 1.1 provides basic diagnostic information about the most common types of depression in the primary care setting. The DSM-IV is the primary source for information presented in Table 1.1. Adjustment disorders are common, particularly among individuals living in disadvantaged life circumstances. Stressors triggering development of adjustment disorders may be single events (e.g., divorce, job loss) or on-going problems (e.g., living in a crime-ridden community or suffering from a chronic, disabling general medical condition). Major Depressive Disorder is characterized by one or more Major Depressive Episodes. An episode of major depression requires the presence of depressed mood *or* loss of interest or pleasure in most or all activities for a 2-week period, and four or more of the following symptoms.

- Change in appetite or weight
- Insomnia or hypersomnia
- Psychomotor agitation or retardation
- Decreased energy
- Feelings of worthlessness or guilt
- Difficulty thinking, concentrating or making decisions
- Recurrent thoughts of death or suicidal ideation, plans, or attempts

Symptoms of depression need to represent a change in functioning for the person and be newly present or clearly worse in comparison with the patient's pre-episode status. Additionally, symptoms must persist for most of the day every day for at least 2 consecutive weeks and be accompanied by clinically significant distress or impairment in social, occupational, or other important areas of functioning. In milder episodes, the patient's functioning may appear to be normal, but is requiring much more effort on the patient's part. In more severe episodes, the patient is unable to perform basic role functions, such as caring for a child or completing work responsibilities.

Table 1.1
Diagnostic Features of Selected Mood Disorders

Depressive Disorder	Diagnostic Features
Adjustment Disorder • with Depressed Mood • with Mixed Anxiety and Depressed Mood	A response to an identifiable psychosocial stressor Developed within 3 months of the stressor Characterized by marked distress or significant impairment in social or role functioning Resolves within 6 months of termination of the stressor
Major Depressive Disorder	Characterized by one or more Major Depressive Episodes
Dysthymic Disorder	Characterized by at least 2 years of depressed mood for more days than not Accompanied by additional depressive symptoms Does not meet criteria for a Major Depressive Episode
Mood Disorder Due to a General Medical Condition	Characterized by prominent, persistent disturbance in mood that is a direct physiological consequence of a general medical condition
Substance-Induced Mood Disorder	Characterized by a prominent, persistent disturbance in mood that is a direct physiological consequence of alcohol abuse, a prescribed medication, or exposure to toxins.

Table 1.2

General Medical Conditions Associated with Development of Mood Disorders

Disease Category	Diseases Conditions
Degenerative Neurological Conditions	Parkinson's disease, Huntington's disease
Cerebrovascular disease	Stroke
Metabolic conditions	Vitamin B_{12} deficiency
Endocrine conditions	Hyper- and Hypothyroidism, Hyper- and Hypoparathyroidism, Hyper- and Hypoadrenocorticism
Autoimmune Conditions	Systemic lupus erythematosus
Viral or other infections	Hepatitis, Mononucleosis, Human immunodeficiency virus
Certain cancers	Carcinoma of the pancreas

Dysthymic disorder is characterized by a "down in the dumps" mood more days than not for at least 2 years and at least two of the following additional symptoms: poor appetite or overeating, insomnia or hypersomnia, low energy, low self-esteem, poor concentration, or difficulty in decision-making, and feelings of hopelessness. In that these symptoms are incorporated into the person's way of life, the person may not volunteer the information. A diagnosis of dysthymia requires that the person not have had an episode of major depression during the initial 2-year period of dysthymic symptoms. If the patient had an episode of major depression during a 2-year period of dysthymic symptoms, the diagnosis is Major Depressive Disorder, Chronic. After the initial dysthymic period, episodes of Major Depression maybe superimposed on dysthymia. When this occurs, the person is said to suffer from "double depression."

The diagnosis of Mood Disorder Due to a General Medical Condition is important in the primary care setting. Various medical conditions may cause mood symptoms. Table 1.2 summarizes disease categories and specific diseases that may cause depressive symptoms in medical patients.

You may differentiate Substance-Induced Mood Disorder from primary mood disorder by evaluating the onset, course, and other factors. For drugs of abuse, a history of intoxication or withdrawal needs to be established. Mood symptoms may develop up to 4 weeks after the cessation of substance use. Various medications (e.g., stimulants, steroids, L-dopa, antidepressants) may induce mood disturbance, particularly manic-like mood disturbances. Other somatic treatments for depression (e.g., electroconvulsive therapy or light therapy) can also stimulate manic-like disturbances.

Patients may present with other types of mood disorders in the primary care setting. Other disorders include the bipolar disorders and cyclothymic disorders. Bipolar disorders involve manic, hypomanic and mixed episodes of mood disturbance. Cyclothymic disorder is characterized by at least 2 years of episodes of hypomanic symptoms that are less severe than in manic episodes and episodes of depression that do not meet criteria for a Major Depressive Episode.

Table 1.3
The Distribution of Mood Disorders in Primary Care Patients

Mood Disorder	Total Sample No. (%)
Any mood disorder	260 (26%)
Major depressive disorder	115 (12%)
Dysthymia	78 (8%)
Partial remission or recurrence of major depressive disorder	63 (6%)
Minor depressive disorder	64 (6%)

Prevalence

Epidemiological studies suggest a trend toward increasing rates of depression in America during the past 15 years. The Epidemiologic Catchment Area (ECA) Study conducted in the 1980's with 20,000 adults aged 18 and older suggested a lifetime prevalence for Major Depressive Disorder of 7.8% (10.5% for women and 5.2% for men). In 1990-1991, the **National Co-Morbidity Study** (NCS) group conducted structured interviews with a representative national sample of adults aged 18-55. **Results suggested the lifetime prevalence of Major Depressive Episode to be 21.3% for females and 12.7% for males, for an overall rate of 17.1%.** The corresponding rates for 12-month prevalence were 12.9%, 7.7%, and 10.3% respectively (Kessler, McGonagle, Zhao, 1994). Zung (1993) studied over 75,000 primary care patients and found the prevalence of clinically significant depressive symptoms to be 20.9%. In an internal medicine clinic that served as a primary facility for indigent patients, Rucker found that 32% of the patients were moderately to severely depressed. Azocar (1994) studied patients in waiting rooms of women's public health clinics and found that 37% had a mood disorder (21% major depression, 14.5% minor depression, 14.5% dysthymia).

Using the Prime M-D ("Primary Care Evaluation of Mental Disorders"), primary care providers diagnosed mood disorders in primary care patients at the prevalence rates listed in Table 1.3 (Spitzer & Williams, 1995). The Prime M-D is a structured interview designed to help primary care providers diagnose the most common mental disorders in primary care in a *time-effective* manner and according to accepted diagnostic protocols.

Responsiveness to Treatment

Effective treatments exist for all forms of depression. Brief psychotherapeutic interventions are helpful to patients with Adjustment Disorders involving mood disturbance. These may include patient participation in educational classes to help in development of specific skills needed to effectively address the stressor(s) precipitating the mood change. Major Depressive Disorder may be treated by antidepressant medications, several specific psychotherapeutic approaches, or combined treatments. Few studies have evaluated the efficacy of treatments for dysthymia. Both medications and brief therapies are promising. About one-half of dysthymic patients do not respond to antidepressant medication and others develop side effects or are simply too fearful to take medications (Markowitz, 1994). Several clinical trials investigating treatments for dysthymia are underway. These will advance understanding in this area in the near future. Patients suffering from Mood Disorder Due to a General Medical Condition as well as patients with Substance-Induced Mood Disorder will likely respond to treatments with established efficacy for treatment of Major Depressive Disorder. Of course, patients with Substance-Induced Mood Disorder require attention to targets of treatment other than mood disturbance, including the use of problematic non-prescribed or prescribed substances causing the disturbance. Likewise, patients with Mood Disorder Due to a General Medical Condition may benefit from supplementary treatment designed to improve skills for coping with the underlying medical condition.

Costs of Depression

Costs of depression include impaired worker productivity, family distress, and greater physical health concerns. Depression is associated with significant losses in multiple domains of role functioning and emotional well-being. Stewart and colleagues (1993) reported that the decrements in functioning by depressed primary care patients were as severe as those suffered by patients seen in mental health settings. In addition, she reported several small yet significant differences between primary care and mental health patients. Specifically, patients of mental health specialists had worse mental functioning and more limitations in social activities. **Patients of medical practitioners had worse physical functioning, more pain, more psychophysiologic symptoms, and worse perceptions of health in general.** Well-being, or subjective assessment of health and quality of life, and functional status, or the capacity to perform tasks and activities, are basic concerns for depressed patients, their families, and providers, as well. These are also concerns for health care policy makers, as reduced functioning results in significant costs to society due to loss of productivity and associated use of health care services.

Wells and colleagues (1989) found that patients with either current depressive disorder or subthreshold depressive symptoms had worse physical, social, and role functioning, worse perceived current health, and greater bodily pain than did patients with no chronic conditions. **Among medical patients, there was little difference in the degree of loss of functioning between patients with a diagnosis of depression and those with subsyndromal depression. Most remarkably, the functioning of depressed patients was comparable to or worse than that of patients with major chronic medical conditions, such as unstable angina, advanced arthritis and diabetes.** Also, the effects of depressive symptoms and medical conditions on functioning appeared to be "additive." For example, a patient with advanced coronary artery disease and depression was likely to have twice the loss in social functioning compared to that associated with either condition alone. **Decrements in well being and role functioning are associated with increased medical utilization** (Broadhead, Blazer, George, & Tse, 1990; Johnson, Weissman, & Klerman, 1992). When health care costs and loss in worker productivity are combined, the costs of depression add up significantly. **The National Institute of Mental Health places the economic costs of depression at $27 billion annually.** Sturm and Wells (1995) suggest that the primary care setting is the most economically viable setting for improving depression care.

Current Treatment By Primary Care Providers

Training in primary care in the past decade has included more attention to the psychological and social issues of patients. In a national survey, Orleans and colleagues (1985) concluded that **family physicians used some type of verbal therapy with roughly two-thirds of the patients they believed to have a significant psychiatric disorder.** While this therapy was not "psychotherapy" per se, it may have included use of practical strategies that improve symptoms of depression, such as supportive problem-solving. Over half of the patients seen for depression in primary care clinics receive antidepressant therapy (Olson and Klerman, 1987). Robinson and colleagues (1994) suggest that **physicians commonly use cognitive behavioral strategies in conjunction with antidepressant therapy in treating depression.**

While practice patterns vary considerably, physicians and other primary care providers play a critical role in identifying and treating the major health problems posed by depression. Howard

(1992) suggests that primary care physicians routinely provide the following mental health treatment services.

- active listening
- advice giving
- adding perspective
- confirmation of the appropriateness of patient concerns
- medication management
- referral to mental health specialists

Outcomes for health care systems and for the country in general will improve as primary care providers become more consistent in using the most effective approaches to diagnosis and treatment. The most promising treatments within the primary care setting include supportive counseling, problem-solving therapy, and pharmacotherapy.

Supportive Counseling

Supportive counseling is a common treatment for depression in primary care. Unfortunately, this approach has not been studied systematically. More highly effective forms of counseling in primary care will probably reflect features from psychotherapy models designed for very brief contacts. A group of mental health practitioners in Milwaukee have studied brief counseling interactions for a number of years (deShazer, et al., 1986). This group specializes in family practice. They suggest that counseling efforts focus on solutions. **The provider empathizes with the patient while moving the dialogue towards the construction of clear, simple, specific behavioral change plans.** Their methods have been used successfully by public school employees. School teachers and counselors, like primary care providers, work within the confines of the 15-minute hour. While this promising approach is yet to be tested in the primary care medical setting, patient satisfaction with the approach in the mental health outpatient setting is consistently high.

Problem Solving

Mynors-Wallace and colleagues (1995) reported that **primary care physician delivery of problem-solving therapy was as effective as antidepressant therapy with primary care patients who had major depression.** Patients who received problem-solving treatment tended to be more satisfied with treatment and more likely to complete treatment than patients receiving antidepressant medication. However, an older antidepressant medication, with more side effects than new medications, was used in this study.

The primary care physicians in this study participated in a brief training and used a structured manual to deliver six 30-minute treatments over a 12-week period. The primary care physicians were supervised by psychiatrists. Problem solving therapy may be particularly well suited for the primary care setting because primary care patients are often struggling with specific life circumstance problems and because the approach is simple and straight-forward.

Pharmacotherapy

Primary care physicians write 80% of the antidepressant prescriptions in the United States (Olfson and Klerman, 1987). Unfortunately, patients frequently do not adhere to prescribed medications. Furthermore, primary care providers tend to prescribe antidepressants at dosages that are lower than recommended by guidelines (Olfson and Klerman, 1993; Simon, et al., 1993; Katon, et al., 1992). Further, **primary care physicians may often prescribe medications to patients with milder forms of depression, even though evidence documenting efficacy of pharmacological treatment for minor depression is lacking** (Katon, et al., 1995). Primary care physician prescribing practices and patient adherence do appear to improve significantly when on-site mental health consultants provide training and patient education materials (Katon, et al., 1995). Primary care physicians may be able to enhance adherence to antidepressant therapy by providing simple and specific educational messages about medications. Also, discussions about scheduling pleasant events have been related to improved adherence early in the course of pharmacotherapy (Lin, et al., 1995).

Current Treatments by Mental Health Providers

Treatment of depression in specialty settings has been studied extensively during the past 25 years. The following discussion provides a brief overview of the types of therapies currently practiced by mental health providers and the efficacy data available on these therapies. **More extensive reviews of literature are available in practice guidelines published by the American Psychiatric Association (APA) and by the Depression Guideline Panel of the Agency on Health Care Policy and Research (AHCPR).** Additionally, several reviews of these published guidelines are available to help practitioners evaluate recommended guidelines (Persons, Thase, & Crits-Christoph, 1996; Schulberg, & Rush, 1994; Munoz, et al., 1994).

Cognitive Therapy

Research evaluations of cognitive therapy include over twenty randomized controlled trials. **Numerous controlled studies have found cognitive therapy to be comparable or superior in efficacy to pharmacotherapy** (Rush, et al., 1977; Elkin, et al., 1989; Blackburn, et al., 1981; Hollon, et al., 1992; McKnight, et al., 1992; Murphy, et al., 1984), interpersonal therapy (Elkin, et al., 1989), behavior therapy (Murphy, et al., 1984; Thompson, Gallagher, & Breckenridge, 1987; Gallagher & Thompson, 1982, Shaw, 1977), and behavioral marital therapy (Jacobson, et al., 1991; O'Leary, & Beach, 1990). Also, four studies conducted in the United Kingdom have shown cognitive therapy to be statistically significantly more effective than treatment as usual or protocol pharmacotherapy provided by general practitioners (Scott, & Freeman, 1992; Ross, & Scott, 1985; Teasdale, et al., 1984; Scott, 1990). Two meta-analyses provided documentation of cognitive therapy's efficacy as compared with waiting-list, alternate psychotherapeutic and pharmacotherapy control conditions (Dobson, 1989; Robinson, Berman, & Neimeyer, 1990).

Behavior Therapy

Behavior therapy appears to be an effective treatment for depression (Murphy, et al., 1984; Thompson, Gallagher, & Breckenridge, 1987; Gallagher & Thompson, 1982; Shaw, 1977). A recent study investigated the components of cognitive behavioral therapy (Jacobson, et al., 1996). Components included behavioral activation (BA), behavioral activation and teaching patients skills to modify automatic thoughts (AT). These two components were compared with the complete cognitive therapy protocol (CT), which included BA, AT, and strategies focusing on change of core schema. The component treatments were as effective as the complete treatment at the termination of acute treatment and at the 6-month follow-up. Also, the components were just as effective as the complete treatment in altering negative thinking and dysfunctional attributional styles. Behavioral activation strategies, as well as more education-related approaches to modifying depressive thoughts, are much more parsimonious than cognitive therapy. For that reason, they may represent a less expensive alternative to cognitive therapy. **Behavioral activation and psychoeducational interventions appear to be more "user friendly" for primary care professionals.**

Interpersonal Therapy

Interpersonal therapy was demonstrated to be an effective treatment for depression in the NIMH Treatment of Depression Collaborative Research Program (Elkin, 1989). Schulberg, et al., (1996) evaluated the effectiveness and feasibility of providing interpersonal therapy to depressed patients in a primary care setting. This study compared patients receiving interpersonal psychotherapy or pharmacotherapy with clinical management to usual care patients. **Among treatment completers, approximately 70% of patients participating in the full pharmacotherapy or psychotherapy protocol were judged as recovered at eight months, while only 20% of the usual care patients were recovered.** Unfortunately, *drop-out* rates were somewhat high among patients in enhanced treatment conditions. Interpersonal therapy is probably quite appropriate for primary care patients in that as many as 60% report relationship problems as precipitants to the depression (Robinson, et al., 1994). However, less lengthy or time intensive versions of therapy may be required in order to retain more patients for the full course of treatment.

Group Therapy

Group cognitive therapy and group behavior therapy have repeatedly been shown to result in statistically significant changes in depressive symptomatology (Nezu & Perri, 1989; Fleming & Thornton, 1980; Nezu, 1986). Group cognitive therapy has also been demonstrated to result in statistically significantly better results than usual care as provided by general practitioners (Ross & Scott, 1985; Scott & Stradling, 1990).

Pharmacotherapy

Large clinical trials have established the efficacy of antidepressant medications in treating Major Depressive Disorder. **All antidepressants appear to be equally effective** (Cunningham, et al., 1994). Newer antidepressants have fewer side effects than older antidepressants, and dropout rates are slightly higher among patients taking older antidepressant medications (Song, et al., 1993; Schweizer, et al., 1994). **Current studies concerning pharmacological treatment of depression are exploring use of *cost-effective* strategies to obtain higher rates of patient adherence.** Hunkler, Kirsch, and Meresman (1996) are investigating the use of nurses in a telephone support intervention to promote patient adherence to newer antidepressant medications. Perhaps the higher cost of new medications can be offset, in part, by changes to patterns of care. Antidepressant therapy is also effective with some dysthymic patients (Markowitz, 1994). **The efficacy of antidepressant therapy for milder forms of depression has not been established** (Elkin, 1989).

Combined Treatment

While some empirical evidence supports the belief that combined pharmacological and psychotherapeutic treatment is superior to single modality treatment, the evidence is not strong enough to warrant recommendation of combination treatment for all patients (Conte, et al., 1986; Hollon, Shelton, & Loosen, 1991; Persons, 1993; Manning & Frances, 1990). **Several research studies have found that depressed patients who received behavior therapy in combination with antidepressants improved more rapidly than those who received behavior therapy alone. However, combined treatment was not more effective by the completion of treatment** (Roth, et al., 1982; Wilson, 1982).

New Integrated Approaches

Integrated models for treating depression in the primary care setting are multifaceted and involve changes to the health care system. **Interventions need to be multifaceted in order to yield significant improvements to care.** The key "facets" include a focus on patient education materials, protocols that help providers incorporate daily use of highly effective behavioral and medication treatment approaches, and provision of on-site mental health professionals to assist with patients and provide on-going educational experiences for primary care providers. **Integrated models need to change the basic structure of health care in the primary care setting. The mental health provider needs to become a valued and long-term member of the primary care team.** Effective integrated models need to address the following seven areas to maximize clinical, patient satisfaction and cost outcomes required in today's health care market.

Improvement Targets

1. **Educational Materials**

   Better education of patients will create more informed consumers who are empowered to comply with treatment. A National Mental Health Association survey reported that 6 of 10 adults know "little or nothing" about depression. In fact, a significant proportion of the public may actually be misinformed about depression (*News Update*, 1992). For example, the same survey found that 43% of the public saw depression as a sign of personal weakness.

2. **Physician Relationship**

   The patient-physician relationship is becoming less patriarchal and more collaborative. Integrated treatment models often employ a biopsychosocial model of depression care. This approach invites the patient to be an *active* participant in choosing and planning treatment. **A patient is more likely to comply successfully with a treatment plan that (1) evolves from a strong educational program, (2) allows her/him a free choice of treatments and (3) requires a clear commitment.** The model proposed in this book gives patients a choice between behavioral and psychopharmacological treatments, as both appear to be equally effective.

3. **Patient Compliance**

   Between 20 and 59% of depressed primary care patients stop taking prescribed medication within three weeks of the initial prescription (Johnson, Weissman, & Klerman, 1992). Patient adherence to medication treatment can be improved by helping providers become more skillful in medication selection and dosing and more consistent in follow-up. Also, patients become more adherent when they have more knowledge about medications and specific plans for using behavioral compliance strategies. The Agency for Health Care Policy and Research (AHCPR) developed a guideline for treatment of depression in primary care. This guideline offers useful information on medication selection, dosing, switching, augmenting, and continuation. The AHCPR guideline is available free of charge. It is an excellent resource concerning medication guidelines. **Our book is consistent with AHCPR guidelines and moves the guideline into an "implementation mode."**

   Patient compliance with behavioral interventions is a second target for improvement in the general area of patient compliance. **While primary care providers may often give excellent advice, patient follow through may be limited because of the patient's poor memory and/or difficulties with concentration or attention during visits with the provider.** A protocol may help providers improve patient adherence to behavioral health plans. This book offers a protocol to help primary care providers move from "giving advice" to using brief, effective behavioral techniques and educational materials that structure the patient's responsibilities and lead to better follow-through with behavioral treatment.

4. **Clinical Management Protocols**

Clinical management is somewhat of a "black box." Adding consistent use of behavioral methods to the "black box" of clinical management enhances the impact of other interventions. Furthermore, primary care providers are more likely to feel satisfied with the care they provide when it includes behavioral techniques that work within the limitations of the "15-minute hour." **As primary care providers become more confident in use of behavioral approaches, they may be less likely to prescribe unnecessary antidepressants.** According to Elkin, et al. (1989), **patients on the mild end of the spectrum in the NIMH Collaborative study of depression had an equal response to placebo treatment and active antidepressant therapy. Several studies have suggested that about half of the primary care patients identified as having probable major depression in actuality have minor depression** (Katon, 1995; Robinson, 1996). Indeed, behavioral treatment may be a more appropriate initial treatment than antidepressant therapy for this large subset of patients with milder forms of depression. When antidepressant treatment is necessary, inclusion of behavioral interventions may broaden the impact of antidepressant treatment. Lin and colleagues (1995) suggested that use of selected behavioral treatments by the primary care physician improved patient adherence to antidepressant therapy. Strategies for improving clinical management will be described in Chapter 2.

5. **Prevention and Chronicity Management**

In many ways, depression in primary care is a "chronic" disorder. Almost 75% of patients who are recognized by primary care providers as depressed report multiple previous episodes. **Early identification and treatment may help some depressed patients avoid future episodes. On-going monitoring and use of effective relapse prevention strategies may reduce risk of deterioration in even chronically depressed patients. Further, treatment of patients with mild symptoms may help prevent development of more disabling symptoms** (Muñoz, et al., 1995).

6. **Team Work**

Health care is truly multifaceted, and no single discipline possesses all of the skills and knowledge necessary for providing the highest possible quality of care. Seventy percent of the members of the American Psychological Association report that they work in a health psychology field. McDaniel (1995) describes these providers as ready to collaborate with primary care providers to develop and deliver comprehensive, multidisciplinary health care services.

Collaboration means "working together in a joint effort" toward common goals. Ada Sue Hinshaw, former director of the National Institute of Nursing Research, (1995) suggests that collaborative team members function as coscholars and shift leadership roles as need be and in response to the expertise required at any given point. When experts from different fields work together, the team is "multidisciplinary." Ms. Hinshaw suggests that **the following characteristics are important benchmarks for successful multidisciplinary teams: merging of expertise, division of labor, collegiality, and distribution of power.**

When mental health professionals and primary care providers work in the same practice setting, they have more opportunities to coordinate treatment and learn from each other. Work with depressed patients is rich with rewards when you can share supportively and intellectually with treatment team members. Also, **older patients and male patients may find**

use of mental health services more "acceptable" when they are provided by a team member "down the hall" from the primary care physician. On-site services help patients feel that their care is coordinated, and this improves patient confidence in treatment.

7. **Continuity Between Primary Care and Specialty Care Treatments**

Treatment selection for depressed patients needs to derive from a systematic assessment method that (1) includes important health care outcomes and (2) applies to all potential treatment settings. Patients obtain the best care in a system that provides "seamless" treatment based on a common assessment and treatment model. **Primary care teams that integrate behavioral health services are in the strongest position to effectively manage depressed patients within the larger health care system.** An on-site mental health consultant can become the conduit for coordinating care with mental health providers in external locations.

While mental health and primary care providers may agree as to the benefits of collaborative, team treatment of depression, few models for achieving the ideal form for integrated care are available. Further, there are barriers that may slow spontaneous development of effective models. McDaniel (1995) suggests that differences between primary care and mental health providers in training, theoretical paradigms, professional "languages," and working styles may obstruct successful collaboration efforts. This book presents a model for addressing barriers to integration efficiently and successfully.

Figure 1.1

Integrated Care Program

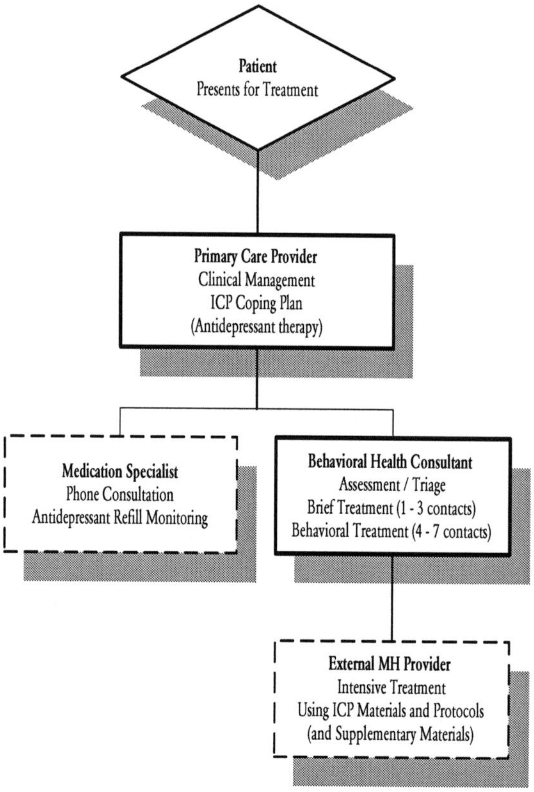

Table 1.4
ICP Treatment Team Members and Responsibilities

Team Member	Responsibility
Primary Care Providers	• Assessment • Patient Education • Clinical Management • Antidepressant Therapy
Behavioral Health Consultants	• Assessment • Behavioral Treatment with More Severely Depressed Patients • Behavioral Medicine Interventions with Medically Ill Patients • Conduct Group and Classroom Treatments • Train Health Care Providers • Coordinate with External Mental Health Providers
Liaison Medication Specialists	• Medication Consultation with Complex Patients

The Integrated Care Program

The Integrated Care Program (ICP) is a comprehensive model for treating depression. It **helps providers bridge the gap between clinical guidelines and implementation strategies.** Figure 1.1 depicts the relationship of patients to providers and describes the responsibilities of ICP team members. Table 1.4 provides additional information on provider responsibilities. Numerous disciplines may participate in the ICP team, including primary care physicians, physician assistants, nurse practitioners, nurses, psychologists, pharmacists, psychiatrists, and master's level therapists. Ideally, most team members will work together in the primary care setting. The ICP recommends specific methods for addressing assessment, clinical management, behavioral health consultation services, antidepressant therapy, intensive treatment by external mental health providers, and managed care issues. In this model, mental health providers enter primary care centers behaving like humble and curious visitors and become auxiliary members of the primary care team. This book attempts to help primary care providers improve recognition, diagnosis and treatment outcomes through changes in their own patterns of care and through collaboration with mental health colleagues. Additionally, the book helps mental health providers measure and pace their steps in moving into the primary care setting.

The ICP is based upon "state of the art" evidence and many years of clinical experience. Together, we have nearly 69 years of experience in treating depressed primary care patients. Our favorite years have been the past 7, when we have worked as a team. In the ICP, primary care provider and mental health provider roles and responsibilities are clearly defined. Providers select specific treatments that are supported by educational materials for patients and treatment delivery protocols for providers. Research indicates that this approach results in improved outcomes for patients with major depression. It also appears to improve outcomes for patients with less severe symptoms of depression, but to a more limited extent. **Further, studies show that both primary care and mental health providers, as well as patients, prefer a model like the ICP to traditional methods of treatment.**

The "spirit" for implementing the ICP is that of a "scientist practitioner" (Barlow & Hayes, 1984). We have intentionally stopped short of setting firm limitations on disciplines and rigid rules for determining treatment approach and level of intensity. Evaluate the resources available to you. Use "cost modeling" to determine your most viable options. Then, set up a plan and collect data on all relevant aspects of your version of the ICP, including multiple patient, provider and system outcomes. Continue to make changes to your program as suggested by your results. And remember to enjoy and learn from your new colleagues.

Summary and Helpful Hints

There are many approaches that you may explore in an effort to improve your recognition and treatment of depression. Integrated models are multifaceted. Evaluate resources in your setting and adapt the ICP model to make it work for you and your team members.

Many primary care providers may not have mental health providers available in their clinics. Many mental health providers may not yet have primary care settings in which to work. It is hoped that this book will help you find each other and start a collaborative, integrated program. As you continue to explore this area of your profession, keep the following points in mind.

1. Depression is highly prevalent in primary care.
2. There are several types of depression, and diagnosis of subtypes may improve your treatment selection.
3. You are most likely to improve your cost outcomes in treating depression by making changes within the primary care setting.
4. Medications and several types of psychotherapy (i.e., cognitive therapy, behavioral therapy, interpersonal therapy, problem-solving therapy) are equally effective.
5. Combination treatment is probably not necessary as a "first-line" approach to treating depression.
6. Seven targets for improving depression outcomes in primary care include: educational materials, patient-physician interactions, improved patient compliance, improved clinical management, prevention or management of chronicity, creation of multidisciplinary treatment teams, and maximizing continuity between primary care and specialty care treatments.
7. Integrated models for treating depression in the primary care setting are multifaceted and involve changes to the primary care system.

References

American Psychiatric Association (1993). Practice guideline for major depressive disorder in adults. *American Journal of Psychiatry*, 150, Supplement.

American Psychiatric Association (1994). *Diagnostic and statistical manual of mental disorders, 4th Ed.* Washington, D.C.: American Psychiatric Association.

Azocar, P. (1994). *Depression Prevalence in Primary Care.* A presentation at the National Institute of Mental Health Conference: Treatment of Medical Disorders in General Medical Settings, McLean, Virginia.

Barlow, D.H., Hayes, S.C., & Nelson, R.O. (1984). *The scientist practitioner: Research and accountability in clinical and educational settings.* Boston: Allyn and Bacon.

Belar, D.D., & Deardorff, W.W. (1995). *Clinical health psychology in medical settings: A practitioner's guidebook.* Washington, D.C.: American Psychological Association.

Blackburn, I.M., Bishop, S., Glen, A.I.M., Walley, L.J., & Christie, J.E. (1981). The efficacy of cognitive therapy in depression: A treatment trial using cognitive therapy and pharmacotherapy, each alone and in combination. *British Journal of Psychiatry*, 139, 181-189.

Broadhead, W.E., Blazer, D.G., George, L.K., & Tse, C.K. (1990). Depression, disability days, and days lost from work in a prospective epidemiologic survey. *Journal of the American Medical Association*, 264, 2624-2528.

Conte, H.R., Pluthchik, R., Wild, K.V., & Kasrasu, T.B. (1986). Combined psychotherapy and pharmacotherapy for depression. *Archives of General Psychiatry*, 43, 471-479.

Cunningham, L.A., Borison, R.L., Carman, J.S., et al. (1994). A comparison of venlafaxine, trazodone, and placebo in major depression. *Journal of Clinical Psychopharmacology*, 14, 99-106.

Depression Guideline Panel. (1993). *Depression in primary care: Vol. 1. Detection and diagnosis.* (Clinical Practice Guideline, No. 5, AHCPR Pub. No. 93-0550). Rockville, MD: U.S. Department of Health and Human Services, Public Health Service, Agency for Health Care Policy and Research.

Depression Guideline Panel. (1993). *Depression in primary care: Vol. 2. Treatment of major depression* (Clinical Practice Guideline, No. 5, AHCPR Pub. No. 93-0551). Rockville, MD: U.S. Department of Health and Human Services, Public Health Service, Agency for Health Care Policy and Research.

Dobson, K.S. (1989). A meta-analysis of the efficacy of cognitive therapy for depression. Journal of *Consulting and Clinical Psychology*, 57, 414-419.

Elkin, E., Shea, M.T., Watkins, J.T., Imber, S.D., Sotsky, S.M., Collins, J.F., Glass, D.R., Pikonis, P.A., Leber, W.R., Docherty, J.P., Fiester, S.J., & Parlaff, M.B. (1989). National Institute of Mental Health Treatment of Depression Collaborative Research Program: General effectiveness of treatments. *Archives of General Psychiatry*, 46, 971-982.

Fleming, B.M., & Thornton, D.W. (1980). Coping skills training as a component in the short-term treatment of depression. *Journal of Consulting and Clinical Psychology,* 48, 652-654.

Gallagher, D.E., & Thompson, L.W. (1982). Treatment of major depressive disorder in older adult outpatients with brief psychotherapies. *Psychotherapy*, 19, 482-490.

Hinshaw, A.S., & DeLeon, P.H. (1995). Toward Achieving Multidisciplinary Professional Collaboration. *Professional Psychology: Research and Practice*, 26(2), 115-116.

Hollon, S.D., Shelton, R.C., & Loosen, P.T. (1991). Cognitive therapy and pharmacotherapy for depression. *Journal of Consulting and Clinical Psychology*, 59, 88-99.

Hollon, S.D., DeRubeis, R.J., Evans, M.D., Wiemer, J.J., Garvey, J.G., Grove, W.M., & Tuason, V.B. (1992). Cognitive-therapy and pharmacotherapy for depression: Singly and in combination. *Archives of General Psychiatry*, 49, 774-781.

Howard, K.I. (1992). The psychotherapeutic service delivery system. *Psychotherapy Research*, 2 (3), 164-180.

Hoy, E., Curtis, R., & Rice, T. (1991). *Change and growth in managed care.* Health Aff (Millwood), 10, 18-36.

Hunkler, E., Kirsch, A., & Meresman, J. (1996). Personal communication with staff at Kaiser Permanente Department of Research, Oakland, CA.

Jacobson, N.S., Dobson, K., Fruzzetti, A.E., Schmaling, K.B., & Salusky, S. (1991). Marital therapy as a treatment for depression. *Journal of Consulting and Clinical Psychology*, 59, 547-557.

Jacobson, N.S., Dobson, K.S., Truax, P.A., Addis, M.E., Koerner, K., Gollan, J.K., Gortner, E., & Prince, S. E. (1996). A component analysis of cognitive-behavioral treatment for depression. *Journal of Consulting and Clinical Psychology*, 64(2), 295-304.

Johnson, D.A.D. (1973). Treatment of depression in general practice. *British Medical Journal*, 11, 18-20.

Johnson, J., Weissman, M.M., & Klerman, G.L. (1992). Service utilization and social morbidity associated with depressive symptoms in the community. *Journal of the American Medical Association*, 267, 1478-1473.

Katon, W., Von Korff, M., Lin, W., Bush, T., & Ormel, J. (1992). Adequacy and duration of antidepressant treatment in primary care. *Medical Care*, 30, 67-76.

Katon, W., Von Korff, M., Lin, E., Walker, E., Simon, G., Bush, T, Robinson, P., and Russo, J. (1995). Collaborative management to achieve treatment guidelines: Impact on depression in primary care. *Journal of the American Medical Association*, 273, 1026-1031.

Katon, W., Robinson, P. Von Korff, M., Lin, E., Bush, T., Ludman, E., Simon, G., & Walker, E. (1996). A multifaceted intervention to improve treatment of depression in primary care. Submitted to *Archives of General Psychiatry.*

Kessler, R.C., McGonagle, K.A., Zhao, S., et al. (1994). Lifetime and 12-month prevalence of DSM-III-R psychiatric disorders in the United States. *Archives of General Psychiatry*, 51, 8-19.

Knesper, D.J., & Pagnucco, D.J. (1987). Estimated distribution of effort by providers of mental health services to U.S. adults in 1982 and 1983. *American Journal Psychiatry*, 144, 883-888.

Lin, E.H.B., Von Korff, M., Katon, W., Bush, T., Simon, G.E., Walker, E., & Robinson, P. (1994). The role of the primary care physician in patients' adherence to antidepressant therapy. *Medical Care*, 33(1), 67-74.

Magil, M.K., & Garrett, R.W. (1988). Behavioral and psychiatric problems. In R.B. Tayler (Ed.), *Family Medicine* (3rd ed., pp. 534-562). New York: Springer-Verlag.

Manning, D.W., & Frances, A.J. (1990). Combined therapy for depression: Critical review of the literature. In *Combined pharmacotherapy and psychotherapy for depression.* Edited by Manning, E.W., Frances, A.J. Washington, DC, American Psychiatric Press, 1990.

Markowitz, J.C. (1994). Psychotherapy of dysthymia. *American Journal of Psychiatry*, 151(8), 1114-1120.

McDaniel, S.H. (1995). Collaboration between psychologists and family physicians: Implementing the biopsychosocial model. *Professional Psychology: Research and Practice*, 26 (2), 117-122.

McKnight, D. L., Nelson-Gray, R.O., & Barnhill, J. (1992). Desamethasone suppression test and response to cognitive therapy and antidepressant medication. *Behavior Therapy*, 1, 99-111.

Muñoz, R.F., Hollon, S.D., McGrath, E., Rehm, L.P., & VandenBos, G.R. (1994). On the AHCPR Depression in Primary Care Guidelines: Further considerations for practitioners. *American Psychologist*, 49, 42-61.

Muñoz, R.F., Ying, Y.W., Bernal, G., Pérez-Stable, E.J., Sorenson, J.L., Hargreaues, W.A., Miranda, J., & Miller, L.S. (1995). Prevention of depression with primary care patients: A randomized controlled trial. *American Journal of Community Psychology*, 23, 199-222.

Murphy, G.E., Simons, A.D., Wetzel, R.D., & Lustman, P.J. (1984). Cognitive therapy and pharmacotherapy. *Archives of General Psychiatry*, 41, 33-41.

Mynors-Wallace, L., Gath, D.H., Lloyd-Thomas, A.R., & Tomlinson, D. (1995). Randomized controlled trial comparing problem solving treatment with amitriptyline and placebo for major depression in primary care. *British Medical Journal*, 310, 441-446.

Narrow, W.E., Reigier, D.A., Rae, D.S., et al. (1993). Use of services by persons with mental and addictive disorders: Findings from the National Institute of Mental health Epidemiologic Catchment Area Program. *Archives of General Psychiatry*, 50, 95-107.

Nezu, A.M. (1986). Efficacy of a social problem-solving therapy approach for unipolar depression. *Journal of Consulting and Clinical Psychology*, 54, 196-202.

Nezu, A.M., & Perri, M.G. (1989). Social problem-solving therapy for unipolar depression: An initial dismantling investigation. *Journal of Consulting and Clinical Psychology*, 57, 408-413.

News Update (1992). Survey on Depression Shows Public Has Much to Learn. *EAP Digest*, January/February.

Nickelson, D.W. (1995). The future of professional psychology in a changing health care marketplace: A conversation with Russ Newman. *Professional Psychology: Research and Practice*, 26 (4), 366-370.

O'Leary, K.D., & Beach, S.R.H. (1990). Marital therapy: A viable treatment for depression and marital discord. *American Journal of Psychiatry*, 147, 183-186.

Olfson, M., & Klerman, G.L. (1987). The treatment of depression: Prescribing practices of primary care physicians and psychiatrists. *The Journal of Family Practice*, 35 (6), 627-635.

Olfson, M., & Klerman, G.L. (1993). Trends in the prescription of psychotropic medications: The role of physician specialty. *Medical Care*, 31, 559-564.

Orleans, C.T., George, L.K., Houpt, J.L., & Brodie, H.K.H. (1985). How primary care physicians treat psychiatric disorders: A national survey of family practitioners. *American Journal of Psychiatry*, 142, 52-57.

Persons, J.B. (1993). Outcome of psychotherapy for unipolar depression. In *Effective Psychotherapy: A Handbook of Comparative Research*. Edited by Giles T. New York, Plenum, 1993.

Persons, J.B., Thase, J.E., & Crits-Christoph, P. (1996). The role of psychotherapy in the treatment of depression: Review of two practice guidelines. *Archives of General Psychiatry*. In Press.

Reiger, D.A., Goldberg, I.D., & Taube, C. (1978). The de facto U.S. mental health service system. *Archives of General Psychiatry*, 35-685-693.

Robins, L.N., & Regier, D.A. (Eds.) (1991). *Psychiatric disorders in America: The Epidemiologic Catchment Area Study*. New York, NY: Free Press.

Robinson, L.A., Berman, J.S., & Neimeyer, R.A. (1990). Psychotherapy for the treatment of depression: A comprehensive review of controlled outcome research. *Psychological Bulletin*, 108, 30-49.

Robinson, P., Bush, T., Von Korff, M., Katon, W., Lin, E., Simon, G.E., & Walker, E. (1994). Primary care physician use of cognitive behavioral techniques with depressed patients. *Journal of Family Practice*, 40(4), 352-357.

Robinson, P., Bush, T., Von Korff, M., Katon, W., Simon, G., Walker, E., & Lin, E. (1996). Educational materials for depressed primary care patients and subsequent use of suggested coping strategies. Submitted for publication.

Robinson, P., Katon, W., Von Korff, M., Bush, T., Ludman, E., Simon, G., Lin, E., & Walker, E. (1996). Use of coping strategies by depressed primary care patients: Results of a randomized controlled trial. In preparation for submission.

Ross, M., & Scott, M. (1985). An evaluation of the effectiveness of individual and group cognitive therapy in the treatment of depressed patients in an inner city health centre. *Journal of General Practice*, 35, 239-242.

Roth, D., Bielski, R., Jones, M., Parker, W., & Osborn, G. (1982). A comparison of self-control therapy and combined self-control therapy and antidepressant medication in the treatment of therapy and antidepressant medication in the treatment of depression. *Behavior Therapy*, 13, 133-144.

Rush, A.J., Beck, A.T., Kovacs, M., & Hollon, S. (1977). Comparative efficacy of cognitive therapy and pharmacotherapy in the treatment of depressed outpatients. *Cognitive Therapy Research*, 1, 17-38.

Rucker, L., Fye, E.B., & Cygan, R.W. (1986). Feasibility and usefulness of depression screening in medical outpatients. *Archives of Internal Medicine*, 146, 729-731.

Schulberg, H.C., Block, M.R., Madonia, M.J., Scott, C.P., Rodriguez, E., Imber, S.D., Perel, J., Lave, J., Houck, P.R., & Coulehan, J.L. (1996). Treating major depression in primary care practice: Eight-month clinical outcomes. *Archives of General Psychiatry*. In press.

Schulberg, H.C., & Rush, A.J. (1994). Clinical Practice Guidelines for Managing Major Depression in Primary Care Practice. *American Psychologist*, 49(1), 34-41.

Schweizer, E., Feighner, J., Mandos, L.A., & Rickels, K. (1994). Comparison of venlafaxine and imipramine in the acute treatment of major depression in outpatients. *Journal of Clinical Psychiatry*, 55, 104-108.

Scott, A.I.F., & Freeman, C.P.L. (1992). Edinburgh primary care depression study: Treatment outcome, patient satisfaction, and cost after 16 weeks. *British Medical Journal*, 304; 883-887.

Scott, M.J., & Stradling, S.G. (1990). Group cognitive therapy for depression produces clinically significant reliable change in community-based settings. *Behavioral Psychotherapy*, 18, 1-19.

Shapiro, S., Skinner, E., Kessler, L., Von Korff, M., German, P., Tischler, G., Leaf, P., Benham, L., Cottler, L., & Regier, D. (1984). Utilization of mental health services. *Archives of General Psychiatry*, 41, 971-978.

Shaw, B.F. (1977). Comparison of cognitive therapy and behavior therapy in the treatment of depression. *Journal of Consulting and Clinical Psychology*, 45, 543-551.

Simon, G., Von Korff, M., Wagner, E.H., & Barlow, W. (1993). Patterns of antidepressant use in community practice. *General Hospital Psychiatry*, 15, 399-408.

Song, L., et al. (1993). Selective serotonine reuptake inhibitors: Meta-analysis of efficacy and acceptability. *British Medical Journal*, 306, 683-690.

Stewart, A.L., Sherbourne, C.D., Wells, K.B., Burnam, A., Rogers, W.H., Hays, R.D., & Ware, J.E. (1993). Do depressed patients in different treatment settings have different levels of well-being and functioning? *Journal of Consulting and Clinical Psychology*, 61(5), 849-857.

Strum, R., & Wells, K. (1995). How can care for depression become more cost-effective? *Journal of the American Medical Association*, 273, 51-58.

Teasdale, J.D., Fennell, M.J.V., Hibbert, G.A., & Amies, P.L., (1984). Cognitive therapy for major depressive disorder in primary care. *British Journal of Psychiatry*, 144, 400-406.

Thompson, L.W., Gallagher, D., & Breckenridge, J.S. (1987). Comparative effectiveness of psychotherapies for depressed elders. *Journal of Consulting and Clinical Psychology*, 55, 385-390.

Wells, K.B., Stewart, A., Hays, R.D., Burnam, A., Rogers, W., Daniels, M., Berry, S., Greenfield, S., & Ware, J. (1989). The functioning and well-being of depressed patients: Results from the Medical Outcomes Study. *Journal of the American Medical Association*, 262(7), 914-919.

Wilson, P.H. (1982). Combined pharmacological and behavioural treatment of depression. *Behavior Research and Therapy*, 20, 173-184.

Wise, R.N. (1995). Commentary: Underdiagnosis of depression in general practice. *Mind/Body Medicine*, 1(1), 23.

Zung, W.W.K., Broadhead, W.E., & Roth, M.E. (1993). Prevalence of depression in primary care. *Journal of Family Practice*, 37, 337-344.

Chapter 2

Screening and Assessment in Primary Care

Improving depression treatment outcomes in primary care requires attention to the processes of screening and diagnosis, as well as other clinical management activities. This chapter suggests strategies to help you detect depressive symptoms and accurately diagnose specific depressive disorders. In this chapter, you will learn the following.

- Populations to target in screening efforts
- How to use visit type as a clue to screen
- Self-report inventories that are useful screeners
- Assessment targets and associated methods

Instructions for Speed Readers: Allow 15 minutes to read and study this chapter. Critical information is printed in bold in all sections of the chapter. Slow down for a more careful study of assessment targets that you do not address on a regular basis.

Improving Screening Procedures

While the prevalence of depression in primary care is high, screening all patients is not feasible. The average primary care encounter is over in less than 15 minutes. Strategies for improving recognition in primary care are useful to the extent that they can work within the time and cost constraints of primary care. **Strategic screening protocols may help busy providers identify patients who warrant more time-consuming diagnostic interviews.** Selective screening may focus on specific population parameters or type of primary care visit.

Target Populations

Dr. Douglas Jacobs (1995) was an investigator in the National Depression Screening Day Project. He and his associates screened 40,000 patients for depression in 1992 and 1993. Based upon his extensive experience, **he recommends that depression screening be limited to medical patients who present with one or more of the following.**

1. Report a recent loss or are undergoing severe stress.
2. Report vague somatic symptoms.
3. Express any expected somatic or emotional symptoms of depression.
4. Report a family history of depression, suicide, or mental illness.
5. Report a history of self-medicating behavior, including use of alcohol and nicotine.
6. Report a history of self-destructive behavior.
7. Are currently taking certain medications, particularly antihypertensives, hormones, histamine-2 receptor blockers, anticonvulsants, and levodopa.
8. Have a major illness such as stroke, coronary artery disease, or cancer.
9. Are in the postpartum period.
10. Have chronic pain.

You may place posters in primary care clinics that invite patients to screen themselves using this list of 10 risk factors. The poster also needs to encourage patients to discuss depression or demoralization with primary care providers. Patients often spend time waiting in registration areas and in pharmacies, as well as waiting rooms. All of these areas may be used to "educate" patients about depression.

Visit Types

Another method for defining patients at risk for depression is to use the existing literature on the prevalence of depression associated with the *type* of primary care visit. Based upon a screening study of 986 primary care patients, Olfson and Leon (1994) reported the prevalence rates of depression by type of visit listed in Table 2.1. They suggested an overall prevalence rate of 14.3%. When you extrapolate from this figure, **you can estimate that around 4 patients in a 30-patient day are experiencing major depression.** One avenue for implementing a visit-based screening protocol is to develop a schedule template, which places higher risk patients on certain days of the week or times of the day. For example, you might **set up several mornings for scheduling monitoring visits for patients with chronic medical problems. In addition, you could develop a poster for your exam room that reminds you of the incidence of depression among patients with chronic medical illnesses.** This type of change to the healthcare context may help both providers and patients to better identify depression.

Table 2.1
Prevalence of Depression by the Type of Primary Care Visit

Visit Type	% with Major Depression
Chronic Medical Problems	16%
New Illness	15.7%
Follow-Up Care	14.3%
Routine Physical	5%

Screening Methods

Once you decide that a patient is experiencing significant symptoms of depression, you may use a self-report inventory to help you assess the overall severity of the problem. Self-report inventories are parsimonious and offer norms to help busy providers quickly assess severity level. **The Beck Depression Inventory-Short Form fits the requirements of primary care** (Beck & Beck, 1972). Most patients complete the one-page, 13-item questionnaire in less than five minutes. Additionally, normative data are available for primary care patients. **The Geriatric Depression Scale has a "yes\no" format and uses language that may increase accuracy of diagnosis of depression in older patients** (Yesavage, et al., 1983). Other self-rating scales worthy of mention include the Center for Epidemiological Studies--Depression Scale (CES-D) (Radloff, 1977) and the Zung Self-Rating Depression Scale (Zung, et al., 1965). All of these instruments are easy to use and sensitive to depression symptom severity. Results of self-report screening instruments can alert the busy primary care provider to the need to spend more time diagnosing symptoms of depression.

Assessment Targets and Methods

Symptoms

The various depressive disorders discussed in Chapter 1 are diagnosed, in part, by determining the presence or absence of a specific number of symptoms experienced by the patient over a certain period of time. Symptoms may be measured in several ways. Structured interviews, as well as symptom checklists, help you conduct a thorough evaluation. Spitzer and colleagues (1994) developed a structured interview format for primary care providers to use in diagnosing common mental disorders, including depression. **Symptom checklists may help busy providers be thorough and time-effective.** Therefore, you may want to make a checklist for your patients to use to indicate persistent symptoms of depression prior to visits with you. Patients can complete checklists independently. This allows you more time to focus on the severity of functional impairments associated with the symptoms. Additionally, some providers use an overview of symptoms as an aid in selecting an initial antidepressant medication. **Symptom checklists also help you evaluate patient response to treatment at follow-up appointments.** We suggest that you include the following symptoms on your checklist.

1. Anger or Irritability – often during the day
2. Sadness – often during the day
3. Sleep Problems: ☐ too much; ☐ slow to go to sleep; ☐ waking in middle of night; ☐ early morning waking
4. Interest Problems – a lack of interest in others and in activities you usually enjoy
5. Guilt, self critical thoughts, feeling inadequate or worthless
6. Energy Problems – tired most of the time
7. Concentration Problems
8. Appetite Changes: ☐ significantly greater; ☐ significantly less; ☐ weight gain; ☐ weight loss
9. Psychomotor Problems: ☐ very "slowed down" or ☐ very "speeded up"
10. Pain Problems – more aches and more pain
11. Suicidal thoughts

While anger/irritability and pain are not included in DSM-IV (APA, 1994), they are common among depressed primary care patients. Anger may be more common among depressed men, who may present for care in the primary care setting more often than in the specialty setting (Robinson, et al., 1994; Nolen-Hoeksema, 1990). Primary care patients also tend to have more medical illness burden, including pain. For this reason, we suggest that you include both symptoms on your checklist.

Primary care providers may have more difficulties in spontaneous recall of psychological symptoms of depression because their training encourages a focus on physical symptoms. Therefore, you may want to **focus formal and informal education efforts in your primary care clinic on helping providers better recognize and explore psychological symptoms of depression.** Jacobs and colleagues (1995) screened 40,000 patients for depression in 1992 and 1993. For both years, he identified the same five psychological symptoms of depression as the most common symptoms of patients whose scores indicated the presence of depression, including severe depression. **Ninety-one percent of those people who scored positive for moderate or**

severe depression suffered from all five of the psychological symptoms, whereas only 49% reported suffering from physical symptoms, including fatigue, rapid heartbeat, constipation, changes in appetite, weight loss, and sleep disturbance. Table 2.2 presents these five psychological symptoms. You may want to print these as a letterhead for primary care provider notepads or present this information in a lunch-hour educational program.

Table 2.2
91% Of 40,000 Patients Who Scored Positive For Moderate Or Severe Depression Suffered From All 5 Of These Symptoms

1. Difficulty in doing things done in the past
2. Feeling hopeless about the future
3. Difficulty in making decisions
4. Feeling worthless and not needed
5. No longer enjoying the things that used to be enjoyable

Coping

Use of active coping strategies buffers the impact of stress and helps lessen symptoms of depression (Burns, et al., 1991). Discussion of coping strategies seems well suited to the primary care provider-patient relationship. Most primary care patients report multiple life stresses and, therefore, find discussion of coping strategies helpful. Robinson (1995) found that depressed patients often reported that their primary care physicians suggested behavioral coping strategies in visits where antidepressant therapy was initiated. Further, Lin reported that physician discussion of

Table 2.3
Use of Coping Strategies by Depressed Primary Care Patients

Coping Strategy Suggested by Primary Care Provider	% of Patients
Identifying activities you already do that help improve your mood	61
Participating in pleasurable activities	40
Using problem-solving techniques for problems you are having in life, such as problems with your job or relationships	34
Noticing negative thoughts and replacing them with more positive thoughts	32
Participating in activities that boost your confidence	27

behavioral coping strategies was associated with better patient adherence to prescribed medications (Lin, et al., 1994). Table 2.3 summarizes the percentages of depressed patients who reported that their physician suggested use of coping strategies during a visit when antidepressant therapy was initiated. Unfortunately, existing scales for measuring use of coping strategies address research purposes better than clinical needs. They are too lengthy for day-to-day use in a practice setting. You may want to construct a list of coping strategies you plan to recommend to patients. **Begin to routinely assess how frequently patients are employing your recommended strategies in their daily lives so that you can assess the impact of your coping education efforts.** Over the years, we have evolved a list of 7 coping strategies. We may only recommend two or three strategies to an individual patient, as patients differ in coping styles and prefer to use strategies consistent with their style. For example, some older patients find psychological acceptance strategies of more interest, while younger patients prefer strategies that increase experience of pleasure and social interactions. The purpose of assessing patient use of coping strategies is to detect low overall rates and, through behavioral planning, to increase overall frequency of use of coping strategies. We routinely assess frequency of use of the following seven coping strategies:

1. Participating in pleasurable activities
2. Participating in activities that boost your confidence
3. Simply being aware of an uncomfortable thought, feeling, or emotion without struggling with it.
4. Participating in activities that help you relax
5. Using problem-solving techniques for problems you're having in life such as problems with your job or relationships
6. Noticing negative thoughts and replacing them with more realistic thoughts
7. Participating in creative activities

We have explored the psychometric properties of a similar checklist of coping strategies and found it to be a sensitive measure of patient response to brief cognitive behavioral interventions in primary care (Robinson, 1996).

Functional Limitations

Depressed patients often experience considerable difficulties performing responsibilities associated with life roles. They may have difficulties meeting their own basic needs. Those with chronic medical problems may adhere less well to medical self-management plans. Patients with moderate to severe depression tend to perform poorly in family, social and work settings. They often falter in their efforts to work with their painfully negative emotional states.

We recommend that your assessment of patients with moderate to severe depression include evaluation of family/marital dysfunction, work/productivity limitations, social limitations, emotional experiencing limitations, and psychobiological limitations, including ability to effectively address health problems. You may use a Likert scale to assess severity of limitation in each area (e.g., 0 = Absent/Nonpathological; 1 = Moderate; 2 = Debilitating; 3 = Incapacitating; 4 = Imminently dangerous). Dr. Michael Goodman and his colleagues (1992) present a system for assessing functional impairments in their book, *Managing Managed Care.*

Patient Satisfaction

Patient satisfaction is an important assessment target area for several reasons. First, **satisfied patients are more likely to adhere to planned treatments**, whether behavioral or pharmacological. Second, **satisfied patients are more likely to continue with you as their provider**, and this is of concern in today's health care market. Finally, **you experience more satisfaction with your job** when your patients are satisfied with your care. You can devise you own questions for measuring patient satisfaction. Generally, you will want to ask about the patient's satisfaction with the assessment, the plan, and the results of treatment. Generally, patients are more than willing to provide this information. Older patients may need a little extra support in order to give negative feedback. It is best to have someone other than a provider collect information on satisfaction.

Summary and Helpful Hints

Assessment in primary care needs to be multifaceted. Assessment also needs to be sensitive to the effects of treatments used most in primary care. Spend a few minutes reviewing your own practice setting and deciding what changes in screening and assessment processes will work best for you at this time. Remember the following points.

1. Use educational materials, such as posters in waiting rooms, to improve patient recognition of depressive symptoms.
2. Focus provider education efforts on targets that are most likely to improve on-going detection of depression (e.g., presence of psychological symptoms).
3. Be practical and creative in devising assessment methods for your setting. The bottom line is that you use them!
4. Place your routine assessment instruments on clinical computing work stations.

References

American Psychiatric Association. (1994). *Diagnostic and statistical manual of mental disorders, 4th Ed.* Washington, D.C.: American Psychiatric Association.

Beck, A.T., & Beck, R. W. (1972). Screening depressed patients in family practice: A rapid technique. *Postgraduate Medicine, 52,* 81-85.

Burns, D.D., & Nolen-Hoeksema, S. (1991). Coping styles, homework compliance, and the effectiveness of cognitive-behavioral therapy. *Journal of Consulting and Clinical Psychology, 59*(2), 305-311.

Goodman, M., Brown, J., & Deitz, P. (1992). *Managing managed care: A mental health practitioner's survival guide.* Washington, DC: American Psychiatric Press, Inc.

Jacobs, D.G., Kopans, B. S.. & Reizes, J.M. (1995). Revaluation of Depression: What the general practitioner needs to know. *Mind/Body Medicine, 1*(1), 17-22.

Nolen-Hoeksema, S. (1990). *Sex differences in depression.* Stanford, CA: Stanford University Press 1990.

Olfson, M., & Leon, L. (1993). Prevalence of depression in primary care patients according to visit type. A presentation at the NIMH Treatment of Mental Disorders in General Medical Settings Conference. Rockville, MA.

Robinson, P., Afari, N., & Bush, T. (1994). Depressed men in primary care: Preliminary results of an on-site intervention to improve care. *Group Health Forum, Winter,* 1994.

Robinson, P., Bush, T., Von Korff, M., Katon, W., Simon, G., Walker, E., & Lin, E. (1996). Brief report: Impact of Multifaceted Treatment on Behavioral Coping by Depressed Primary Care Patients. In preparation for submission.

Radloff, L. (1977). The CES-D scale: A self-report depression scale for research in the general population. *Applied Psychological Measurement, 1,* 385-401.

Spitzer, R.L., Williams, J.B., Kroenke, K., Linzer, L., deGruy, F. V., Hahn, S.R., Brody, D.. & Johnson, J.G. (1994). Utility of a new procedure for diagnosing mental disorders in primary care: The PRIME-MD 1000 Study. *Journal of the American Medical Association, 272*(22), 1749-1756.

Yesavage, J.A., Brink, T.L., Rose, T.L., & Lum, O. (1983). Development and validation of a geriatric depression screening scale: A preliminary report. *Journal of Psychiatric Research, 17*(1), 37-49.

Zung, W.W., Richards, C.B., & Short, M.M. (1965). Self-rating depression scale in an outpatient clinic. *Archives of General Psychiatry, 13,* 48-65.

Chapter 3

Assessment in the Integrated Care Program

This chapter describes assessment protocols and procedures used in the Integrated Care Program (ICP). These will help you select a level and type of care, track patient progress, and determine when to continue and stop treatment. We present examples to illustrate use of depression assessment and medication assessment protocols. In this chapter, you will learn the following.

- The components of the Depressive Symptoms Assessment System (DSAS)
- When and how to use the Level 1 and 2 depression assessment protocol
- How to link assessment results to specific treatment options
- When and how to complete the medication assessment protocol

---

Instructions for Speed Readers: Allow 1 hour to read, study, and practice protocols. Critical information is printed in bold in all sections of the chapter. **Take time to complete the depression assessment forms and the medication assessment form, as if you were a patient.** Role play being a provider of care and a patient using these protocols.

Depressive Symptoms Assessment System (DSAS)

Accurate assessment is critical for improving the quality of care for depressed patients. In the Integrated Care Program, we suggest that practitioners use the Depressive Symptoms Assessment System (DSAS). The DSAS helps you select treatments that fit the level of severity. You may save money by refraining from prescribing antidepressant medications to patients with milder forms of depression. Additionally, you may save patients a great deal of suffering by on-going assessment efforts that help you promptly intensify treatment when symptoms fail to improve or worsen. **On-going assessment also helps you know when to stop active treatment, discontinue antidepressant therapy and begin a relapse prevention program.**

The DSAS involves two levels of assessment. The first level focuses solely on determination of symptoms. The second includes assessment of patient functioning in multiple life roles. We believe that separating symptoms and functional impairment is effective for several reasons. First, having two levels simplifies assessment. Many patients only need the initial level of assessment. This level is obtained by patient self-report. The initial level of assessment is also adequate for assessing treatment response during initial phases of treatment. **Simplicity in assessment protocols helps providers use them accurately and consistently.** The second level of assessment is more complex and needs to be reserved for moderately to severely depressed patients. **The two-tier system encourages providers to adjust health care resources to patient needs.**

Table 3.1 provides an overview of assessment protocols. Take a few minutes to study Table 3.1. Copies of assessment forms are located in Appendix A, as well as later in this chapter when they are used in case examples. The DSAS Level 1 assessment is parsimonious and time-effective. It yields adequate information for treatment planning and treatment response monitoring for patients who are less impaired by their depression. Typically, these will be dysthymic patients and patients with milder forms of major depression. The Level 2 protocol requires you to establish the degree of functional impairment suffered by the patient. Level 2 is useful with patients who have moderate to severe depression. Both protocols can be placed on clinical computing stations to allow for on-going data entry and to show providers and patients the patterns of change in symptoms over time. **Use of self-report inventories is optional but recommended where feasible.**

Table 3.1
Depressive Symptoms Assessment System (DSAS)

DSAS Form	For Patients With	Assessment Areas	Provider Responsibilities
Level 1 Depression Assessment	Mild Symptoms	• Symptoms Checklist • Use of Coping Strategies • BDI-SF* or GDS**	Briefly discuss self-assessment results and plan to reassess in 1-month; plan treatment & evaluate patient satisfaction with plan.
Level 2 Depression Assessment	Moderate to Severe Symptoms	• Symptoms Checklist • Use of Coping Strategies • Emotional Experience • Living According to Values • Functional Limitations	Evaluate severity of functional limitations, plan treatment, evaluate patient satisfaction with plan, & plan post-treatment evaluation.
Medication Assessment Questionnaire **(MAQ)**	Moderate to Severe Symptoms and Prefer Medication Treatment	• History of medication use • Current medication use • Interest in antidepressant treatment • Beliefs about psychotropic medications • Side effect concerns • Knowledge about antidepressant treatment	Evaluate patient responses. Discuss history, interest, beliefs, concerns about side effects and basic knowledge about medication use.

*BDI-SF is Beck Depression Inventory - Short Form. **GDS is Geriatric Depression Scale.

Levels One and Two Depression Assessment

The Level 1 and 2 assessment protocols use a questionnaire that evaluates the presence of eleven specific symptoms and patient use of seven specific coping strategies known to buffer stress. Most patients can complete this one-page questionnaire independently. The Level 1 questionnaire is designed for patients with mild symptoms of depression. Patients who receive Level 1 assessment will usually require less hands-on clinical management. For these patients, you will develop a behavioral treatment plan and schedule a return visit for 2 to 4 weeks later. If the patient is improving at the return visit, no further intervention is needed. If the patient is not improving or is more symptomatic at the return visit, you will conduct a Level 2 assessment and plan more intensive treatment.

Conducting a second evaluation after 4 weeks is useful with patients with mild symptoms because many will improve with minimal treatment. Those who have not improved or have worsened may be candidates for more intensive treatment. Improvements in symptoms of depression in *untreated* patients are minimal after 4 weeks. This has been demonstrated in studies using a placebo treatment condition to evaluate the efficacy of antidepressant therapy (Cunningham, et al., 1994; Fontaine, et al., 1994).

Level 2 includes assessment of the patient's functional limitations in the areas listed in Table 3.2. The provider interviews the patient to assess the extent of impairment. Level 2 also includes a few more questions for the patient to complete independently. These questions relate to the patient's ability to work with emotional experience and to participate meaningfully in seven areas of daily living. These questions facilitate behavioral treatment planning and assist with evaluating the impact of behavioral plans. They relate closely to skills and exercises suggested in the self-management workbook, *Living Life Well: New Strategies for Hard Times* (Robinson, 1996). Patients who use this workbook may elect to respond to these questions on a weekly basis, as is suggested in the workbook.

Complete Level 2 assessment activities in your initial visit with patients who report 5 or more symptoms on the one-page Level 1 form. On occasion, patients with only four symptoms of depression may report significant problems with functioning (e.g., poor work performance, difficulties with managing medical problems, or substance abuse). This type of patient often warrants a Level 2 assessment. Use clinical judgment to answer the question "How much is this patient 'impaired' in functioning by her/his symptoms of depression?" This will help you decide between staying with the basic, Level 1 assessment or moving onto the more comprehensive, Level 2 assessment. Level 2 patients require more assessment time and more structure and intensity in follow-up. They are also candidates for medication assessment and treatment.

The Medication Assessment Questionnaire (MAQ)

The Medication Assessment Questionnaire (MAQ) helps you thoroughly evaluate and address all aspects of medication adherence risk prior to initiating antidepressant treatment. Take a moment to locate the MAQ in Appendix B. A second copy illustrating a patient's responses is presented in a later section of this chapter. Patients may complete the MAQ at any point in treatment when medication becomes an option. For patients with Major Depressive Disorder who prefer medication treatment, the MAQ will be completed at the beginning of treatment. Patients with Major Depressive Disorder who are initially ambivalent or negative about medication treatment may complete the MAQ after starting behavioral treatment in the ICP. Patients with milder forms of depression will probably not complete the MAQ, as they are not usually candidates for antidepressant therapy. Patients may respond to MAQ questions at home prior to an appointment, in a "phone appointment," or in a waiting area at the clinic just prior to a visit.

The MAQ targets five areas of crucial importance to the patient's compliance with antidepressant treatment, including the patient's: (1) *history* of use of antidepressants, (2) *interest* in use of medications, (3) *beliefs* about medications, (4) *attitudes* toward specific side effects and (5) accurate basic *knowledge about antidepressant therapy*. The MAQ also asks the patient about current use of antidepressants and experience of benefits and side effects. This will expedite your work with patients who are already taking antidepressant medications prescribed by other providers of care. Guidelines regarding optimal use of the MAQ precede the case example presented later in this chapter.

Table 3.2
Level 2 Assessment: Functional Limitations

Area	Limitation*
Family Limitations	Family dysfunction
	Family dysfunction with substance abuse
	Marital/relationship dysfunction
	Marital/relationship dysfunction with violent behavior
Work and Productivity Limitations	Work dissatisfaction
	Work performance problems
	Educational performance deficits
	Inadequate survival skills
Social Limitations	Assaultiveness
	Manipulativeness
	Social withdrawal
	Oppositionalism
	Uncommunicativeness
	Verbal aggressiveness
Emotional Experiencing Limitations	Self-mutilation
	Substance abuse
	Hopelessness
	Suicidal thoughts/behavior
Psychobiological Limitations	Altered sleep
	Decreased concentration
	Decreased frustration tolerance
	Dysphoric mood
	Mood lability
	Psychomotor agitation
	Psychomotor retardation
	Concomitant medical condition
	Medical treatment noncompliance
	Inadequate health care skills

*Rated on a scale of 0 = Absent/Nonpathological; 1 = Moderate; 2 = Debilitating; 3 = Incapacitating; 4: Imminently dangerous.

Assessment Drives Treatment Selection

ICP assessment results suggest an appropriate treatment. **In fact, you may attach the ICP Treatment Plan form to Level 1 and Level 2 assessment results. The ICP Treatment Plan is located in Appendix C. It allows you to indicate your selected treatment *and* document start, review and completion dates associated with the selected treatment.** Additionally, this page provides a record of your work with the patient during the relapse prevention phase and a place for recording the patient's satisfaction with treatment.

Treatment Options in the Integrated Care Program

The ICP has the following four treatment options.

1. Primary Care Clinical Management with or without Antidepressant Treatment
2. Services from the On-Site Behavioral Health Consultant
3. Consultation with Medication Specialist
4. Brief Mental Health Treatment Delivered Externally

Treatment options associated with particular assessment results are presented in Table 3.3. As the severity of depression increases, more treatment options may be selected. **Within each treatment option, use your clinical judgment to determine the *treatment intensity* (e.g., adjusting frequency of clinic visits and/or adding phone visits).** Primary care providers vary in their interest and skill in treating more significantly depressed patients. If you are not confident in planning treatment with a patient, involve an on-site behavioral health consultant or an external mental health provider. Your consultant may be able to help you develop a strong clinical management plan after seeing the patient once or twice. Alternatively, the consultant may determine that the patient needs to participate in the ICP Behavioral Treatment protocol or, in rare instances, to participate in an even more intensive treatment located outside the primary care clinic. When faced with a patient with severe impairments, contact your behavioral health consultant for emergency assistance. **Antidepressant therapy may be a part of any treatment option in the ICP.**

Provider Responsibilities in the Integrated Care Program

Primary care providers may complete the depression assessment and medication assessment protocols in the ICP without any assistance from a mental health specialist. However, some primary care providers will ask on-site mental health specialists to complete depression and medication assessments for selected patients who require more time. This will ease the burden of work on the primary care team.

Procedures in the Depressive Symptoms Assessment System (DSAS)

Patients can complete self-report inventories at home and mail them to the clinic, complete them in the waiting area prior to a medical visit or complete them in an exam room during the visit. Structured phone interviews concerning symptoms of depression and use of coping strategies can be reliably conducted by nurses and other primary care staff. **Most patients will complete the Level 1 assessment process in 5 minutes, while the Level 2 assessment requires 10 minutes or more.** Many of these instruments can be entered into computer formats with touch screens.

Table 3.3
Treatment Options in the Integrated Care Program*

Assessment Results Suggest	Treatment Options
Mild to Moderate (2 to 4 symptoms, low coping use score)	Primary Care Team Clinical Management protocol
Moderate Symptoms (5 or more symptoms, low coping use score) *and* Moderate Difficulties with Functioning (scores 10-15 on functional assessment)	On-Site Behavioral Health Consultant Services, including ☐ Brief Treatment protocol or ☐ Behavioral Treatment protocol
Severe Symptoms (6 or more symptoms, low coping use score) *and* Severe Difficulties with Functioning (scores 16+ on functional assessment, has 1+ areas rated imminently dangerous)	More intensive implementation of Behavioral Treatment protocol *Consider* Specialty Treatment Delivered Externally
Complex or Poor Response to Antidepressant Treatment (no improvement after 4 weeks of treatment)	Consultation with Medication Specialist *Consider* Specialty Treatment Delivered Externally

*Antidepressant Therapy may accompany any treatment option.

The Initial Visit

When patients present with **depression as a chief complaint**, you may complete the ICP depression assessment protocol in the initial visit. If results warrant immediate planning efforts and you *and* the patient have time, you may complete the medication assessment protocol in the initial visit as well. When patients present **for medical care** and you suspect depression, you may complete the depression assessment protocol or simply give it to patients to complete after the visit and mail to the clinic. When you receive mail-in assessment information, you can plan timely follow-up, which may include a treatment-planning phone appointment with the patient.

Follow-Up Visits

Ask patients to complete the single-sheet, Level 1 form just prior to each follow-up visit with you. Follow-up assessment results will help you adjust your treatment plan. When results suggest little progress or a worsening of symptoms, intensify your treatment. When results suggest improvement, commend the patient on progress and start a discussion regarding phases of active treatment and relapse prevention support. **For patients using medication, suggest that assessment results will help the two of you make any needed changes to the medication plan *and* decide when to start tapering medications.**

Treatment Completion Visit

The treatment completion visit is the visit when assessment results indicate that a positive response to treatment has occurred and you are ready to move into relapse prevention work. You may select your own specific cut-point for "positive response." Two good rules of thumb are:

1. the patient no longer meets criteria for the depressive disorder for which you started treatment, and/or

2. the patient is 50% improved.

You may show the patient how assessment results demonstrate improvement. After acknowledging the patient's efforts and progress, complete a written relapse prevention plan with the patient.

Relapse Prevention Visits

Patients need to complete the one-page, Level 1 depression assessment form monthly during the relapse prevention phase of treatment. This phase commences at the completion of active treatment and continues for the following six months. This is the time period when risk of relapse is greatest. Stress the importance of on-going assessment to patients. When the patient begins to taper from medication, you may suggest that he or she complete the basic depression assessment weekly for a month. Early detection of increasing symptoms supports prompt corrections to lifestyle and medication plans.

ICP Level 1 Assessment: An Example

Nina was a 51 year old accountant who sought care from her primary care provider regarding headaches. She explained that her headaches had increased since her menstrual periods had stopped and related that she had recently married. When asked about her marriage, she explained that the marriage was going well enough, but that she felt somewhat inadequate and unattractive. She explained that she had gained 20 pounds over the past 3 years and that she often ate out of frustration. She began to cry and reported that her father was dying in another country. As the interview continued, she explained recent difficulties at work and discomfort with the idea of using any kind of medication, including hormone replacement therapy. Nina's primary care provider, Dr. Bush, asked her to respond to the Level 1 assessment questionnaire. Her responses are recorded on the Sample ICP Level 1 Assessment Form.

Nina indicated four symptoms of depression, a somewhat low rate of use of coping strategies, and a score of 8 on the BDI-SF (low end of the moderate range). Dr. Bush asked Nina if she would like to set up a behavioral plan to improve her mood. Nina indicated she would prefer this to "taking pills." When Dr. Bush explained the biopsychosocial model, Nina asked several questions about menopause and depression. She was interested in the booklet, *Seven Ways to Cope*, and asked Dr. Bush if there were other materials she might read. Dr. Bush recommended that Nina read *Living Life Well: New Strategies for Hard Times.*

Dr. Bush selected a behavioral treatment for Nina because her symptoms were mild. Additionally, Nina had a history of coping well with multiple stresses and was interested in behavioral rather than pharmacological treatment. When Nina came for her follow-up visit with Dr. Bush, she indicated success in implementing her behavioral treatment. Her responses to the Level 1 assessment form indicated a 50% reduction in her symptoms and a significant increase in the frequency of employing coping strategies. Dr. Bush helped Nina develop several new behavioral plans to implement during the next three-month period. They planned to reassess Nina's progress three months later.

Sample: ICP Level 1 Assessment

Level 1 ICP Assessment (Patient Completes)		
Patient: *Nina Carlisle*	**Provider(s):** *Bush*	
Dear Patient: Please respond to the following questions. If you need help with any of the questions, ask your doctor or nurse.		
Mark an "X" by any symptom that has troubled you *more days than not* during the past ☐ one or ☒ two (*check one*) week(s).	Today's Date 1/18/96	Return Visit Date 1/29/96
1. Anger or Irritability – often during the day	☒	☐
2. Sadness – often during the day	☒	☐
3. Sleep Problems: ☐ too much; ☐ slow to go to sleep; ☐ waking in middle of night; ☐ early morning waking	☐	☐
4. Interest Problems – a lack of interest in others and in activities you usually enjoy	☐	☐
5. Guilt, self critical thoughts, feeling inadequate or worthless	☒	☐
6. Energy Problems – tired most of the time	☐	☐
7. Concentration Problems	☐	☐
8. Appetite Changes: ☒ significantly greater; ☐ significantly less; ☒ weight gain; ☐ weight loss	☒	☐
9. Psychomotor Problems: ☐ very "slowed down" or ☐ very "speeded up"	☐	☐
10. Pain Problems – more aches and more pain	☐	☐
11. Suicidal Thoughts	☐	☐
How often have you used the following coping strategies in the past ☐ one or ☒ two (*check one*) week(s). **0 = Not at all; 1 = Once; 2 = Several times; 3 = Almost Daily; 4 = Daily**		
1. Participating in pleasurable activities	1	
2. Participating in activities that boost your confidence	1	
3. Simply being aware of an uncomfortable thought, feeling, or emotion without struggling with it.	2	
4. Participating in activities that help you relax	2	
5. Using problem-solving techniques for problems you're having in life such as problems with your job or relationships	0	
6. Noticing negative thoughts and replacing them with more realistic thoughts	1	
7. Participating in creative activities	2	

ICP Level 2 Assessment: An Example

Elana Miller was a single mother with a history of alcohol and drug abuse. She had moved from another state recently after the sudden death of her husband. She lived in the basement of her mother's home with her young son. Elana worked as a full-time secretary. She spent an additional ten hours a week caring for her mother who was in poor health. Elana's son, Emilio, was an exceptionally bright child, who was struggling with the loss of her father.

Elana presented to her primary care physician, Dr. Jones, with complaints of pelvic pain, headaches, insomnia, and the fear that she was "going to loose her mind." Elana completed the Level 1 assessment. She indicated persistent problems with irritability, sadness, disturbed sleep, loss of interest, guilt, low energy, diminished concentration, and suicidal ideation.

Dr. Jones asked Elana how she was doing in her efforts to work, parent, and care for her mother during this very difficult time for her. She indicated significant problems at work, including frequent conflicts with co-workers, receiving formal reprimands concerning mistakes and working additional hours to complete her responsibilities. Additionally, she reported arguments with her mother and difficulties with buying food, preparing regular meals and getting her son through a predictable daily routine. She was leaving her son often with a neighbor while she sat at home and read or watched television. Elana had "given up" on house cleaning and felt ashamed to tell Dr. Jones that her son was trying to clean and cook for them. Elana's responses to the ICP Level 2 Assessment questions and Dr. Bush's ratings are recorded on the following Level 2 samples.

Elana checked eight persistent symptoms of depression. She was using very few coping strategies to buffer her numerous life stresses. Her emotions were very intense and she resisted all of her feelings. She indicated that she was living her values in the sense that she was providing an income and she spent time with her son. The two read together every evening, and she was responsive to many of his questions about the world. Dr. Bush's ratings on page 3 indicated at least moderate impairment in all major areas of role functioning. She denied any plan concerning suicide, but noted a longing for a "way out." She indicated strong urges to return to use of alcohol.

Dr. Jones helped Elana make a behavioral plan to improve the quality of her life in several small yet significant ways. Additionally, she helped Elana start antidepressant therapy. Dr. Jones' follow-up included a phone call appointment three days later and a clinic visit one week later. Elana completed the Level 1 assessment form at the follow-up appointment. Results indicated that irritability, sleep, and concentration were less problematic. Additionally, results suggested some improvement in Elana's use of coping strategies to improve her quality of life. Dr. Jones and Elana added several new components to their behavioral plan. Elana agreed to continuing her medication as well and returning to see Dr. Jones in two weeks.

Sample: ICP Level 2 Assessment

Level 2 ICP Assessment – Page 1 (Patient Completes)		
Patient: *Elana Miller*	**Provider(s):** *Jones*	
Dear Patient: Please respond to the following questions. If you need help with any of the questions, ask your doctor or nurse.		
Mark an "X" by any symptom that has troubled you *more days than not* during the past ☐ one or ☒ two (*check one*) week(s).	Today's Date 5/11/96	Return Visit Date
1. Anger or Irritability – often during the day	☒	☐
2. Sadness – often during the day	☒	☐
3. Sleep Problems: ☐ too much; ☐ slow to go to sleep; ☒ waking in middle of night; ☐ early morning waking	☒	☐
4. Interest Problems – a lack of interest in others and in activities you usually enjoy	☒	☐
5. Guilt, self critical thoughts, feeling inadequate or worthless	☒	☐
6. Energy Problems – tired most of the time	☒	☐
7. Concentration Problems	☒	☐
8. Appetite Changes: ☐ significantly greater; ☐ significantly less; ☐ weight gain; ☐ weight loss	☐	☐
9. Psychomotor Problems: ☐ very "slowed down" or ☐ very "speeded up"	☐	☐
10. Pain Problems – more aches and more pain	☐	☐
11. Suicidal Thoughts	☒	☐
How often have you used the following coping strategies in the past ☐ one or ☒ two (*check one*) week(s).		
0 = Not at all; 1 = Once; 2 = Several times; 3 = Almost Daily; 4 = Daily		
1. Participating in pleasurable activities	0	
2. Participating in activities that boost your confidence	0	
3. Simply being aware of an uncomfortable thought, feeling, or emotion without struggling with it.	1	
4. Participating in activities that help you relax	1	
5. Using problem-solving techniques for problems you're having in life such as problems with your job or relationships	2	
6. Noticing negative thoughts and replacing them with more realistic thoughts	1	
7. Participating in creative activities	0	

Level 2 ICP Assessment – Page 2 (Patient Completes)

Which of these emotions have you experienced on a daily basis during the past week and with how much intensity (1 = "not intense" to 10 = "very intense") and willingness (1= "I cannot tolerate this feeling" to 10 = "I accept this feeling completely")?

Today's Date: 5/11/96			Return Visit Date:		
	Intensity of Feeling	Willingness to Feel		Intensity of Feeling	Willingness to Feel
1. Sadness	1. 7	1. 10	1. Sadness	1.	1.
2. Anger	2. 7	2. 8	2. Anger	2.	2.
3. Fear	3. 8	3. 10	3. Fear	3.	3.

Please record a number beside each activity to indicate how much you "lived your values" in that area *during the past week*. Use this rating scale:

1 2 3 4 5 6 7 8 9 10

Did not live what I value … *Lived according to my values*

	Today's Date: 5/11/96	Return Visit Date:
1. Enjoying Things Alone	1. 2	1.
2. Accomplishing Things Alone	2. 1	2.
3. Talking with Others	3. 3	3.
4. Contentment with Work	4. 3	4.
5. Sensual Experience	5. 1	5.
6. Fun with Others	6. 1	6.
7. Images of a Better Future	7. 1	7.

For Health Care Provider's Use

If additional measurement used, indicate whether:

☒ *Beck Inventory – Short Form or* ☐ *Geriatric Scale*

☐ *Other:* ____________________

The Beck Inventory – Short Form has the following norms:

0 - 4 = None or minimal; 5 - 7 = Mild; 8 - 15 = Moderate; 16+ = Severe

Today's Date	Score	Return Visit Date	Score
5/11/96	19		

Level 2 ICP Assessment – Page 3 (Provider Completes)

Note: After reviewing the patient's responses on pages 1 and 2, complete the following assessment to determine the impact of a patient's symptoms on her/his functioning. Interview the patient to clarify the extent of limitation. The format allows you to rate each area today and again at treatment completion. **Critical areas of functioning are in bold font** and need greater weighting in planning treatment intensity.

Today's Date	Return Visit Date	**Functional Limitations / Severity Ratings:** 0 = Absent/Nonpathological; 1 = Moderate; 2 = Debilitating; 3 = Incapacitating; 4: Imminently dangerous*
5/11/96		
***Severity Rating (0 - 4)**		***Family Limitations*** **(Check if limitation is present)**
1. 1	1. ____	1. ☒ Family dysfunction
2. 0	2. ____	2. ☐ Family dysfunction with substance abuse
3. 0	3. ____	3. ☐ Marital/relationship dysfunction
4. 0	4. ____	4. ☐ **Marital/relationship dysfunction with violent behavior**
***Severity Rating (0 - 4)**		***Work and Productivity Limitations*** **(Check if limitation is present**
1. 0	1. ____	1. ☒ Work dissatisfaction
2. 2	2. ____	2. ☒ Work performance problems
3. 0	3. ____	3. ☐ Educational performance deficits
4. 0	4. ____	4. ☐ **Inadequate survival skills**
***Severity Rating (0 - 4)**		***Social Limitations*** **(Check if limitation is present)**
1. 0	1. ____	1. ☐ **Assaultiveness**
2. 0	2. ____	2. ☐ Manipulativeness
3. 2	3. ____	3. ☒ Social withdrawal
4. 1	4. ____	4. ☒ Oppositionalism
5. 1	5. ____	5. ☒ Uncommunicativeness
6. 1	6. ____	6. ☒ Verbal aggressiveness
***Severity Rating (0 - 4)**		***Emotional Experiencing Limitations*** **(Check if limitation is present)**
1. 0	**1.** ____	**1.** ☐ **Self-mutilation**
2. 0	**2.** ____	**2.** ☐ **Substance abuse**
3. 1	3. ____	3. ☒ Hopelessness
4. 1	**4.** ____	**4.** ☒ **Suicidal thoughts/behavior**
***Severity Rating (0 - 4)**		***Psychobiological Limitations*** **(Check if limitation is present)**
1. 1	1. ____	1. ☒ Altered sleep
2. 1	2. ____	2. ☒ Decreased concentration
3. 1	3. ____	3. ☒ Decreased frustration tolerance
4. 1	4. ____	4. ☒ Dysphoric mood
5. 1	**5.** ____	**5.** ☒ **Mood lability**
6. 1	**6.** ____	**6.** ☒ **Psychomotor agitation**
7. 1	**7.** ____	**7.** ☒ **Psychomotor retardation**
8. 0	**8.** ____	**8.** ☐ **Concomitant medical condition**
9. 0	9. ____	9. ☐ Medical treatment noncompliance
10. 0	**10.** ____	10. ☐ **Inadequate health care skills**

Using the MAQ

The following guidelines will help you use the MAQ protocol successfully.

1. **Assess patient history of use of antidepressants.**

The first sections of the MAQ enable the patient to summarize pertinent information regarding her/his prior and current experience with antidepressant medication. Patients often have tried an antidepressant previously. Those who have no prior experience may have friends or loved ones who have tried antidepressant medications. You may save considerable time and energy by identifying patients with histories of successful antidepressant treatment. **Patients with a positive response in the past often prefer to re-start the "proven" medication.** The provider does not need to spend as much time with remaining areas of the MAQ with these patients.

Patients who report histories of unsuccessful treatment are at higher risk for treatment failure. Spend more time planning with these patients. Help the patient recall specific information about any previous medication trials. Avoid a blaming attitude. Focus on reassuring the patient. **Identify how the present treatment plan will address the problems encountered in the previous negative experience.** Patients with negative prior experiences often benefit from a brief supportive phone appointment two or three days after the start of medication.

2. **Assess patient interest in using medications.**

When a patient does not have a strong interest in medication treatment, explore psychotherapeutic treatment as an alternative. A patient may develop a stronger interest in medication treatment after several weeks of behavioral treatment. This section of the MAQ also asks the patient to identify specific benefits desired from use of antidepressant medication. Knowing these desired outcomes, you are ready to **help the patient find a positive focus for evaluating the success of medication treatment**. Usually, patients are not equally troubled by each symptom of depression. For example, a patient in a high stress job may be particularly concerned about concentration difficulties. A parent with young children may be most concerned about irritability and frequent crying. Patients can usually identify a "target benefit" when you ask, "What would you most like the medication to help you with--your ___ or ___?" **Asking a patient to focus on slight improvements in this target area may prevent the patient from over-focusing on undesirable side effects.** Additionally, information about the patient's initial target benefit may help a prescriber select specific medications. Patients may select new target benefits after initial targets respond to treatment.

3. **Address patient beliefs about medications.**

A checklist of beliefs about medication is incorporated into the MAQ. Patients usually require only 2 or 3 minutes to read the items and to indicate which beliefs might influence antidepressant therapy. Encourage the patient to note beliefs that are weak as well as strong. **Discussion of all endorsed beliefs--weak or strong--will facilitate successful antidepressant treatment**. Discuss the endorsed beliefs with the patient collaboratively. Your approach needs to be one that says to the patient, "I understand your beliefs and I am curious about how you came to hold these beliefs." The following questions are usually acceptable to patients.

- "Is this belief based on an experience you have had?"
- "Did a friend or loved one suggest this belief to you?"
- "Are any of your personal experiences inconsistent with this belief?"

- "Does holding this belief help you or hold you back at the present moment?"

You can present additional evidence as needed to help the patient realistically evaluate the validity of an endorsed belief. You may note that there are many "gray areas" involved in the decision to use anti-depressants. Avoid arguments about "right" and "wrong." Offer factual information to help the patient more correctly evaluate a belief that interferes with successful use of medications. When a patient's belief is founded upon factual information, you may help the patient feel more empowered to respond to the belief with autonomy and choice. For example, a patient may endorse the belief, "My family would not want me to use a medication like this." After determining that this belief has validity in terms of the person's experience, you might note that the person probably has the right to keep some things about his own life private. You might then ask if using an antidepressant might be one of those private areas.

4. **Assess patient attitudes toward specific side effects and readiness to use strategies for coping with possible side effects.**

Explain to the patient that there is "bad news" and "good news" in starting antidepressant therapy. The "bad news" is, of course, the initial experience of troubling side effects. The "good news" is the beneficial effects within 2 to 6 weeks of starting the medication. The second page of the MAQ allows you to assess which side effects would be most distressing for your patient. It also offers practical strategies for coping with those side effects. **Avoid selecting a medication with a side effect that interacts with an area of vulnerability for a particular patient.** Select a medication with side effects which the patient can likely tolerate. Then, educate the patient about potential side effects. Explain that most side effects decrease significantly over time. **Give the patient a choice concerning building slowly or quickly toward a therapeutic dose.** This may help the patient feel more empowered to cope with side effects. Help the patient identify a specific strategy for each anticipated side effect. Always use the MAQ as a reference in discussing side effects and planning specific coping strategies.

5. **Assess basic knowledge about antidepressant therapy.**

Depressed patients often have difficulties with concentration and memory, and primary care visits where antidepressant therapy is initiated are typically brief. **The MAQ concludes with four critical messages** about antidepressant medications. Patients who are able to recall these four units of information are more likely to adhere to medications than patients who do not (Lin, et al., 1994). These messages include: (1) It will take 2 to 3 weeks for you to begin to experience beneficial effects from the medication; (2) You will need to take the medicine every day; (3) Stop the medicine only when you decide with your provider that it is time to stop; and (4) Call the clinic if you are concerned about an unpleasant sensation that you think might be related to your medication. These messages are again repeated in the booklet *Using Medications Successfully*.

MAQ Assessment: An Example

Sam was a 42 year old attorney in a highly stressful job. He had received a "demotion" several months ago. Sam worried excessively about finances and meeting his deadlines at work. He explained, "I just can't turn my mind off." Sam reported a successful response to antidepressant treatment in an initial episode of depression "about 5 years ago" at the time of a divorce. He had used a more sedating antidepressant, which helped him with sleep, but had annoying side effects. Sam was very worried about side effects. He described a highly pressured work situation. Also, he felt his current spouse would see him as "weak" if he told her he was taking an antidepressant. Sam told his doctor, "I just can't be 'doped up' at home or at work. I'm already in trouble with my boss and I can hardly function now. I'll gladly pay for any medicine that can help me without giving me a lot of side effects." Sam's responses to the Medication Assessment Questionnaire are indicated on the following sample MAQ.

Sam's responses to the MAQ helped Dr. Brubakken obtain critical information quickly and use it to plan effectively. Dr. Brubakken helped Sam reconsider his beliefs about medications and plan effective strategies for coping with anticipated side effects. Dr. Brubakken recommended a medication with minimal side effects. Also, he asked Sam to phone his office to report his progress every three days during the first nine days of treatment, as Sam was mildly high risk for antidepressant treatment failure.

Sam adhered successfully to his medication and behavioral plans. He returned to the clinic for a visit with Dr. Brubakken two weeks later. Assessment on the Level 1 form indicated significant improvement. He felt more calm and confident. He was using more coping strategies. Specifically, he had started jogging and reading the newspaper on a daily basis. He reported increased productivity at work and more enjoyment in social situations. He saw no need for frequent follow-up. Dr. Brubakken asked him to return for a follow-up assessment four to six weeks later.

Sample: MAQ Assessment

ICP Medication Assessment Questionnaire – Page 1

Dear Patient: Your answers to the following questions will assist you and your primary care provider in developing an effective treatment plan.

Patient:	Provider(s):	Today's Date:
Sam Baker	Brubakken	11/18/95

Have you used an antidepressant medication previously? ☒ Yes ☐ No

If Yes, what medication did you use? Don't remember - something that ended with "ine"

When? 1991 - during divorce

For how long? 3 months

Did you have any side effects? ☒ Yes ☐ No

If Yes, what? Very dry mouth, constipation

How much did you benefit from the medication? Use a scale ranging from 0 to 100%, where 0 is "feeling very bad" and 100% is your "normal." How much *did* you improve when you used this medicine? 70%

Are you taking an antidepressant medication now? ☐ Yes ☒ No

If Yes, what medication are you taking? ______

When did you start taking this medication? ______

What symptoms have not yet improved? ______

Are you having any troubling side effects with this medicine? ☐ Yes ☐ No

If Yes, what? ______

How much have you benefited from the medication? Use a scale ranging from 0 to 100%, where 0 is "feeling very bad" and 100% is your "normal." How much improved are you right now? ______

Do you want to take an antidepressant medication? ☒ Yes ☐ No

If yes, what specific symptoms do you want the medication to address?

Sleep, nerves, concentration

Sometimes we have beliefs about medications that make using medications successfully more difficult. Put an "X" by any of the following statements that you believe, even a little, concerning medications or drugs prescribed by doctors for treatment of anxiety and depression.

	X	Belief
1.	☒	These kinds of drugs are not the answer to problems in one's life.
2.	☒	These kinds of drugs are a crutch.
3.	☐	I would be the one to get severe side effects.
4.	☐	I should be able to get by without using these kinds of drugs.
5.	☐	I could get addicted.
6.	☒	My family would not want me to use these kinds of drugs.
7.	☒	I will not be able to work if I take these kinds of drugs.
8.	☐	These kinds of drugs are overused.
9.	☒	It is harmful to take too many different kinds of drugs.
10.	☒	These kinds of drugs should not be taken long-term.
11.	☐	Drugs that doctors prescribe for anxiety and depression are dangerous.

ICP Medication Assessment Questionnaire – Page 2		
Antidepressant medications often have side effects. Following is a list of common side effects and strategies for coping effectively with the side effects. Side effects tend to lessen after several weeks of use of a medication. **Put an "X" by any side effect that you would have difficulties tolerating.**		
Side Effect		**Coping Strategy**
1. ☐	Dry Mouth	Drink plenty of water, chew sugarless gum, & use sugarless drops.
2. ☒	Constipation	Eat more fiber-rich foods or take a stool softener.
3. ☒	Drowsiness	Get fresh air and take frequent walks. Try taking your medicine earlier in the evening. If you are taking your medicine in the day ask you doctor if you can take it at night.
4. ☐	Wakefulness	Take medications early in the day. Learn more about insomnia. Take a warm bath and have a light snack before bed.
5. ☐	Blurred Vision	Remind yourself that this will be a temporary difficulty. Contact your doctor if it persists.
6. ☒	Dizziness	Get up more slowly; drink plenty of fluids. If you are worried, call your doctor.
7. ☒	Feeling Speeded Up	Tell yourself, "This will go away within three to five days." If not, call your doctor or nurse.
8. ☒	Sexual Problem	Talk with your doctor.
9. ☐	Nausea or Appetite Loss	Take the medicine with food. Eat small healthy meals.
The following information is important. Do you have any questions about any of these instructions? (1) It will take 2 to 3 weeks for you to begin to experience beneficial effects from the medication. (2) You will need to take the medicine every day. (3) Stop the medicine only when you decide with your provider that it is time to stop. (4) Call your doctor if you are concerned about an unpleasant sensation that you think might be related to your medication.		

Summary And Helpful Hints

This chapter provides forms and protocols to help you improve your assessment of depressed patients. As you evaluate the usefulness of the suggested techniques, keep the following points in mind.

1. Using accurate and efficient depression assessment methods allows you to select an appropriate initial treatment and modify your level of care as needed during the course of treatment.
2. The ICP offers two levels of assessment: one for patients with mild depression and one for patients who are more severely depressed. The Level 1 assessment form is adequate for most primary care patients.

3. You may need to adjust your assessment approaches for use with older patients, who may prefer that you say "the blues" rather than "depression."
4. Using the MAQ with patients may yield considerable savings of both time and other health care costs in the near future (e.g., fewer premature medication stops, fewer medication switches).
5. While a few patients may balk at completing the ICP questionnaires, most will view it as an important part of their treatment.

References

Cunningham, L.A., Borison, R.L., Carman, J.S., Chouinard, G., Crowder, J.E., Diamond, B.I., Fischer, D.E., & Hearst, E. (1994). A comparison of venlafaxine, trazadone, and placebo in major depression. *Journal of Clinical Psychopharmacology*, *14*(2), 99-106.

Fontaine, R., Ontiveros, A., Elie, R., Kensler, T.T., Roberts, D.L., Kaplita, S., Ecker, J.A., & Fahidi, G. (1994). A double-blind comparison of Nefazodone, Imipramine, and placebo in major depression. *Journal of Clinical Psychiatry*, *55*(6), 234-241.

Lin, E.H.B., Von Korff, M., Katon, W., Bush, T., Simon, G.E., Walker, E., & Robinson, P. (1994). The role of the primary care physician in patients' adherence to antidepressant therapy. *Medical Care*, *33*(1), 67-74.

Chapter 4

Clinical Management by the Primary Care Provider: An Overview

This chapter suggests specific strategies for improving clinical management services in the primary care setting. We present information to help you improve behavioral and pharmacological treatment within the confines of the "15-minute hour." Additionally, this chapter provides information to help you work with on-site and externally located mental health providers. In this chapter, you will learn the following.

- The "Quality Triad" of primary care clinical management
- Strategies that foster patient commitment to treatment
- Information to help you improve pharmacological treatment
- Techniques for changing levels of care, including what to say to patients who are tapering from antidepressant therapy
- How to make and support a relapse prevention plan

Instructions for Speed Readers: Allow 20 minutes to read and study this chapter. Critical information is printed in bold in all sections of the chapter. Slow down for a more careful study of sections that present information on strategies that are "new to you."

The Quality Triad

In the primary care setting, clinical management of depression always involves attention to the patient's life circumstances and the patient's ability to cope effectively. Depressed patients need help in responding to acute stressors (e.g., job loss) and in addressing lifestyle problems (e.g., chronic marital conflict). Antidepressant medications can improve depressed mood, increase energy and improve sleep and appetite. Behavior change strategies help patients address important life problems or lifestyle issues that trigger or maintain depression. Typical examples include lack of daily exercise, failure to engage in leisure or recreational activities, withdrawal from social and family get-togethers, and "workaholism." Most studies show that when these behavioral risk factors are addressed, the likelihood of a future episode of depression decreases dramatically. Effective clinical management requires primary care providers to be skillful in targeting key areas for behavior change *and* in prescribing antidepressants within the confines of the "15 minute hour." **The "Quality Triad" involves attention to three critical processes in behavioral *and* pharmacological treatment. These are:**

- Education
- Collaborative Planning
- Monitoring

Chapter 5 introduces the Coping Plan, which is a format to help you apply the Quality Triad in your day-to-day treatment of depressed patients.

Education

Patient education materials can be used to support interventions focused on problem-solving, lifestyle change and antidepressant treatment. Depressed patients often suffer from concentration and memory problems. A depressed patient may nod in agreement to a primary care provider's advice or information concerning medication use, yet fail to remember this after the appointment. An educational booklet in combination with a written treatment plan provides the depressed patient with structure needed to comply with treatment and make significant changes in behavior.

Educational materials need to be interactive. Interactive materials invite the patient to respond in writing to questions posed or exercises suggested in the materials. Interactive materials used in the ICP model include two booklets, (*Seven Ways to Cope*, *Using Medications Successfully*) and a more comprehensive patient workbook *Living Life Well: New Strategies for Hard Times.*

An effective educational strategy involves (1) asking patients to read educational materials and (2) requesting that patients bring written responses to educational materials to follow-up appointments. This strategy improves the probability that the patient will read the materials and complete exercises suggested by materials. In addition, this clinical management strategy helps the provider save time. Providers can read patient written responses quickly, which allows more time for collaborative development of treatment plans.

Using patient education strategies not only de-mystifies depression for your patient but helps enlist him or her as a "partner" in the treatment process. The biopsychosocial model is a good conceptual framework for primary care clinical management. The model can be used as an educational tool in all phases of treatment. In starting treatment, you may explain to a patient that depression influences all aspects of human functioning. Depression affects the human biologically, psychologically and behaviorally. Further, depression occurs most often in response to specific stresses, such as illness or loss. Stress, like depression, affects the entire person. Interventions can target the depressed person's biology, mental activity, or behavior. The model allows the patient to choose among equally effective treatments: antidepressant therapy and/or behavioral interventions.

You may use the biopsychosocial model to help you explain why combining medication and behavioral treatment may be useful when symptoms are more severe. Most patients grasp the idea of how medications and behavioral treatments have an additive impact.

There are other ways to introduce the biopsychosocial model to patients. For example, you may explain to the patient that "depression is a problem in living" (Lewinsohn, 1984). When life "serves up" many problems to a person, her/his physiology changes. Of course, the body and mind change and behavioral adaptations may be ineffective. Medications target the bodily symptoms or physiologically experienced symptoms of depression, which include poor sleep, appetite changes, concentration difficulties, irritability, and fatigue. Behavioral interventions improve mental symptoms, including positivity of thoughts, hopefulness, concentration, and calmness. Also, behavioral interventions improve functional impairments associated with depression. Functional impairments include use of avoidant coping strategies to solve problems of living and lack of participation in activities that bring pleasure, a sense of connection with others, and a sense of mastery. **Drawing the "mind-body-behavior circle" (Figure 4.1) on a prescription pad may help the patient to understand the mechanics of depression and how various interventions will help.**

Drawing the depression spiral (Figure 4.2) may help focus the patient on the concept of how mind, body, and behavior interact to improve or worsen symptoms of depression. You may offer several examples to the patient of how even a simple intervention can have dramatic positive

Figure 4.1: Biopsychosocial Model of Depression

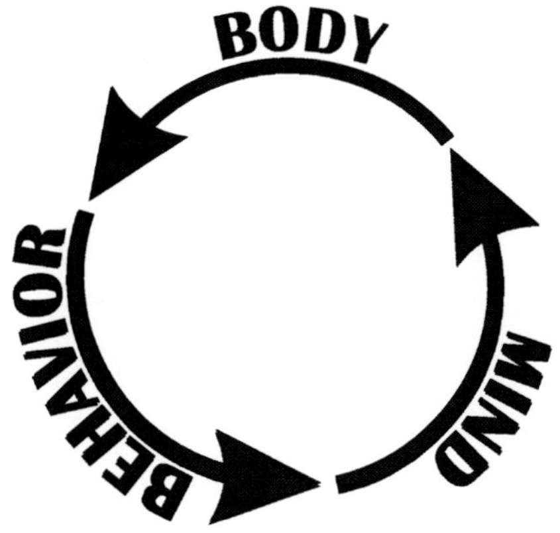

effects. Explain that a depressed person who follows through on a plan to call a friend may enjoy the conversation and decide to accept an invitation to dinner. The enjoyment experienced in the phone call may result in an "energy boost." The person may decide to prepare a dessert to take to the dinner which provides a sense of accomplishment. This behavior change may help create more positive thoughts. At the dinner party, she may have interactions with others that are enjoyable and have positive effects on her biology and mood. The depression spiral can also be drawn on a prescription pad and given to the patient as a reminder of the biopsychosocial model.

Figure 4.2: The Depressive Spiral

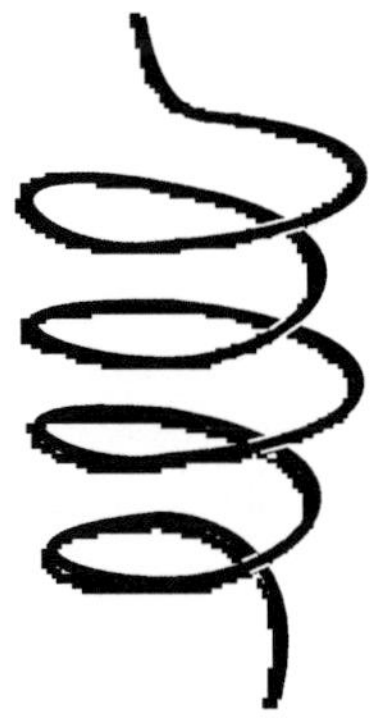

Drawing the "mind-body-behavior circle" or the "depression spiral" makes your educational work with the depressed patient multi-sensory. Adding the visual aspect to patient education improves comprehension. Additionally, drawing educational aids gives providers something to do with their hands other than write prescriptions when depressive symptoms are not severe enough to warrant antidepressant treatment.

Collaborative Treatment Planning

Collaborative treatment planning fosters a commitment to compliance and builds buy in. Patients are much more likely to implement treatment plans that evolve from cooperative efforts. The patient-provider relationship is becoming more collaborative, and patients expect providers to offer treatment options and discuss advantages and disadvantages of each option. Even more dependent depressed patients benefit when the clinical management process requires the patient to make decisions and commit to plans. **Whether the treatment is behavioral or pharmacological, the patient and provider need to make a jointly agreed upon plan.** The strongest plans evolve from interactions where the process flows from a general goal (e.g., change a daily activity to improve mood; start an antidepressant medication) to a specific plan (e.g., spend 20 minutes reading a good book after work; take medication X at X dosage for the next 7 days) that is revised as necessary by both parties (e.g., change into comfortable clothes, sit in favorite chair and read 20 minutes; take medication X at X dosage with food in the morning for the next 7 days and reward self for remembering with a dinner out on Sunday).

Collaboration continues even after you establish a highly specific treatment plan. **Remember to check the patient's level of commitment to the plan as a final step in planning.** You accomplish this by asking the patient about her/his perception of the "attainability" of the goal. We recommend the use of scaling questions. The following is an example of a scaling question that helps you clarify the patient's subjective sense of confidence about actually implementing your plan.

> *"How confident are you that you can actually implement the plan we just made? Use a scale of 0% confidence to 100% confidence to describe your confidence in our plan at this moment."*

Using scaling questions like this can help providers detect situations where a behavioral health plan is likely to fail. **When a patient indicates less than 70 or 80% confidence, change the plan in a way that will foster more confidence. A strategy for making changes to plans expediently involves "cutting the plan in half."** For example, you might say, "Maybe we were planning for you to do too much this week. How about we cut the plan in half (e.g., have you take two walks instead of four walks)?" Scaling questions are also helpful in evaluating the viability of a medication treatment plan. Asking your patient to rate her/his confidence in sticking with a medication in spite of initial side effects can reveal whether there is a significant risk of non-compliance.

Even with the best collaboration, patients sometimes fail to complete the planned treatment. When this occurs, "collaborative" planning requires you to share the responsibility for the failure of the plan. Sharing the burden with the patient helps the patient "open up" to more cooperative planning with you. Following are phrases you might use when patients fail to adhere to a treatment plan.

> *"Well, I guess we didn't completely anticipate what could happen when we made our plan."*
> *"You know, I really should have seen the weakness in the plan."*
> *"I guess part of the plan worked and part didn't. We were partially successful."*
> *"Let's learn from this."*
> *"We can make a stronger plan now."*

Monitoring

Always follow-up on treatment plans. If the plan is behavioral, ask about the specific plan made in the last visit. **Ask questions in a way that helps the patient "paint a picture" of what happened when she/he implemented the plan.** Acknowledge the patient for implementing any part of the plan. Behavior change is difficult even when patients are not depressed. Behavior change by depressed patients is worthy of a strong, sincere compliment from you.

Initiation of antidepressant therapy is really a behavior change, as well. Monitor the patient's success in starting medications carefully. Ask specific questions, such as: "How many days did you remember to take the medication?" or "When you remembered to take the medication, what did you use as a clue?" Be positive. Numerous patients may avoid follow-up if they believe you will criticize them or be disappointed by their failure. When patients avoid needed follow-up, symptoms often worsen. Eventually, treatment becomes more time-intensive and costly.

Monitor improvement in symptoms that are associated with the patient's implementation of the treatment plan. **Depressed patients have difficulty with positively acknowledging themselves. You have many opportunities to provide positive input as you provide on-going monitoring.** Remember to help patients see the "gray" areas represented by "small changes" or partial successes in implementing treatment plans.

Monitoring procedures are important in all phases of treatment. The acute phase of treatment usually lasts three to eight weeks. The objective of monitoring during the acute phase is to determine the viability of initial treatment plans. The maintenance or continuation phase of treatment proceeds from the second or third month to the eighth month of treatment. Monitoring efforts become less intensive. The objective is to assess the completeness of a patient's recovery. The relapse prevention phase of treatment may overlap with the maintenance or continuation phase. **The purpose of relapse prevention monitoring is to determine the patient's ability to incorporate strategic behavioral changes into her or his lifestyle.** Relapse prevention monitoring needs to continue for one year after the initial diagnosis of an episode of major depression.

Behavioral Treatment

Most depressed patients are experiencing problems in their lives and are employing ineffective strategies for solving on-going problems. Ineffective strategies are usually strategies that help the patient temporarily avoid the problem, but make it worse in the long run. When a patient comes to the primary care provider with symptoms of depression, he or she is really saying, "I am suffering, and my attempts to cope are not working for me." Your job involves helping the patient plan new ways to cope with problems of living. When patients learn to use effective coping strategies to address problems of living, symptoms of depression lessen. Burns (1991) notes that better coping appears to moderate the impact of life stress. Mynors-Wallis and Gath (1995) report that **depressed primary care patients who receive training in problem-solving from primary care providers improve as much as depressed patients who use antidepressant medications.** Helping patients develop effective coping strategies is a very powerful treatment. In other investigations, patients starting antidepressant therapy reported that their providers often suggested coping strategies (Robinson, et al., 1994). Approximately 30 to 40% of patients reported interactions with physicians concerning use of the following coping strategies.

- Planning pleasurable activities
- Solving life problems
- Identifying and changing depressive thoughts
- Planning activities that boost confidence

You can raise that percentage to 90% or even 100% in your practice.

Treatment based on the use of coping strategies is perhaps even more critical for patients with milder forms of depression because antidepressant therapy does not appear to be an effective treatment for minor depression. For example, research indicates that providing patients with minor depression access to an on-site liaison psychiatrist does not result in significantly better outcomes than those from usual treatment, even though medication adherence rates improve significantly (Katon, et al., 1995). Antidepressant therapy, even at AHCPR guidelines, is not associated with improved coping. Unfortunately, minor depression is the diagnosis given to half or more of the depressed patients seen by primary care physicians. Minor depression in medical patients may not be completely "minor," as it is associated with significant losses in role functioning and greater use of medical services. Brief behavioral treatment delivered in the primary care clinic does significantly improve use of coping skills and can reduce severity of depressive symptoms (Robinson, 1996). Finally, research and consumer "focus group" studies suggest that patients with milder forms of depression view treatment that focuses on coping strategies to be highly satisfying and "empowering."

Behavioral Techniques for the 15-Minute Hour

Since primary care providers have limited time for enlisting the active participation of depressed patients, brief counseling approaches need to be used. De Shazer and Kim-Berg (1986) developed a counseling approach that seems particularly well suited for 15-minute therapeutic encounters. Solution-focused treatment relies on the use of questions that help the patient shift from a focus on "problems" to a focus on "solutions." Table 4.1 presents definitions and examples of solution-focused questions. These questions help the busy provider gently and clearly interrupt a depressed patient's lamentation.

Several other techniques are useful in working with patients on coping and lifestyle problems. These include the following.

1. **Identify the patient's problem-solving strengths**, e.g., "hard worker," "smart," "good observer," "good self-control."
2. **Compliment the patient.** Direct your compliments to the patient's strengths and to the patient's efforts to solve problems. Your positive input may be the only compliment the patient receives that day. To the patient who uses his "self-control to get to work," you might respond, "Good for you. I wish all of my patients had such good control!" Be attentive and genuine.

Commitment

The most effective behavioral intervention is one that defines several small goals designed to improve the patient's mood and/or life circumstance. The main rule in this type of intervention is to "*accumulate small positives.*" Experiencing success in achieving even small goals can have a dramatic impact on depressed mood." Behavioral plans need to be very specific. A plan to "go to a movie" is not specific. A plan to go to the 2:00 matinee at the neighborhood theater on the next Saturday of the month is specific. Specific plans can be written briefly, for example: "2:00 movie this Saturday, Moore Theater." In general, behavioral plans need to be small in order to be realistic. This is because the depressed patient is low on energy, as well as interest and enthusiasm. A plan to "be a better mother" is neither small nor realistic. Alternatively, "read a chapter from the children's favorite book each night at 7:00 for the next three nights" is small and realistic. Again, these types of plans can be written briefly, for example, "Read *Shiloh* to children, 7 PM, 3 nights." After you establish a plan or goal with a patient, check the patient's perception about the "attainability" of the goal. Scaling questions discussed earlier in this chapter are quite useful in assessing patient commitment to treatment plans.

Table 4.1
Solution-Focused Therapy Techniques

Question	Definition	Example
Exception Questions	A question that asks the patient to evaluate exceptions to the problem, or times when the problem was not present or was less troublesome.	"Can you think of a time in your life when you felt better? What was different then?"
Miracle Questions	A question that asks the patient to consider a hypothetical or imagined solution to a problem.	"If you went to sleep tonight and a miracle happened and you no longer had this problem, what would you notice the next day?" "What would you notice first that would tell you the miracle had happened?" "Next?"
Coping Questions	A question that asks the patient to identify specific coping strategies s/he uses to stabilize adjustment to difficult life circumstances.	"How, when things are so bad, are things not worse?" "What is it that you do to cope?"

Pharmacological Treatment

The AHCPR Guidelines for Treatment of Depression in Primary Care offer excellent suggestions for selecting medications, dosing, augmenting, switching, tapering, and establishing maintenance treatment regimes in antidepressant therapy. When you and your patient decide that medications need to be included in the treatment plan, we recommend that you use the AHCPR Guideline as a technical reference. Chapters 3, 4, and 5 in this book will prepare you to provide effective assessment and clinical management services to depressed patients. The "coping model" can help you work with patients to achieve a high level of adherence and satisfaction with pharmacological treatment. **Patients need help in this area because medication use is a *new* behavior that is difficult to initiate.** This is particularly true for patients who are experiencing substantial life circumstance problems. As a group, depressed patients have significant problems with concentration, memory and follow-through. As many as half of the patients started on antidepressant therapy in the primary care setting stop treatment prematurely during the first month. This section presents information to help you apply a coping strategy approach to insure successful use of medications.

Anticipating Problems

Success with antidepressant therapy depends on a thorough initial assessment and development of a written plan addressing important areas of concern. **Some patients are more at risk for poor outcomes. These include patients with bipolar disorder, patterns of alcohol dependence or histories of substance abuse.** Always rule out bipolar disorder prior to initiating antidepressant treatment. Additionally, ask the patient about current and past patterns of use of alcohol or other mind-altering substances. **Suicidal patients also present certain challenges.** Antidepressant treatment may or may not be helpful to patients with prominent suicidal ideation, as not all suicidal patients are depressed. Additionally, certain classes of antidepressant medications can provide a lethal method for suicidal behavior. Therefore, evaluate suicidal patients thoughtfully and consider use of strategies to assure patient safety, such as those suggested by Chiles and Strosahl (1995). These include:

- Assure that the available means for suicidal action have been removed from the patient's home.
- Form a 24 hour crisis plan with the patient.
- Reduce the length of anti-depressant prescription to 7 days.
- Schedule brief follow-up phone contacts with the patient every other day.

Optimal Patient Evaluation and Education

Patient education needs to flow from evaluation of a patient's readiness to use medications successfully. In Chapter 3, we presented a medication assessment protocol (i.e., the Medication Assessment Questionnaire or MAQ). You may save time in educational efforts when you have information that helps you focus your educational work with patients. The questions in Table 4.2 will help you target educational efforts. To assess beliefs that might obstruct treatment, have the patient complete the MAQ, which can be reproduced from Appendix B. In the long run, you may save time by discussing these beliefs and presenting evidence for the patient to use in re-evaluating unsubstantiated beliefs prior to staring treatment. Explain to the patient that knowing more about antidepressant medications enhances patient success. Take time to help the patient plan for any anticipated side effects.

Table 4.2
Potential Targets for Patient Education

Target	Example Questions
Patient's Beliefs	*"Let's look at your beliefs for a moment."*
Patient's Basic Knowledge about Antidepressants	*"While your doctor probably told you these things, I want to make sure that you know that: (1) It will take 2 to 3 weeks for you to begin to experience beneficial effects from the medication; (2) You will need to take the medicine every day; (3) Stop the medicine only when you decide with your doctor that it is time to stop; (4) Call your doctor if you are concerned about an unpleasant sensation that you think might be related to your medication."*
Patient's Skills for Tolerating Side Effects	*"How have you been able to tolerate other types of medications that have side effects, e.g., the upset stomach that you may experience with antibiotics or pain medicines?" "What have you used in the past to cope with ___ (dry mouth, feeling 'speeded up,' constipation)?"*

Antidepressant therapy proceeds more smoothly when patients receive educational materials and written instructions. When educational information is available in written form, patients can review the details if and when the need arises. Written information needs to include the medication name, beginning dose, when to take the medication, titration plan, target symptoms the patient plans to monitor, any anticipated side effects and associated coping strategies the patient plans to implement.

Other Guidelines for Pharmacological Treatment

The following guidelines may help you with medication issues.

Guideline 1: Work with the patient to select a tolerable medication and help the patient work toward the target dose with minimal experience of unpleasant side effects. Table 4.3 provides usual therapeutic dosing ranges and estimates of magnitude of side effects for commonly prescribed antidepressants. Thoughtful selection of the initial medication may help you avoid

Table 4.3
Dosing Ranges and Side Effects of Commonly Prescribed Medications

	Therapeutic Dose Range (mg/day)		Side Effects*		
Medication	**Minimal Dose**	**Maximum Dose****	**Sedative Effects**	**Anti-cholonergic Effects**	**Orthostatic Hypo-tension**
Imipramine	75	300	+++	+++	++++
Desipramine	75	300	+	+	++
Nortriptyline	40	200	+	+	++
Trazodone	150	600	++++	0	+
Fluoxetine	10	40	0	0	0
Sertraline	50	150	0	0	0
Paroxetine	20	50	0	0	0

* Magnitude of side effect ranges from 0 = "absent or rare" to ++++ = "relatively common."
**Target Dose is usually one-half of the maximum dose.

problems with compliance and medication switching. Always review the patient's past history of anti-depressant use, looking for areas of side effect "vulnerability." Try to select agents that have a lower profile in these areas. Older patients are more "medication sensitive," and respond to dosages toward the lower end of the ranges presented in Table 4.3. Side effects may be avoided or minimized by use of a slower titration plan. You can always help a patient through a slower start-up period by helping her or him develop and implement a strong behavioral plan.

At present, there is a controversy regarding selection of "newer" versus "older" antidepressant medications. Older and newer medications appear to be equally effective in lessening symptoms of depression. However, newer medications appear to have fewer troubling side effects. Patients are less likely to switch from medications that have fewer side effects (Simon, 1996). Newer medications cost significantly more than older medications. However, there may be significant health care costs associated with the higher rates of switching medications associated with use of older medications. Many patients come to their providers with considerable information (and misinformation) about types of antidepressant medications. You will need to work with the complexities presented by discovery of newer and more palatable medications.

Guideline 2: Help the patient reach a therapeutic level. Table 4.3 provides the usual therapeutic dosages for commonly prescribed antidepressants. **The therapeutic dosage is usually one-half of the maximum dose.** Patients vary in their ability to metabolize antidepressant medications. Consider increasing the patient's dosage if the:

- Patient is not improving and is on a low dose.
- Patient is not recovered, is below the therapeutic dosage *and* is not complaining of side effects.
- Patient is at therapeutic dose, but lower than the maximum *and* still symptomatic.

Guideline 3: Describe the overall course of treatment to the patient. Explain to the patient that she/he will likely use antidepressant medication for 4 to 7 months after a positive response occurs. Additionally, explain that you will consider a change in medication if no positive response occurs after 4 to 8 weeks of treatment. Tell the patient that you will help them develop a plan for tapering when it is time to stop the antidepressant. It is important that you emphasize the role of antidepressant treatment in relationship to behavioral treatment. You might say, "Our job in the next 4 to 7 months is to use the 'window' created by medications to help you learn strategies for decreasing your risk of depression in the future."

Guideline 4: Aggressively track treatment response. Evaluate response to medication on a regular basis. Most medicines work within 8 weeks. If no benefits are obtained, it is time to make a change. Consider switching or augmenting. Also, consider contacting a medication specialist if no significant results have been obtained after 8 to 12 weeks of active treatment. If the patient cannot come for clinic visits every two to four weeks during the initial dosing period, schedule a telephone review. This can easily be done by nurses using a depression symptom checklist. Aggressive follow-up will allow you to make timely changes in antidepressant therapy. The AHCPR medication guideline provides excellent information on switching and augmenting medications during the course of antidepressant therapy. The following guidelines will help you with monitoring.

- Monitor response every 1 to 2 weeks during the first 6 weeks of treatment. (Monitoring may be coordinated by phone.)
- Assess the patient's treatment response in a visit six to eight weeks after diagnosis.
- If the patient is clearly better at the six to eight week visit, continue the medication for six months and then evaluate for discontinuation.
- If the patient is somewhat better at the six to eight week visit, consider an increase in dosage and re-evaluate three to four weeks later.
- If the patient is not better at the six to eight week visit, consider changing the medication regime and re-evaluate three to four weeks later.
- If patient is not better at the twelve week visit, seek a consultation with a medication specialist.

Guideline 5: Consult with a medication specialist when the need arises. Consider calling the medication specialist when either of the following occurs:

- Patient is at a therapeutic dose for twelve weeks and is still symptomatic.
- Patient has any of the following side effects at severe levels: dizziness, speech blockage, urinary retention, weight gain (10+ pounds).

Guideline 6: Look for signs that the patient is ready to discontinue medication. The following are positive signs for cessation of medication:

- Episode of depression is resolved and is the first for patient.
- Social stresses are resolved (e.g., patient has adjusted to job change).
- Medical illness is improved.

Guideline 7: Plan discontinuation with patients. The following suggestions are compatible with AHCPR recommendations:

- Continue patients for 4 to 7 months after the time they are symptom-free or at least 80% improved.
- Taper tricyclic antidepressants by decreasing by 25 mg. to 50 mg. every 1 to 2 weeks.
- Schedule a one-month return visit after tapering begins to check for relapse.
- Ask patients to use a depression symptom checklist to monitor symptoms.
- Stress the importance of following relapse prevention plans concerning use of behavioral coping strategies.

Guideline 8: Consider longer-term treatment (up to 12 months) for treatment-responsive patients who:

- Have chronic depression.
- Have had three or more episodes of major depression.
- Have chronic unresolved social stresses.
- Have chronic pain.

Mileposts for Monitoring Progress

On-going monitoring will help you make timely changes to your clinical management plan. Table 4.4 provides information on how to "station" your progress checks. In general, follow-up visits need not be frequent or lengthy to be effective. All follow-up visits allow you to assess whether you have reached certain "mileposts" in delivering successful treatment. More mildly depressed patients may only require one follow-up visit. This visit needs to occur within four weeks of the initial visit. More severely depressed patients will require more visits over a longer time period.

Discontinuation and Relapse Prevention

The goal of all treatment for depression is to stabilize the patient's mood state, restore functioning to pre-episode levels, and to "wean" the patient off medication or behavioral treatment. Many primary care providers report that recognizing depression and getting patients started on appropriate treatment is not as big of a challenge as knowing when and how to get patients to stop treatment. This is particularly true of medications, because of the "passive" nature of medication-only treatments. This underscores the importance of including behavioral planning and lifestyle change strategies in treatment for patients participating in pharmacotherapy. When behavioral treatment does not accompany pharmacological treatment, patients tend to attribute all improvements to the medication and to develop a corollary belief that he or she "can't live with the medication."

In responsive patients, discontinuation usually occurs six to nine months after treatment began. In discussing a discontinuation plan, develop a specific tapering plan. Give the tapering plan to the patient in written form. Be optimistic and encourage the patient to believe in her/his ability to buffer future stresses through skillful behavioral coping. Cite specific examples of the patient's skill in creating a non-depressed lifestyle in recent months. Also, suggest that the patient

Table 4.4
Sequence of Visits

Follow-up Contact	Phase of Treatment	Weeks or Months After Initial Visit	Goals
First	Acute	2-4 weeks	Behavior Plan Review Side Effects Titrate
Second		6-8 weeks	Review Behavior Plan Assess Side Effects Evaluate Efficacy of Medication Write Relapse Prevention Plan Consider Medication Switch or Augmentation
Third (optional)	Continuation	12-16 weeks if second follow-up indicated positive response	Review Behavior Plan Switch or Augment Update Relapse Prevention Plan
Fourth		16-28 weeks if second follow-up indicated positive response	Review Behavior Plan Tapering Trial Update Relapse Prevention Plan

monitor symptoms of depression weekly during the first month after stopping medication treatment. Further, encourage the patient to intensify behavioral planning efforts when and if symptoms of depression become more significant.

The greatest single cost associated with treating depression is probably failure to prevent recurrences. Repeat episodes are not only preventable, but are often associated with greater functional impairment and may require more intensive treatment. **When you conclude that it is time to discontinue active treatment, take time to complete a written relapse prevention plan with the patient. The plan should addresses the 6-month period after completion of active treatment. Most patients relapse during this critical period.** Relapse prevention plans need to address the following four areas.

- monitoring of symptoms
- practice of coping strategies
- lifestyle goals
- emergency plans

Patients who are participating in antidepressant therapy need to update their relapse prevention plan with you prior to the start of tapering from medication.

You can create a relapse prevention form by simply writing the above areas as sub-headings on your usual medical record charting form. "Monitoring of Symptoms" refers to patient use of a method of assessing symptoms of depression on a regular basis. Some patients will use a depression symptom checklist. Others will prefer something more brief, such as simply rating their mood on a scale of 1 to 10 (1= not good and 10 = very good). It is a good idea for patients to complete monitoring on the same day every week, for example, on Sunday mornings. Suggest that the patient monitor symptoms weekly for the first month after treatment stops and then move to a monthly monitoring practice.

In the "Practice of Coping Strategies" section, indicate the patient's commitment to continue using strategies that have helped during active treatment. For example, a patient who started an exercise program and found it useful will have "continue exercise program" on her/his relapse prevention plan. A patient who started going to a book club group on Friday evenings will have "continue with book group" on her/his relapse prevention plan. When a patient has started strengthening a skill area, such as personal assertion, the relapse prevention plan might read, "Start an assertiveness training class this month."

In the "Lifestyle Goals" section, list 2 or 3 activities the patient plans to pursue in order to firmly establish a pattern of progress. Lifestyle goals, of course, flow from a patient's values. A patient with a pattern of "workaholism" may value adequate rest and set a lifestyle goal of participating in more restful and restorative activities. The "Lifestyle Goals" section of her relapse prevention plan might list these behavioral goals: "Take a long walk in the woods on Saturday mornings, sleep late on Sundays."

The "Emergency Plan" section includes directions for the patient to follow if monitoring results suggest a significant and stable worsening of mood and other symptoms of depression. Planning details in this critical area will need to be individualized, as in other areas. For example, a patient who finds trips to the ocean curative might have "take a trip to the ocean" (or mountains or to a specific friend's home) in the Emergency Plan. Other common elements of the Emergency Plan relate to involving a trusted friend in supporting the patient's use of the relapse prevention plan. Often, patients will have "call Dr. X to review my relapse prevention plan" in the Emergency Plan section.

It is wise to label discontinuation as a "field experiment." Discontinuation is an opportunity for the patient to test her/his behavioral coping strategies in a structured way. Plan a return visit for six months later with the patient and congratulate her/him for staying with the relapse plan.

Depressed primary care patients are vulnerable to relapse even after "graduating" from the 6-month relapse prevention phase of treatment. Given a higher probability of relapse for two years, annual monitoring is probably a time-effective strategy. Annual monitoring supports early detection and treatment. Early onset of treatment is linked with speed of recovery from an episode of depression (Frank, Karp, & Rush, 1993). Additionally, on-going monitoring allows you to re-initiate active treatment quickly--a move that can help you avoid expensive and mildly effective interventions, such as hospitalization.

Involving Behavioral Health Providers

The primary care team is the "hub of the wheel" in the treatment of depression. As such, primary care providers are in the best position to provide on-going monitoring of patients and to decide when and how to use available mental health providers. Table 4.5 summarizes potential services that specific mental health professionals may provide for primary care providers and their depressed patients.

Some of you will have behavioral health professionals available on-site in your clinic. Psychologists have a training background in behavioral health, pharmacotherapy and research. Given the diversity and depth of their training, they are capable of offering a wide range of primary care behavioral health consultation services. Psychologists may help primary care providers complete more extensive assessments and provide more in-depth behavioral treatment

Table 4.5
Roles and Tasks for Mental Health Providers Who Work in Primary Care

Discipline	Role	Tasks
Psychologists	On-going program development and evaluation	Program evaluation Generate accountability information
	Supervision and training	On-going supervision and training of MLTs*
	Patient assessment and treatment	Assessment Behavioral interventions with difficult patients
	Coordination of external mental health and emergency services	Crisis Assessments Triage
Medication Specialists (Psychiatrist, ARNP)	Consultation with primary providers regarding complex patients	Phone and person-to-person consultation with primary care prescribers regarding medically complex or treatment-resistant patients
	Set up system for monitoring of antidepressant refills	Monthly monitoring of antidepressant refills and generation of reports to primary care prescribers Quarterly half-hour workshops
Master's Level Therapist	Delivery of treatment services	Completion of behavioral health treatment protocols, including phone follow-ups with patients. Psychoeducational groups Liaison for community resources

*MLTs: Master's Level Therapists

than is possible when the primary care provider works alone. Psychologists may also assist primary care providers by training and supervising master's level therapists and by setting up outcome assessment programs for the clinic. Primary care providers and on-site psychologists can access medication specialists through "on-demand" phone calls and/or by invitations for periodic on-site case reviews. The category of medication specialist includes psychiatrists, prescribing nurse specialists, psychiatric physician assistants, and, in some areas, clinical pharmacists. Some clinics may be fortunate enough to have weekly or monthly on-site consultation available from psychiatric nurses or psychiatrists. "Curbside consultations" with on-site mental health professionals may occur daily and may be initiated by both primary care and mental health providers. A "knock on the door anytime" policy needs to prevail.

Many primary care providers will not have the much needed benefit of having on-site mental health professionals available. The clinical management system described in this book may still help you improve quality of care for your depressed patients. You can use protocols and forms suggested in this book without having on-site mental health partners. You may also ask mental health professionals in your community with whom you work to use protocols and treatments recommended for mental health providers. Continuity in assessment and treatment is a critical dimension in improving depression treatment outcomes. Create as much continuity as possible with your present resources.

Working with Behavioral Health Care Consultants

Behavioral health care specialists provide consultation and training to primary care providers and direct services to patients. The role of behavioral health consultant may be filled by psychologists or master's level therapists with strong backgrounds in behavioral and pharmacological treatment. You may use behavioral health consultants in the following ways.

- Phone or brief in-person consultation regarding depressed patients
- Brief direct consultations with depressed patients (one to three contacts)
- Delivery of a behavioral treatment package (four to seven contacts)
- Triage for external services, including consultation with medication specialists

You may communicate the nature of your request for assistance using a brief code (e.g., bt for brief treatment and BT for Behavioral Treatment). When you request Brief Treatment, the consultant will help in developing a primary care clinical management plan and return the patient to you for active treatment. When you request Behavioral Treatment, the consultant will implement a behavioral treatment program involving 4 to 7 contacts and return the patient to you with a relapse prevention plan. You will be in charge of monitoring the relapse prevention plan, unless you make other arrangements with your consultant. When you use your behavioral health care consultant for triage, she/he will "keep you in the loop" at all times by charting the patient's progress. **When external treatment is concluded, the behavioral health provider will assure that the patient returns to you with a written relapse prevention plan.**

Working with Medication Specialists

Medication specialists provide consultation, supervision, and training to the primary care provider and the behavioral health consultant. Medication consultation may occur by phone, in direct contact with the patient or with the primary care provider, or in the context of a health care team staff meeting. Only a small minority of depressed primary care patients need a direct consultation with a medication specialist. If you have a medication specialist on-site in your clinic, patients requiring direct consultation will not have to go to an external facility for these services and you can have on-site multi-disciplinary team meetings. An on-site medication specialist can enrich your treatment program by providing didactic presentations on new medications, innovative strategies for dosing and combining medications, the latest information on drug-drug interactions, etc. If you do not have an on-site medication specialist, you may contract for telephone consultation services.

To maximize the impact of medication consultations, formulate a specific question prior to contacting the medication specialist. Relate pertinent information briefly. Over time, consultations will become more relaxed and efficient.

In addition to consultation and training, the medication specialist may help you develop a tracking and profiling system for patients receiving antidepressant treatment. The tracking service needs to identify and follow patients taking antidepressants. Tracking data need to include the following: start date for treatment, type of medication, therapeutic dosage, and planned length of treatment.

In summary, the medication specialist role includes the following responsibilities.

- Availability for phone consultations
- On-going supervision and training of behavioral health consultants concerning medication issues
- Direct consultations with complex patients
- Brief monthly workshops
- Monitoring of antidepressant prescription patterns on selected patients and relating refill information to primary care prescribers

Less than 5 to 10% of depressed primary care patients will need direct consultation with a medication specialist. Reserve direct consultation services for medically complex patients and the small minority of patients who fail to respond to at least two different anti-depressant medications and behavioral treatments.

Working with External Mental Health Providers

The most severely impaired depressed patients may need intensive treatment in an external location. Ideally, this treatment will be consistent with the protocols and forms you are using in the primary care setting. Patients benefit most when care is continuous and seamless. External providers may use group, family or couples sessions in addition to the individual treatment format to help a more seriously depressed patient. Ideally, the external specialist will initiate a coordinated transfer with you or your on-site behavioral health consultant when a patient completes an episode of specialty treatment. The transfer plan should detail the patient's need for follow-up treatment, which, in most instances will be provided exclusively by you, as the primary care provider, and the on-site behavioral health consultant, if one is available. You should monitor patients who are recovering from severe depression thoughtfully. The intensity of your follow-up will depend upon the severity of the patient's initial depression and the degree of recovery during specialty care. More fragile and partially recovered patients should be seen monthly for at least 6 months. Fully recovered patients might be seen at one month, six months, and 12 months after completion of an episode of external treatment.

Summary and Helpful Hints

The "Quality Triad" of primary care clinical management involves patient education, collaborative treatment planning, and monitoring. These three processes are the keys to quality outcomes in treating depressed primary care patients. Review the following points occasionally to help you maintain changes you plan to make in your clinical management of depressed patients.

1. Behavioral treatment planning may be a solo treatment for patients with mild depression.
2. Behavioral treatment needs to accompany pharmacological treatment.
3. Counseling techniques need to fit the 15-minute hour.
4. Use scaling questions to help you assess patient confidence in medication and behavioral treatment plans.
5. Track treatment response aggressively.
6. Track treatment response by phone when feasible.
7. Explain the entire course of treatment to patients at the beginning of treatment and help patients approach medication tapering with confidence.

8. The greatest single cost associated with treating depression is probably the failure to prevent recurrences.
9. Write relapse prevention plans that include plans for monitoring, using coping strategies, working toward specific lifestyle goals, and responding to emergencies.
10. Hold mental health providers accountable for coordinating care with you.

References

Burns, D.D., & Nolen-Hoeksema, S. (1991). Coping styles, homework compliance, and the effectiveness of cognitive-behavioral therapy. *Journal of Consulting and Clinical Psychology, 59*(2), 305-311.

Chiles, J., & Strosahl, K. (1995). *The suicidal patient: Principles of assessment, treatment and case management.* Washington, DC: American Psychiatric Press.

Depression Guideline Panel. (1993). *Depression in primary care: Vol. 1. Detection and diagnosis.* (Clinical Practice Guideline, No. 5, AHCPR Pub. No. 93-0550). Rockville, MD: U.S. Department of Health and Human Services, Public Health Service, Agency for Health Care Policy and Research.

Depression Guideline Panel. (1993). *Depression in primary care: Vol. 2. Treatment of major depression* (Clinical Practice Guideline, No. 5, AHCPR Pub. No. 93-0551). Rockville, MD: U.S. Department of Health and Human Services, Public Health Service, Agency for Health Care Policy and Research.

deShazer, S., Kim-Berg, I., Lipchik, E., Nunnally, E., Molnar, A., Gingrich, W., & Weiner-Davis, M. (1986). Brief therapy: Focused solution development. *Family Process, 25,* 207-221.

Frank, E., Karp, J., & Rush, A.J. (1993). Efficacy of treatments for major depression. *Psychopharmacology Bulletin, 29,* 457-475.

Katon, W., Robinson, P. Von Korff, M., Lin, E., Bush, T., Ludman, E., Simon, G., & Walker, E. (1996). A multifaceted intervention to improve treatment of depression in primary care. *Archives of General Psychiatry.* In press.

Mynors-Wallace, L., Gath, D.H., Lloyd-Thomas, A.R., & Tomlinson, D. (1995). Randomized controlled trial comparing problem solving treatment with amitriptyline and placebo for major depression in primary care. *British Medical Journal, 310,* 441-446.

Robinson, P., Bush, T., Von Korff, M., Katon, W., Lin, E., Simon, G.E., & Walker, E. (1994). Primary care physician use of cognitive behavioral techniques with depressed patients. *Journal of Family Practice, 40*(4), 352-357.

Robinson, P., Katon, W., Von Korff, M., Bush, T., Ludman, E., Simon, G., Lin, E., & Walker, E. (1996). *Use of coping strategies by depressed primary care patients: Results of a randomized controlled trial.* Submitted for publication.

Simon, G. (1996). Personal communication.

Chapter 5

The Integrated Care Program Clinical Management System

This chapter focuses on the Coping Plan, which is a basic structural support for clinical management in the Integrated Care Program. We review critical concepts, describe provider responsibilities and suggest a time table for sequencing of visits. We also describe ICP educational materials and provide an example to illustrate use of the ICP clinical management system. In this chapter, you learn the following.

- How to use the Coping Plan in the initial clinical management visit
- How to use the Coping Plan in follow-up clinical management visits
- How to use ICP educational materials in clinical management visits

---

Instructions for Speed Readers: Allow two hours to read and study this chapter, along with educational booklets and the patient self-help workbook. The educational booklets are presented in the Appendices. The companion self-management workbook is titled *Living Life Well: New Strategies for Hard Times.* **Take time to respond to the Coping Plan questions from the perspective of the patient. Recruit a colleague to role play** a patient with you so that you can practice providing clinical management using the Coping Plan.

Overview of the ICP Clinical Management System

The ICP Clinical Management System involves use of a specific protocol that includes patient educational and treatment planning materials. Additionally, the protocol details responsibilities of the provider and suggests a visit schedule. The system is highly structured in order to help providers develop new patterns of care with a minimal amount of effort. Most patients like this system because it encourages them to become actively involved. There are four critical concepts to convey to patients in clinical management visits. They include the following points.

1. **In the biopsychosocial model, the patient's *behavioral response* to depression is critical.**

   Emphasize the importance of the patient's efforts to cope. Of course, you will be empathetic about the patient's predicament. However, do use the biopsychosocial model to explain to the patient that she/he can make a difference in her/his mood by making small changes to her/his lifestyle. Methods of presenting the biopsychosocial model are presented in Chapter 4.

2. **Behavioral health plans are *experiments* to help the patient discover what lifestyle changes are possible and desirable at this point in her or his life.**

   Explain to the patient that behavioral health plans must be very simple and specific in order to be effective. Also, explain that the patient needs to be 100% confident in behavioral health plans or lifestyle experiments she/he plans with you. Behavioral health planning is hard work. The pay-off is substantial over time.

3. **Using active problem solving strategies will help the patient's mood and level of optimism.**

   Tell the patient that people tend to try to solve problems by avoiding them when they are stressed. Explain that you will help the patient gain psychological strength so that she/he is ready to start using more active, solution-focused strategies again in the near future.

4. **Self-monitoring is crucial.**

   Changes in mood and overall functioning occur in degrees. In order to assess progress, the patient needs to monitor mood or quality of life on a frequent basis. You may recommend that the patient purchase a pocket-sized notebook to record daily mood ratings or quality of life ratings. Also, describe depression as an on-going vulnerability. While episodes of depression do end, they have a way of returning. On-going self-monitoring empowers the patient to detect small changes in mood and respond effectively.

The Coping Plan

The Coping Plan format is the "backbone" of the ICP Clinical Management System. It is a two-page document that helps providers consolidate assessment information, educational booklets and treatment planning. A copy is provided in the Appendix for you to reproduce and use in your daily practice. The Coping Plan enables you to accomplish the following objectives in a time-effective manner that is satisfying to patients.

1. Obtain pertinent information for treatment planning
2. Review educational materials with patients
3. Develop potent behavioral health and medication compliance plans

Ask patients to complete the first page of the Coping Plan prior to the visit. You may give the patient a copy of the ICP Coping Plan prior to your initial clinical management visit or have the patient complete the form in the waiting area after she/he arrives for a clinical management visit. If you and the patient do not have time to start the clinical management protocol in the initial contact, you may give the Coping Plan, ICP depression assessment materials, and the ICP behavioral planning educational booklet to the patient to review at home. When patients are interested in antidepressant treatment, you may also give them the ICP booklet on medications. The ICP educational materials are described in detail in a later section of this chapter.

Give yourself time to develop skill in using the Coping Plan format. If you have a behavioral health consultant in your clinic, ask her/him to give you feedback on your first few efforts to design behavioral plans using the Coping Plan format. **The following guidelines are presented for you to read thoughtfully now and scan just prior to your first experiences in using this approach with depressed patients.**

The Initial Visit

Provider responsibilities in the initial clinical management visit are summarized in Table 5.1. Begin the visit by reviewing the patient's responses to the first page of the ICP Coping Plan. As you evaluate these responses, along with assessment results, you and the patient will select a treatment option. Treatment options are summarized in Table 3.3 (see Chapter 3). The majority of your patients will elect behavioral treatment only or behavioral treatment in conjunction with antidepressant treatment. Some patients will warrant referral to a behavioral health specialist. For a

Table 5.1
Clinical Management Initial Visit

Clinical Management Services	Minutes
Review Assessment Results with Patient	
• Level 1	2 – 4
• Level 2	additional 4
Discuss Patient Responses to Medication Risk Assessment	3
Review and Complete *ICP Coping Plan*	
• Discuss Patient's Responses to Page 1 of Coping Plan	5
• Write Out Plan on Page 2 of Coping Plan	3

small minority, you may need to consult with a medication specialist. Whatever the treatment option, you will use the Coping Plan format to support your clinical management program.

The second page of the Coping Plan is a treatment planning document that helps you and the patient record planned medication and lifestyle goals. Using this format saves you time. This format can be made in duplicate or triplicate forms, so that it serves multiple functions, including documentation of the medical visit and plan, prescription information for pharmacy, and written instructions for the patient. If the patient is not going to use medications, simply cross out the medication section. As you begin to practice the ICP Clinical Management system, use Table 5.1 as a "checklist" to help you complete initial session tasks. Table 5.2 describes specific responsibilities associated with different treatment options.

Interviewing Patients

The Coping Plan format can be used to structure your interview with the patient. Staying with the suggested questions will allow you to move the interview along and cover all areas important to planning in a time-effective manner. Many of the questions will be familiar to you. Others will be new. Devote your interview time to the questions for which the patient's answers are unclear. The following guidelines will help you explore patient responses to each of the Coping Plan questions on page 1 and plan treatment on page 2 of the Coping Plan.

Question 1: *"What is the major problem you would like help with?"*

This question has two purposes. First, it will give you a clear idea as to what you need to do for the patient at that visit. Second, it will help you incorporate the patient's language into your assessment and treatment planning efforts. If a patient wants help with "back pain," your treatment needs to address this request. You may wrap treatment of depression into treatment of back pain by saying that you want to provide treatment for both. If a patient wants help with sleeping, you will plan to help with sleep . . . and depression.

Question 2: "*What do you think is causing your problem?*"

This question will help you adjust your explanation of the biopsychosocial model to the patient's conception of her/his problem. If the patient sees stress as the cause, you may explain how stress "wears down" certain aspects of biological health. If the patient sees

Table 5.2
Initial Visit: Primary Care Clinical Management Activities

ICP Treatment Options	Primary Care Provider Responsibilities
Coping Plan: Behavioral Health Focus Only	Ask patient to read *Seven Ways to Cope* and/or *Living Life Well: New Strategies for Hard Times.* Complete ICP Coping Plan with patient. Plan Return Visit: 2-4 weeks.
Coping Plan: With Antidepressant Therapy	Ask patient to read *Seven Ways to Cope* and/or *Living Life Well: New Strategies for Hard Times* and *Using Medications Successfully.* Ask patient to complete Medication Assessment Questionnaire and review responses with patient. Complete ICP Coping Plan with patient. Plan Return Visit: 2-4 weeks.
Refer to Behavioral Health Consultant	Ask patient to read *Seven Ways to Cope* and/or *Living Life Well: New Strategies for Hard Times.* Complete ICP Coping Plan with patient. Arrange 30-minute visit with BHC. (If starting medication at this visit, ask patient complete Medication Assessment Questionnaire and give patient booklet, *Using Medications Successfully.*) Plan Return Visit: 2 - 8 weeks.
Consultation with Medication Specialist	Phone consultant and discuss issues. Contact patient to discuss results of consultation. (Ask specialist to track refills and provide feedback to you.)
Intensive Treatment by External Mental Health Provider	Ask patient to arrange intensive psychotherapy or to work with the BHC in making arrangements. Plan Return Visit: 2 - 4 weeks. Support Relapse Prevention Plan.

medical illness as the cause, you can explain how biological deficits contribute to behavioral inadequacies in coping with stress. "Build onto" the patient's frame of reference.

Question 3: *"Which of the following do you think is or might be helpful? (Medications, Lifestyle adjustments, Other)"*

For the most part, you will want to center treatment on what the patient believes will be helpful. If a patient is extremely negative about medications and interested in lifestyle change, your plan will focus on lifestyle adjustments.

Question 4: *"What questions do you have about the booklets, Seven Ways to Cope or Using Medications Successfully?"*

If a patient has read the booklets and brought them to the visit, take a moment to thumb through to see what the patient has written in response to exercises in the booklets. Support the patient's efforts. If the patient has not read the booklet(s), ask that she/he do so and that she/he bring the booklet(s) to the next follow-up. When a patient is interested in more information on coping, recommend the book, *Living Life Well: New Strategies for Hard Times.*

Question 5: *"If you have ever had a period of depression before, what helped you start to feel better then?"*

The purpose of this question is to help the patient focus on potential behavioral changes that will yield small, immediate improvements in mood. As you review the patient's answers, ask the patient questions to elicit more details about activities that marked the start of recovery from a previous episode of depression.

Question 6: *"List the activities or thoughts that have helped you feel even a little better in the last two weeks, no matter how brief the time that you felt better (for example, visiting a friend or going for a walk)."*

This question asks the patient to review the past week for "clues" as to what changes in daily activities and/or interpersonal events might generate an upward move on the depression spiral. When a patient has difficulty recalling a time when she/he felt better, stress the wording, "even a little better," or suggest that there may have been times when she/he felt "not quite as bad."

Question 7: *"List the activities you'd be doing or the thoughts you'd be having if you started to feel even a little bit better in the coming weeks."*

This question moves the patient into the framework of generating possible behavioral solutions to lessen depression or improve mood. Encourage the patient to use their imagination. You may even suggest that the patient imagine that "a miracle happened" and she/he felt better. Once the patient moves into the perspective of a "better life," ask her/him to tell you what you or someone else would observe . . . what would she/he be doing differently.

Question 8: *"Who can help you start doing some things that will help you feel better?"*

The patient's response to this question gives you a picture of her/his interpersonal support base. If the patient lists one or more people here, include them as part of the ICP Coping Plan (Page 2) in the Lifestyle and Activities planning section. If the patient is unable to identify a person who she/he believes will support identified behavioral changes, tell the patient you will support her/his change plan. Record your name in the Lifestyle and Activities planning section of the ICP Coping Plan. When a patient has little or no support for behavioral change, it is a good idea to make a brief, supportive call to the patient a few days after the visit. If you are unable to do so, ask another member of the primary care team to provide this support to the patient.

Planning Initial Treatment

Page 2 of the Coping Plan serves two purposes. The first is to provide a written treatment plan for the patient to take home from the appointment. The second is to provide a chart note for the medical record. The second page of the ICP Coping Plan needs to be in a duplicate or triplicate format.

1. "Medication Use" Plan

The medication section lists the most commonly prescribed antidepressants and a format for indicating how the patient is to take the medicine. Additionally, several important educational messages about medication treatment are printed for the patient to review later. These include:

- Most medications are started at a low dosage and increased slowly in order to give your body time to adapt to a new medicine.
- If you are having side effects, you can stay at a specific dosage for a longer period of time until you adapt and then increase the amount.
- Do not stop taking your medication.
- If you have any problems, call your doctor or nurse.

2. "Lifestyle Goals and Activities" Plan:

This section is designed to help you write specific behavioral health plans for the patient. Use these three questions to involve the patient in making a lifestyle change or behavioral health plan.

- What will you do over the next few days to improve your mood?
- What will you do to increase the time you spend with people who can help you feel better?
- Who will support you in working toward these lifestyle changes?

Follow-Up Visits

Provider responsibilities in the follow-up clinical management visits are summarized in Table 5.3. This table also suggests a time frame for completing clinical management activities. Follow-up visits begin with a review of the patient's answers to questions on page 1 of the ICP Coping Plan Follow-Up. As you review the patient's responses to these questions and assessment results, you and the patient will evaluate the effectiveness of your initial treatment plan. The majority of your patients will not require involvement with mental health providers. However, some patients may need the services of a behavioral health specialist. For a small minority, you may improve your outcome by consulting with a medication specialist. Whatever the treatment option, use the Coping Plan Follow-Up format to support your on-going clinical management program.

Table 5.4 suggests a timeline for scheduling follow-up visits with patients you are seeing in the ICP Clinical Management System. Adjust the schedule to meet the follow-up needs of individual patients. At minimum, patients will need two visits and a phone call to assess progress four to six months after diagnosis. Minimal clinical management is reserved for patients with mild symptoms who do not require pharmacological treatment. In some cases, patients and providers may elect to conduct clinical management visits by phone. If a patient mails in responses to the Coping Plan Follow-Up, phone consultations may be brief yet thorough and effective.

Table 5.3
Follow-Up Visits: Primary Care Clinical Management Activities

If Treatment Plan Was:	Then, Follow-Up Tasks Are:	Minutes
Clinical Management: Behavioral Health Focus Only	Look at patient's written responses in the pamphlet. Commend patient on planning efforts. Evaluate impact of Lifestyle Plan on mood. Patient and provider complete Coping Plan Follow-Up format. Evaluate need for further follow-up. If patient is not improving, consider referral to behavioral health consultant and/or discuss use of medications.	15
Clinical Management: With Antidepressant Therapy	Look at patient's written responses in the pamphlets. Commend patient on planning efforts. Evaluate impact of Medication and Lifestyle Plans on mood. Patient and provider complete Coping Plan Follow-Up format. Evaluate need for further follow-up. If patient is not improving, consider referral to the behavioral health consultant and/or consultation with medication specialist.	15
Refer to Behavioral Health Consultant	Review chart note from Behavioral Health Consultant. Plan any needed follow-up.	5
Consultation with Medication Expert	If you have not already discussed results of consultation with patient, do so.	5
Intensive Treatment by External Mental Health Provider	Review evaluation and treatment plan provided by external mental health provider. Plan return visit with patient.	5

Interviewing Patients

As with the Initial Coping Plan, the patient completes page 1 in the waiting room. Begin your follow-up visit by reviewing the patient's responses to page 1 of the Coping Follow-Up Plan. The Follow-Up format helps you quickly assess the patient's adherence to medications, problems with side effects, adherence to lifestyle plans made at the prior appointment, and perceptions about

Table 5.4
Sequence of Visits

Follow-up Contact	Weeks or Months After Initial Visit	Your Tasks
First	2-4 weeks	Coping Plan Follow-up
Second	6-8 weeks	Coping Plan Follow-up Evaluate Efficacy of Medication Consider Medication Switch or Augmentation
Third	12-16 weeks if second follow-up indicated positive response	Coping Plan Follow-up
Fourth	16-28 weeks if second follow-up indicated positive response	Coping Plan Follow-up Tapering trial

what is helping. The format also helps the patient generate information needed to plan additional behavioral or lifestyle changes to improve mood or quality of life. Page 2 of the Follow-Up document is a treatment plan that allows you to address both medication and lifestyle plans in a time-effective manner. It may be used for medical charting, prescription authorization, and providing written instructions to the patient.

Some patients will need only a phone call follow-up, while others will need to come back to the clinic within two weeks. Phone call follow-ups need to be scheduled for a specific time. The following suggestions will help you respond skillfully to patient responses on page 1 of the Coping Plan Follow-Up.

Question 1: *"To what extent have you taken the medication we discussed in our last visit?"*

This question, along with others in this section, allows the patient who is taking medication to indicate the helpfulness of the medicine. Additionally, the patient explains problems she/he is having with the medicine. If the patient's responses indicate a positive response, acknowledge the patient's success and move the interview along. If the patient's responses indicate problems with adherence, explore obstacles in a supportive manner.

Question 2: *"Mark an 'X' beside any difficulties you have had in the past week."*

This item gives the patient an opportunity to use a checklist to indicate experience of possible side effects. Explore any difficulties indicated. Focus your questions about these items on determining the severity of the side effect and the patient's distress concerning it. Patients vary in their tolerance for new and different types of bodily sensations. Work carefully with a patient who is sensitive to bodily sensations and prone to worry. Discuss coping strategies the patient is employing to minimize discomfort associated with the side effect. Empathy is needed here. Reassure the patient that the side effect will diminish over time and suggest additional avenues for coping with bothersome side effects.

Question 3: *"To what extent have you completed the lifestyle changes we discussed in our last visit?"*

Patients are much more likely to adhere to behavioral plans when they believe their provider will follow-up on the plan. Explore the patient's successes in implementing the plan from the last contact. Emphasize that "small steps add up to big steps." When plans have not gone well, explain that "mistakes are a good way to learn." On occasion, the patient's next lifestyle plan may simply be to continue with a previous plan that is highly beneficial. At other times, the next lifestyle plan will be a "revised" version of the prior plan.

Question 4: *"What do you think is helping you the most? (Medications, Lifestyle Adjustments, Other)"*

Determine what the patient sees as helping her/him the most. If the patient indicates medications, emphasize the patient's role in adhering to the prescription. If the patient indicates behavioral changes, compliment the patient on implementing effective plans.

Questions 5, 6, & 7: *"List the activities or thoughts that have helped you feel even a little better in the last two weeks (for example, visiting a friend or going for a walk)." "List the activities you would be doing or the thoughts you would be having if you started to feel a little bit better in the coming weeks." "Who can help you do more things that help you feel better?"*

The patient's responses to these solution-focused questions will help you quickly devise a new behavioral or lifestyle plan with the patient. Use the patient's ideas. Try to create circumstances where friends or loved ones support the patient's behavioral health change efforts.

Question 8: *"What questions do you have about our treatment plan?"*

This question encourages the patient to carefully construct questions prior to the actual visit. Always give the patient an opportunity to pose these questions to you.

Treatment Planning in Follow-Up Visits

On page 2 of the ICP Coping Plan Follow-Up you again have a format for completing both medication and behavioral health or lifestyle plans that can be given to the patient at the end of the visit and placed in the medical chart for documentation of the visit. In the "Medication Use" Section, you may indicate the follow-up plan regarding dosage. Additionally, you may review several more educational messages concerning medications with the patient, as these are provided on the form. These messages include the following.

1. *Remember to use strategies suggested by your doctor for coping with side effects.*
2. *You will be able to evaluate the full benefit of your medication after 4 to 6 weeks of use at your target dose.*

In the "Lifestyle Goals and Activities" section, three statements help you and the patient develop a longer-term behavioral health plan. The following questions will help you involve the patient in effective planning.

1. *Let's come up with a list of two or three activities you will do to create a healthy satisfying lifestyle in the coming month.*

   Remember to be specific in describing planned activities. Also, specify when planned activities will happen.
2. *When will you spend time with people who are helpful to you and who can help you feel better?*

Again, ask the patient to plan, at minimum, one contact per week with one person whose company is enjoyable to them. Social activities are particularly powerful mood elevators.

3. *How will you reward yourself for making these lifestyle changes?*

   Explain that behavioral change is hard work. Help the patient specify a small reward for each week that they complete planned lifestyle changes.

Remember to keep your behavioral plans simple and specific. **In research evaluating the Coping Plan, we noticed a tendency for behavioral plans to become more complex in the follow-up visits. With added complexity, we also noted a tendency for patients to adhere less well to behavioral plans.** When a patient starts to recover, she or he can usually manage more extensive change efforts. However, the patient's confidence is not yet strong. You are advised to restrain patients from committing to behavioral plans that exceed their energy or skill levels.

Patient Education Materials

Unfortunately, most of the available educational materials for depressed patients are not ideally suited for use in a primary care clinical management program. Available pamphlets tend to be overly focused on didactic information about diagnosis and treatment. Few include the important dimension of requiring the patient to "interact" and become a "partner" in the management process. Available self-help books tend to be long and somewhat expensive. Most are designed with "mental health clinic-type" patients in mind. As you may recall from Chapter 1, depressed patients who present to primary care differ from those who present to a mental health setting. Patients who see mental health specialists tend to have worse mental functioning and more limitations in social activities. **Patients of medical practitioners tend to have worse physical functioning, more pain, more psychophysiologic symptoms, and worse perceptions of health in general** (Stewart, et al., 1993). **Few self-help books have been written with the primary care patient as the target audience.** The ICP includes two patient education booklets to support the clinical management system, as well as a workbook designed for the primary care patient and focused on development of self-management skills (Robinson, 1996). These materials include the following.

1. *Seven Ways to Cope* (an interactive booklet)
2. *Using Medications Successfully* (an interactive booklet)
3. *Living Life Well: New Strategies for Hard Times* (a self-management workbook)

Seven Ways to Cope

Seven Ways to Cope is a 23-page booklet that explains specific coping strategies to improve mood and quality of life. The format of the booklet encourages the patient to take an active role in treatment. Prior to an appointment, the patient may complete brief written exercises in the booklet. The patient brings the booklet to the medical appointment. The provider reviews the patient's work in the booklet and provides additional instruction and assistance in planning as needed. Some patients develop strong lifestyle change plans with minimal assistance. They only need support and encouragement from the provider. *Living Life Well: New Strategies for Hard Times* provides additional information and exercises for skill work on strategies suggested in the booklet *Seven Ways to Cope.* You can recommend the *Living Life Well* book to patients at the time you present the *Seven Ways to Cope* booklet. Explain to patients that the *Living Life Well* book provides a more comprehensive structure for promoting behavior change and gives examples and illustrations that facilitate learning and application of strategies. Table 5.5 provides a summary of the contents of *Living Life Well: New Strategies for Hard Times.*

Table 5.5
Living Life Well: New Strategies for Hard Times

Chapter	Coping Strategy
1. Hoping . . . planning . . . doing	• Making a written Behavioral Health Plan • Generating hope by revising your explanation of your present situation
2. Attending your mind and making value-based choices	• Identifying avoided psychological experiences • Choosing a method of self-observation • Acceptance practice procedures • Using acceptance procedures in daily life
3. Appreciating your mind and body	• Muscle relaxation techniques • Imagery techniques • Cultivating psychological neoteny
4. Solving problems	• Applying steps of formal problem solving to a difficult situation in my life
5. Responding to interpersonal conflicts	• Daily Caring Moment Exercise • Awareness of feelings • Respectful expression of feelings • Caring Days • Blending exercise • Use of formal guidelines for conflict resolution
6. Expressing yourself . . . assertively and creatively	• Strengthening beliefs in basic assertive rights • Strengthening practice of basic assertive rights • Identifying creative expression activities • Practicing creative expression activities
7. Continuing to live well . . . planning your lifestyle	• Writing a Behavioral Health Plan for the next 6 months that helps maintain and further gains made in using this book

Using Medications Successfully

Using Medications Successfully is a 12-page booklet that explains use of medications in treating the syndrome of depression. The booklet asks the patient to respond to questions, and a provider may instruct the patient to bring the booklet to medical visits for discussion. The booklet addresses questions commonly asked by patients who are starting antidepressant therapy. Also, the booklet identifies common problems patients have in adhering to prescribed medications and presents a variety of strategies for coping successfully. Use this booklet when a patient expresses an interest in antidepressant therapy or when you actually start antidepressant therapy with a patient.

Living Life Well: New Strategies for Hard Times

Living Life Well: New Strategies for Hard Times is a self-management workbook designed for depressed primary care patients. It can be used as a "companion reader" to support the strategies suggested in the ICP Behavioral Treatment protocol (See Chapter 7). This book is relatively brief and can be completed in a five- to seven-week period of treatment with a minimum amount of support and guidance. **The book requires eighth-grade reading skills** and presents numerous exercises to help patients develop self-management skills. You may suggest this book to all patients with symptoms of depression who are interested in reading more about coping strategies. **The book may also help patients who are struggling with difficult chronic illnesses to avoid development of more significant symptoms of depression.** Chapter 1 presents strategies for increasing hopefulness and confidence. Chapter 2 presents acceptance strategies that are crucial for patients who are struggling with difficult life problems that are unlikely to change soon. Acceptance strategies are also important for patients who suffer from intense anxiety or who have problematic habits, such as alcohol dependence, substance abuse or patterns of over-eating. Chapter 3 introduces the patient to relaxation techniques and imagery techniques, both of which may be helpful to patients who need to adhere to challenging medical procedures. Chapter 4 provides a review of problem solving skills, and Chapter 5 helps the patient evaluate the extent to which she/he needs to strengthen skills for resolving interpersonal conflicts. Chapter 6 presents strategies for effective personal assertion and creative expression. The book concludes by helping the patient develop a relapse prevention plan, which provides a safety net for the following 6 months, when relapse is most likely. Table 5.5 presents a list of coping strategies covered in each chapter of *Living Life Well.* Patients who want a basic program for developing self-management skills may limit their work to Chapters 1, 2, 3, 4, and 7. An "enhanced" program includes completion of Chapters 5 and 6. Patients who are struggling with interpersonal difficulties need to include Chapters 5 and 6 to improve their "psychological resilience."

Anticipating Problems

Use of time can be a problem in clinical management of depression. Many depressed patients are literally "slowed down." The ICP system suggests several ways to help you use time effectively with depressed patients. First, patients can complete self-report assessments in the waiting room. Second, the Coping Plan format can be used to support telephone-based treatment, which can be "backed-up" by mailed communications.

Another possible problem is working with a globally negative depressed patient in a brief visit format. When a patient is extremely negative, try to accept her/his negativity and "validate" it. You can state that the "dimension of time" is often skewed in a depressed state. An extremely negative patient may hear a suggestion that perhaps if she/he can "just hold steady for now," then the difficult things in her/his life may "let up." This may give you an entry into forming a lifestyle plan with a patient that helps her/him "hold on" or "take one small step" during the coming week.

A third possible problem is attempting to coordinate care with an external provider who sees a patient for counseling. This is a particularly difficult situation when the patient appears to be benefiting minimally from the counseling she/he is receiving. You may ask the patient if she/he wants you to coordinate care with her/his counselor. In addition, you may ask your patient to share ICP educational materials with her/his counselor. Educational materials can tell an external counselor a great deal about your treatment approach, which will help her/him provide care to the patient with greater continuity.

The ICP Clinical Management System: An Example

The following case example illustrates how the initial ICP Coping Plan and ICP Coping Plan Follow-Up structure treatment of depression.

Denise's Initial Coping Plan

Denise Bacon was a 44 year old teacher's aide. She worked with handicapped students and received positive feedback from her colleagues. Denise was married and lived with her husband of nine years and their two young children. Denise's husband worked for a trucking company, and he was required to be away from the home about two weeks out of every month. Her husband tended to drink alcohol excessively when he was at home. Denise had used Alanon with positive results shortly after the birth of her second child. She had also used Weight Watchers with good results. Denise had a history of recurrent depression and had used medications successfully in the past. She was about 40 pounds overweight and tended to use food to satisfy emotional needs. Recent stresses included cutbacks in the school district that employed Denise, discovery that her oldest child had learning problems, increased marital conflict, and increased use of alcohol by her husband.

Denise provided the following information on the Coping Plan format while she was waiting to see Dr. Dacey, her primary care physician of the past four years. Dr. Dacey worked with Denise to select a medication and to plan participation in the most potent mood-elevating activities in the Lifestyle Goals and Activities section of the Coping Plan. Dr. Dacey decided to employ a slow titration strategy because of Denise's concerns about side effects. They planned a return visit for sixteen days later.

Sample: ICP Coping Plan

ICP Coping Plan – Page 1			
Name *Denise Bacon*	Number *00234089*	Date of Birth *5/10/52*	Date of Visit *1/11/96*

Dear Patient: Your answers to the following questions will assist you and your primary care provider in developing a helpful treatment plan.

1. What is the major problem you would like help with?

   anger, irritability, depression, anxiety

2. What do you think is **causing** your problem? (Check all that apply.)
   ☒ Physical disorder or illness; ☒ Stress; ☐ Other
   Describe cause(s):

   PMS, husband drinks too much, I may get laid off my job, kids

3. Which of the following do *you* think is or might be **helpful**? (Check all that apply.)
   ☒ Medications; ☒ Lifestyle adjustments; ☒ Other
   Describe:

   Go back to Weight Watchers

4. If you have read the booklets, "*Seven Ways to Cope*" or "*Using Medications Successfully*," what questions do you have about them?

   Can you combine medicines? My girlfriend is using two antidepressants.

5. If you have ever had a period of depression before, **what helped** you start to feel better then?

   Started going to Weight Watchers. Saw my friends. Left the kids with my husband more.

6. List the activities or thoughts that have helped you feel even a little better in the past two weeks, no matter how brief the time that you felt better (for example, visiting a friend or going for a walk).

   Thinking that I am good at my job and that I won't get laid off. Also, taking my kids to the movie last Saturday.

7. List the activities you'd be doing or the thoughts you'd be having if you started to feel even a little bit better in the coming week.

   Go back to Weight Watchers. Go to an Alanon meeting.

8. Who can help you start doing some things that help you feel better?

   Joey, my neighbor

ICP Coping Plan – Page 2

Name	Number	Date of Birth	Date of Visit
Denise Bacon	*00234089*	*5/10/52*	*1/11/96*

Dear Patient: Your provider will complete this with you.

Medication Use

☐ None or:

☐ Imipramine	☐ 25 mg	☐ 50 mg	☐ Fluoxetine	☐ 10 mg	☐ 20 mg
☒ Desipramine	☒ 25 mg	☐ 50 mg	☐ Sertraline	☐ 25 mg	☐ 50 mg
☐ Nortriptyline	☐ 10 mg	☐ 25 mg	☐ Paroxetine	☐ 10 mg	☐ 20 mg
☐ Trazodone	☐ 25 mg	☐ 50 mg	☐ Other:		

☒ Dosage Plan:

Step One:	Take	*25 mg*	every day for	*4*	days. Then, . . .
Step Two:	Take	*50 mg*	every day for	*4*	days. Then, . . .
Step Three:	Take	*75 mg*	every day for	*4*	days. Then, . . .
Continuation:	Take	*100 mg*	every day for		months.

Most people find this medication works best when taken: ☒ In AM ☐ In PM

Most medications are started at a low dosage and increased slowly in order to give your body time to adapt. If you are having side effects, you can stay at a specific dosage for a longer period of time while you adjust and then increase the amount. Don't stop taking your medication. If you are having problems, call you doctor.

Lifestyle Goals and Activities

1. What will you do over the next few days to improve your mood?

   Go for a walk with neighbor, Joey, on Thursday. Go to a Weight Watchers meeting. Go to an Alanon meeting, too.

2. What will you do to increase the time you spend with people who can help you feel better?

   Go to coffee with friend at work on Monday.

3. Who will support you in working toward these lifestyle changes?

   Dr. Dacey and Joey

Checkback Date	Time	Provider
1/27/96	*2:00 P.M.*	*Dacey*

Denise's Follow-Up Coping Plan

Denise returned for a follow-up appointment sixteen days later. She had completed most of her behavioral health plan and reported significant improvements in her mood. She was still very discouraged about her marriage and struggling with guilt about her son's learning problems. On the ICP Coping Plan Follow-Up, Denise indicated that she had started reading *Living Life Well.* One of the self-management strategy exercises in the book had proved helpful to her. She was feeling more calm and attributed this to the Desipramine. The medication plan had gone well, and she was confident about continuing to increase her dose. Denise indicated a concern about whether or not she needed counseling on the Coping Plan Follow-Up form. She and Dr. Dacey discussed this. They decided to develop a behavioral and medication plan for the next month and have a follow-up visit in four weeks. If Denise continued to improve, she would not need counseling. If she experienced difficulties in implementing her plans and she did not feel she was making progress, she would seek counseling in addition to her on-going work with Dr. Dacey at that time.

ICP Coping Plan *Follow-Up* – Page 1

Name	Number	Date of Birth	Date of Visit
Denise Bacon	*00234089*	*5/10/52*	*1/27/96*

Dear Patient: Your answers to the following questions will help you and your primary care provider to evaluate your progress and plan further.

1. To what extent have you taken the medication prescribed in your last visit?

Name of Medication	Dose	Number of days taken
Desipramine	***100 mg***	***4***
Any problems	Did it help?	If yes, how?
☐ Yes ☒ No	☒ Yes ☐ No	More calm

2. Mark an "X" beside any of the following difficulties you have had during the past week.

☐ Daytime sleepiness	☐ Dry mouth	☐ Constipation
☐ Blurred vision	☐ Hesitating on urination	☐ Weight gain
☐ Nausea	☐ Appetite Loss	☐ Sexual Problem
☐ Dizziness	☒ Trouble sleeping	☐ Feeling anxious/jumpy

3. To what extent have you completed the lifestyle changes we discussed in our last visit?

   I went for the walk and had coffee with my friend at work. I went to Alanon, but not to Weight Watchers.

4. What do you think is helping you the most? (Check all that apply.)

   ☒ Medications; ☒ Lifestyle adjustments; ☒ Other

   Describe other: ***Got news that my job would be the same for the coming school year***

5. List the activities or thoughts that have helped you feel even a little better in the last two weeks (for example, visiting a friend or going for a walk).

   Walked away from a fight with my husband and took a bath instead. Started reading Living Life Well and practiced an exercise from the second chapter everyday this week.

6. List the activities you'd be doing or the thoughts you'd be having if you started to feel a little bit better in the coming week.

   I'd feel better about my son's learning problems.

7. Who can help you do more things that help you feel better?

   Joey - she wants to read Living Life Well, too

8. What questions do you have about our treatment plan?

   Do you think I need to see a counselor?

ICP Coping Plan *Follow-Up* – Page 2

Name	Number	Date of Birth	Date of Visit
Denise Bacon	00234089	5/10/52	1/27/96

Dear Patient: Your provider will complete this with you.

Medication Use

☐ None or:

☐ Imipramine	☐ 25 mg	☐ 50 mg	☐ Fluoxetine	☐ 10 mg	☐ 20 mg
☒ Desipramine	☐ 25 mg	☒ 50 mg	☐ Sertraline	☐ 25 mg	☐ 50 mg
☐ Nortriptyline	☐ 10 mg	☐ 25 mg	☐ Paroxetine	☐ 10 mg	☐ 20 mg
☐ Trazodone	☐ 25 mg	☐ 50 mg	☐ Other: ________		

☐ Dosage Plan:

Step One:	Take	125 mg	every day for	4	days. Then, . . .
Step Two:	Take	150 mg	every day for	4	days. Then, . . .
Step Three:	Take		every day for		days. Then, . . .
Continuation:	Take	150 mg	every day for	4 - 7	months.

Most people find this medication works best when taken: ☒ In AM ☐ In PM

Remember to use strategies suggested by your doctor for coping with side effects. You will be able to evaluate the full benefit of your medication after 4 to 6 weeks of use at your target dose. If you have any problems, call your doctor or nurse.

Lifestyle Goals and Activities

1. List activities you will do to create a healthy, satisfying lifestyle in the coming month.

   Keep reading Living Life Well. Take a bubble bath on Friday nights.

   Buy myself a magazine when I buy groceries on Thursdays.

2. When will you spend time with people who can help you feel better?

   Walk with Joey on Monday and Wednesday mornings.

   Have lunch with friend at work once a week.

3. How will you reward yourself for making these lifestyle changes?

   Buy flowers on Thursdays.

Checkback Date	Time	Provider
2/24/96	3:30 PM	Dacey

Summary and Helpful Hints

In this chapter, you have learned a protocol for integrating medication and behavioral treatment in clinical management of depression. Continue to review the educational materials and practice using the forms for a week before starting to implement the protocol in your day-to-day practice. Keep the following in mind, as you work to master this new clinical management system.

1. Provide one month of behavioral treatment to patients with minor depression prior to considering pharmacological treatment.
2. Make behavioral plans simple and specific.
3. Make slower titration plans when you use medications with more side effects or when patients are more apprehensive about side effects.
4. Schedule specific follow-up contacts for six to twelve months after diagnosis.
5. When feasible, plan phone contacts in lieu of clinic visits.
6. Always assess patient adherence to behavioral and medication plans. Encourage patients by emphasizing the value of small and partial successes in changing behavior.
7. Use mental health providers as consultants to help you manage more complex patients.

References

Robinson, P. (1996). *Living Life Well: New Strategies for Hard Times.* Reno, NV: Context Press.

Stewart, A.L., Sherbourne, C.D., Wells, K.B., Burnam, A., Rogers, W.H., Hays, R.D., & Ware, J.E. (1993). Do depressed patients in different treatment settings have different levels of well-being and functioning? *Journal of Consulting and Clinical Psychology, 61*(5), 849-857.

Chapter 6

On-Site Behavioral Health Consultation Services in Primary Care

This chapter provides you with an overview of the primary care setting and the potential roles mental health providers may play in this setting. In this chapter, you will learn the following.

- How to start a behavioral health practice in a primary care setting
- The range of behavioral health services needed in the primary care setting
- The difference between consultation and psychotherapy
- How to adapt behavioral treatments to fit the primary care setting
- How to assist with pharmacological treatment
- How to coordinate care with the primary care team
- How to serve the educational needs of primary care providers concerning behavioral health issues

---

Instructions for Speed Readers: Allow 30 minutes to read this chapter and related materials introduced in this chapter. Critical information is printed in bold in all sections.

The Basics

"Getting started" is the most difficult step for a mental health provider who wants to develop an integrated treatment program for depression in a primary care clinic. As a mental health professional, you probably trained in mental health out-patient and hospital settings. Your knowledge about the primary care setting may be limited to your personal history with primary care physicians and your stereotypes about care delivered in the primary care setting. **Take a moment now to check your assumptions about primary care.** Do you assume that all primary care providers will welcome you with open arms? Do you assume that all primary care providers will understand the unique skills that you bring to their patients and to depressed patients, in particular? Do you assume that treatment of depression is a concern for all primary care providers? **Primary care providers vary widely in their interests in and experience with mental health providers and treatments.** Furthermore, primary care providers vary significantly in the types of patients they have in their panels. Some have younger panels; some, older. Some have more females in their panel, while others specialize in treatment of patients with AIDS or diabetes. For the most part, the patient panels of primary care providers vary considerably in the incidence and types of serious physical and mental health problems.

Approach each physician and each patient with as few preconceptions as possible. **Patients vary considerably in severity of impairment and interest in mental health treatment. Your responsibilities are to *consult* with the patient and provider. Humility and curiosity will expedite your learning and multiply your successes.**

Scope of Services

Table 6.1 provides a list of services you may provide in the role of primary care behavioral health consultant. Often, providers only want to discuss a patient with you for a few minutes. These brief consultations often occur in the hallway. A provider may be seeking help in making a diagnosis, refining a treatment plan, or simply hearing your reassurance regarding a management plan with a difficult patient.

Many of the patients referred to you for consultation will only need a single visit. Patients with strong relationships with the primary care health team may use a single consult to develop a specific behavioral coping plan regarding a medical problem. **Sometimes, physicians "who ran out of time" in a medical contact with a depressed patient may refer the patient to you for a single medication risk evaluation.** Patients in an acute crisis may see you only once and you will connect them with community resources, such as Alanon or grief groups. Occasionally, patients will need several follow-up consultations with you. Patients with major mental disorders, such as panic disorder, may complete treatment by using a few additional consultation visits with you.

As a consultant, you may also develop and offer programmatic treatments for disorders seen frequently in the primary care clinic. The Integrated Care Program Behavioral Treatment protocol is an example of a population-based programmatic treatment designed for depressed patients in the primary care setting. This program is derived from treatments with demonstrated efficacy and adjusted to the briefer context of care required in the primary care setting. Lengthier, more complex specialty treatment for other disorders (for example, eating disorders, alcohol dependence, panic disorder, etc.) may be shaped up for the primary care setting. You may also offer programmatic services in group formats. Chapter 8 provides suggestions for group work in the primary care setting.

Table 6.1
Primary Care Behavioral Health Services

1. Consultation with the Primary Care Team
2. Single Consultations with Primary Care Patients
3. Episode of Consultation with Primary Care Patients (1 to 3 contacts)
4. Programmatic Treatment (4 to 7 contacts)
5. Group Treatment
6. Triage
7. Consultation with Medication Specialists
8. Educational Services

Occasionally, primary care consultation will include triage of patients to providers in external locations. **A small minority of patients may need more intensive treatment than is possible in the primary care setting.** In these cases, your responsibilities include patient assessment and collaborative decision-making concerning an adequate treatment option designed to meet mutually agreed upon treatment goals. Also, your role may include arranging for the patient's initial contact with an externally located specialist. You or the primary care provider will talk with the specialist prior to the patient's initial contact to discuss treatment goals and plans, including when the patient will be returning to the care of the primary care team. **Explain to the external provider that you want the patient to return with post-treatment assessment information and a relapse**

prevention plan that can be supported in primary care. Fewer than twenty-five percent of the patients you see will need services from external specialists.

With medically complex or older patients, you may want to consult with a medication specialist. Clinical pharmacists, pharmapsychologists, prescribing psychiatric nurses and psychiatrists may lend expertise to primary care pharmacological treatment. In most circumstances, you may obtain needed advice through a telephone call.

As a behavioral health consultant, you may be asked to provide educational training programs about mental health issues. Usually, requests for training occur after a sustained period of consultation. In the last section of this chapter, we provide guidelines for developing educational workshops and newsletters.

Consultation Versus Psychotherapy

Your "mission" in primary care is different from your charge in the outpatient or hospital setting. You are no longer "taking charge" of patient care. You are providing consultative support to the primary care team. Although you may initiate interventions with a patient, these are designed to reinforce and build upon what is already being done by the primary care team. Basically you act as an advisor to the patient and primary care provider. Your relationship with the patient is that of an auxiliary provider, and your relationship with the patient is limited and temporary. Present yourself as an expert on behavioral health issues. In consultations with patients, assess, support and build upon the current strengths of the patient's relationships with primary health care providers.

Getting Started

Prior to starting a consultation service, attend one or more physician and nurse staff meetings. Introduce yourself briefly. Explain your hours and your start date. **One 4-hour weekly consultation is a minimum commitment.** Offering eight hours per week is better, and two 4-hour schedules are better than one 8-hour consultation period. Written announcements are also useful. Following is an example of an announcement of behavioral health consultation services.

> *My name is Mike Rose. I am a psychologist. I will offer Behavioral Health Consultation Services at the Northland Clinic on Monday mornings and Thursday afternoons starting June 6. Send patients to Linda Smith at Station 3 to schedule appointments with me. All of my appointments are 30-minutes, and I provide written same-day feedback to you. My general consultation services extend up to 3 visits per patient. I limit return visits so that I can consistently see your new referrals within one-week. Feel free to knock on my door when I am with patients.* ***Mike Rose, Ph.D. Voice Mail: 997-4569; Pager: 287-2558.***

Include a photograph of yourself on your announcement. **Print your pager and voice mail numbers in large bold print under your photograph.** Pass out announcements to every physician practice on a weekly basis for a few weeks. When you receive your first referral from a provider, make a point of seeing him/her in person, if only to say, "Thanks for your referral. I left a chart note on your desk." When a referral requires a more complex intervention, take the time needed to collaborate with *all* involved providers.

Once you begin to see patients, there may be unanticipated challenges. Providers may begin their use of your services by referring their most difficult patients. Primary care providers want you to know the extreme mental problems some of their patients face. They also want to see what you can do to help them. **Be sure to say thank you for the referrals, acknowledge the difficulty of their jobs, and be creative in interventions and recommendations.**

Another challenge comes when your schedule is full, and an emergency arises. In a specialty setting, you often have the luxury of an emergency service program. In primary care, "You are it." **Take the emergency and work late. On average, primary care physicians work over 50 hours**

per week. Primary care providers will appreciate your willingness to "roll your sleeves up and get the job done."

A final adjustment that will ease your entry into primary care is to **"be brief" in everything you do.** If you confer with a provider about a patient, be brief. If you give a talk at a professional meeting, be brief. If you pass out handouts, make them practical and brief. If you prepare a behavioral health newsletter, use bullets and short phrases. When you are brief and direct, you have a greater impact in primary care. Table 6.2 provides a checklist to help you "get started."

Table 6.2
A Checklist for "Getting Started"

1. Set up a schedule for at least 4 hours of 30-minute consultations on a weekly basis.
2. Walk around the clinic at the end of the day and distribute a written announcement concerning your start of a practice.
3. Provide legible, same-day, written and verbal feedback on referred patients.
4. State that you have an open-door policy.
5. Assume that physicians also have an open-door policy.
6. Prepare a handout with a photocopy of a photograph of yourself. Include your pager and voice mail numbers in large, bold print on the handout. Suggest that the medical receptionist place the announcement on a provider bulletin board.
7. Accept an emergency and work late.
8. Present a requested talk and/or provide brief, practical, and instructional handouts.
9. Write a weekly newsletter to build interest in programmatic treatment of depression.

The Attitude: Humble and Curious

You are most likely to "find a home" in primary care when you **approach the setting as a humble and curious guest.** With this attitude, you will be attentive to the differences in style between yourself and primary care providers. As a guest, you are responsible for making adjustments so that you "fit in." There are a number of factors about your position that support your being modest. First, what you "know best" will not work in primary care. Secondly, you are not an expert on this context of care. Third, you do not have on-going relationships with the patients, so you most often know less about their history.

There are many reasons for approaching behavioral health consultation with curiosity as well. The field of primary care behavioral health is new. The possibilities are tremendous. Be curious about the world view of the primary care provider. Be curious about diseases, medications, and medical procedures. Be curious about the roles various disciplines play within health care teams, as they may vary from one primary care practice to another. Be inquisitive in a "brief" way, as "brief" is the conceptual frame for primary care.

Adaptations for the 30-Minute Hour

Time is measured in 15-minute units in primary care. In order to see the number of patients needing consultation services, **you will need to provide 15 or 30-minute consultation visits.** Your approach to interview and treatment planning needs to fit this time frame.

Behavioral Treatment

Recent research findings suggest that behavioral activation strategies are simple, straight forward, and equal in power with more complex cognitive strategies (Jacobson, et al., 1996). Most primary care providers had course work that included behavioral psychology. Therefore, basic behavioral interventions are ideal for the primary care environment. Treatment plans need to be concrete and simple, yet powerful. It is best to provide written instructions. Both the patient and the referring primary care provider need copies of the behavioral health plan. For example, a depressed patient might plan to call a friend, go to the library, and review his favorite book of quotations. Record this list in two places: the patient's instruction sheet and the medical chart. If the primary care provider is the next health care provider to see the patient, the provider knows exactly what to ask the patient. **Behavioral health treatments need to be capable of being supported by primary care staff.**

Pharmacological Treatment

Pharmacological treatment of mental disorders is common in the primary care setting. **Your job as a consultant may include assisting patients and providers with pharmacological treatment.** For example, you may assist in evaluating patient interest in and readiness to use medications. Further, you may help educate the patient regarding medications and help the patient plan specific strategies for coping effectively with troubling side effects. If you have not read Chapter 4, do so now. Also, familiarize yourself with the Medication Assessment Questionnaire in the Appendix. You have a professional responsibility to understand pharmacological treatment of mental disorders (Littrell & Ashford, 1995; Buelow & Chafetz, 1996).

Charting

Charting practices will need to fit the primary care setting, where you chart in the medical record. The "data-assessment-plan" format is acceptable in most health care centers. In general, the planning section should be the longest section of your chart note. Avoid including details of personal information that the patient would not want known to all providers. Such details may be shared orally with other providers if important to care plans for the patient. **Chart briefly in legible handwriting and leave your notes with the referring provider on the same day of the consultation.**

The General Consultation Model

As a behavioral health consultant, you may see a variety of primary care patients. Many of your referrals will be facing challenging medical illnesses. Others will suffer chronic pain, anxiety, insomnia, and numerous life circumstance problems. Offering general consultation services gives you a chance to identify primary care providers who have stronger interests in behavioral health services. Physicians and nurses with stronger interests in behavioral health will want you to continue working in their clinic and will probably be mentors for you.

You will need to make personal and practice style adjustments to fit into the primary care setting. Your office will be different. **You may even work in a room with a sink and an exam table.** Furthermore, you may change offices weekly. The following guidelines will help you adjust to the 30-minute visit, which incidentally needs to include patient care, charting, and necessary collaboration with the primary care team.

Initial Visit

Table 6.3 summarizes the initial visit tasks. The ordering of the tasks may vary from patient to patient and consultant to consultant. The patient often feels more at ease with discussing basic information first. You may shift the interview quickly into treatment planning by explaining that you need to ask a series of questions to further determine the nature of the kinds of problems the patient is having. Most patients welcome educational information and skill instruction. **On occasion, you may choose to leave the interview briefly in order to confer with a primary care provider regarding a treatment issue (e.g., start or change of a psychotropic medication).**

Table 6.3
Primary Care Behavioral Health Initial Contact Tasks

Task	Approximate Time
1. Obtain basic information (age, employment, living situation, health concerns, patient's perception of reason for referral, patient's expectation regarding the consultation)	10
2. Ask questions needed to make a diagnosis	5
3. Provide education or training experience	5
4. Make a formal treatment plan	5
5. Charting and collaboration with Primary Care Provider(s)	5

Follow-Up Visit(s)

Follow-up visits need to begin with an evaluation of the plan that resulted from the initial consultation. When a patient has not complied with the plan, explore the obstacles with an attitude of support and interest. Further evaluation may improve the quality of the treatment plan. **Try to prepare the patient for return to care by the primary care team as soon as possible. Stay in the role of *consultant.***

The General Consultation Model: An Example

Henry was a 32 year old computer programmer who experienced a panic attack at his job four weeks prior to his behavioral health consultation. At the consultation, he reported that his "attack" had occurred late at night and that he had called 911 for help and had received care at the Emergency Room. He participated in a thorough medical evaluation, and results suggested he was in good health. While he reported confidence in his physician and the test results, he indicated continued problems. He described hypervigilance and specific worries about recurring symptoms of excessive sweating, heart palpitations, dizziness, fears of loosing control and a sense of being "outside of myself." Henry indicated that he had generally good health habits. He explained that he had lost his father to a heart attack when he was young and that he had a commitment to maintaining good health. Since the panic attack, Henry had stopped his exercise program and his morning cup of coffee, as he associated both with onset of worrisome symptoms. Henry wanted more information about anxiety and ways to stop his symptoms. The behavioral health consultant provided two interventions during the consultation: (1) education regarding the nature of anxiety, physiological arousal and the physical basis of somatic symptoms and (2) an initial exercise in breathing retraining. The chart note included:

Data: Patient is a 32 year old, single computer programmer. Patient referred by Dr. Israel subsequent to patient experience of an initial episode of panic four weeks ago. Patient received care from 911 and a subsequent thorough medical evaluation. Results suggested a healthy adult who is experiencing panic attacks. Patient continues to be hypervigilant and to experience attacks several times a week (characterized by heart palpitations, excessive sweating, dizziness, fears of loosing control and feeling "outside" of his body). Father died of heart attack. Patient is now avoiding exercise and coffee.

Assessment: Panic Disorder

Plan: (1) Patient will read pamphlet on physiological arousal and panic.

(2) Patient will practice breathing retraining exercise introduced today on a daily basis.

(3) Primary Care to reinforce explanation of fear arousal and support breathing practice at medical visits.

(4) Patient will return in 2 weeks for additional work on breathing and cognitions.

(5) Patient will attend a 4-session Mind-Body Class starting next month.

When Henry returned to the clinic, he reported that he had read the handout and purchased a suggested book. Also, he had practiced the breathing exercise daily. He reported fewer and less intense problems with heart palpitations and other symptoms. He wanted to discuss the physiology of "tingling" sensations and hot and cold flashes. Henry also read suggested educational materials and explained that he had changed his explanation about his problem. He no longer believed, "Something is wrong with my body." Instead, Henry explained, "It's simple. I'm stressed out and long overdue for a vacation." He was looking forward to starting the Mind-Body class series the following week. The behavioral health consultant provided two interventions in this follow-up appointment: (1) educational information on symptoms of concern and (2) a second breathing retraining exercise. No further follow-up was planned. The chart note included:

Data: Henry reports compliance with initial behavioral health plan. He is benefiting from education and practice of breathing exercises. His symptoms are of less concern to him today.

Assessment: Much improved.

Plan: (1) Start Mind-Body Class series next week.

(2) Selected reading in *Living Life Well* book.

(3) Continue breathing exercises.

(4) Return if need be in future for "booster" on skills to lower arousal.

Teacher/Student Possibilities

The primary care setting is rich with learning opportunities for all members of a multi-disciplinary team. You will receive new and, sometimes, highly interesting information in your primary care mailbox. We recommend that you start to **read several primary care journals on a regular basis.** Ask questions. Primary care providers enjoy sharing their expertise. As you prepare to "teach your trade," ask what interests them and center your efforts around their requests.

Guidelines for Educational Talks

Primary care providers will learn from your treatment of their patients. They will learn from your chart notes, your hallway consults, and what their patients tell them about consultations with you. They will be interested in behavioral health plans and suggestions about relapse prevention activities. Additionally, you may provide brief lunch hour educational programs and write brief, one-page newsletters. **The key word here is brief.** Lunch talks need to be 20-30 minutes in length. Also, primary care providers enjoy interacting and sharing experiences related to the presentation. Allow time for discussion and questions.

Guidelines for Primary Care Behavioral Health Newsletters

A "recipe" for writing primary care newsletters on depression is as follows.

1. One feature article
2. One instruction regarding behavioral health treatment
3. One reference to the clinic or one of the providers
4. One unit of information about your availability or experience as a behavioral health consultant
5. A little humor

In general, your feature article needs to be in response to a primary care provider's interest or request. **You may run a series on a highly prevalent disorder such as depression, particularly during seasons of the year when the disorder is more prevalent.** This may boost both recognition and treatment. We are enclosing several examples of newsletters at the end of this chapter, and all relate to recognition and treatment of depression.

Summary and Helpful Hints

As a behavioral health consultant in primary care, you will deliver a wide range of services to a diverse group of patients. Keep the following points in mind to ensure your success.

1. Remember to be humble and curious.
2. Chart legibly after every patient contact.
3. Approach every initial visit with the idea that it is a "single" visit.
4. Remember that you are a consultant, and your job is to return the patient to the primary care team with a behavioral treatment plan as soon as possible.
5. Be knowledgeable concerning pharmacological treatment of mental disorders.
6. Scan several primary care journals monthly.
7. Be brief.

References

Buelow, G.D., & Chafetz, M.D. (1996). Proposed ethical practice guidelines for clinical pharmacopsychology: Sharpening a new focus in psychology. *Professional Psychology: Research and Practice, 27*(1), 53-58.

Jacobson, N.S., Dobson, K.S., Truax, P.A., Addis, M.E., Koerner, K., Gollan, J.K., Gortner, E., & Prince, S. E. (1996). A component analysis of cognitive-behavioral treatment for depression. *Journal of Consulting and Clinical Psychology, 64*(2), 295-304.

Littrell, J., & Ashford, J.B. (1995). Is it proper for psychologists to discuss medications with clients? *Professional Psychology: Research and Practice, 26*(1), 238-244.

Strosahl, K. (1996). Confessions of a behavior therapist in primary care: The odyssey and the ecstasy. *Cognitive and behavioral practice, 3*, 1-28.

THE ICP REVIEW

"Experiment" – A Basic Concept in Behavioral Health Care TX of Depression

BY PATTI ROBINSON, *IP Reporter*

SEATTLE. ICP In their initial contacts with depressed patients Behavioral Health Consultants at the Northland Clinic teach patients how to conduct a "behavioral experiment." Patients identify one of seven areas of daily living (e.g., having fun alone, talking with others, contentment with work, accomplishment activities alone, sensory experiencing, etc.) to use as the focus of an initial behavioral experiment designed to improve their quality of life in the targeted area. Patients learn steps to take in planning a successful experiment, including:

1. Choose an activity area.
2. Imagine yourself doing something different in the activity area.
3. Plan a specific time and place to actually engage in that activity.
4. During and after the experiment, watch what happens -- inside you (feelings, thoughts, behaviors) and outside of you (what others say or do).
5. Think about your findings or results.
6. Talk with others about your results and draw conclusions.
7. Plan other experiments.

****

Coming Next Week: The Psychological Theory of Short Term Change

Experiments Improve Mood

BY STEPHANIE HAINS, *IP Reporter*

NORTH SEATTLE. Northland Primary Care Patients have been very successful in improving their mood through planning successful behavioral experiments. For example, one person planned a single family bike ride. Finding this enjoyable, he is now planning weekly family bike rides. Another ICP participant planned to go to a movie alone. While the movie was not as humorous as expected, the popcorn was delicious and she bumped into an old friend coming out of the movie. They had tea together and the net impact of the experiment on her mood was positive. A third participant, who had a pattern of chronic worry, designed a "nature" walk around his neighborhood where he focused on the color, shapes, smells, and textures of plants. Finding this refreshing, he is now pursuing solitary nature walks four or five times a week.

The behavioral experiments designed by patients and consultants in the ICP are as unique as the patients themselves. Experiments that help improve mood are simple, extremely clear, specific, and involve only one small step.

Behavioral Health consultants actually *write out* the planned experiment for the patient and give it to her or him, just as Primary Care doctors may write out prescriptions for antidepressant medications.

THE ICP REVIEW

The Psychological Theory of Short Term Change

BY PATTI ROBINSON, *IP Reporter*

SEATTLE. ICP Behavioral Health Consultants at the Northland Clinic teach patients the meaning of the Theory of Short Term Change. (See attached copy of the visual aid given to depressed patients when this theory is explained.) This theory asserts:

1. Small changes can be made in a very short period of time.
2. Small changes in one's life can create motivation for making larger changes.
3. When the direction of small change is maintained, rather large life changes are inevitable.

Primary Care Doctors Facilitate Big Changes

BY PATTI ROBINSON & EVETTE TRETORN, *IP Reporters*

NORTH SEATTLE. Northland Primary Care Patients have been checking back with their Primary Care Doctors to review their Progress Plans. The Progress Plan is a relapse prevention plan. This plan summarizes the small changes the patient made during his/her work in the ICP and details the changes the patient plans to pursue during the 6-month period after graduating from intensive treatment. Primary Care doctors are facilitating big changes desired by patients when they support the patient Progress Plan. Go for it, doctors! Show your patients you understand The Psychological Theory of Short Term Change.

Change: *Modification* Alteration
Shift Variation **Movement**
T R A N S F O R M A T I O N

****

Coming Next Week:

"The Value of Written Instructions to Patients"

THE ICP REVIEW

The Value of Written Instructions

BY PATTI ROBINSON, *IP Reporter*

SEATTLE. In the Integrated Care Program, depressed patients receive written instructions at the end of each of their visits. Each visit has a specific patient instruction sheet tailored to support the patient's maximum benefit from that visit. Instruction sheets for all visits include two sections: "Medication Plan" and "Behavioral Experiment." The "**Medication Plan**" section gives the patient:

1. the name and dose of the medication prescribed for depression,
2. a list of the side effects they have been experiencing and specific coping suggestions for these particular side effects, and
3. beneficial effects of the medication that they have experienced in the past week and specific beneficial effects they are expecting to experience in the coming week.

The "**Behavioral Experiment**" section includes:

1. the question the patient is seeking to answer by engaging in the experiment (e.g., "Can I change my mood by changing my behavior?"),
2. the "Key Activity" that the patient is addressing in the experiment (one of the seven areas of life satisfaction–enjoyment alone, accomplishment alone, fun with others, talking with others, contentment with work, sensual experience, images of a better future),
3. the "Skill Practice" planned (e.g., rating mood on a daily basis in a small spiral notebook),
4. the specifics of the planned behavioral experiment, and
5. how the patient plans to **reward** herself/himself for following the medication plan and completing the behavioral experiment.

Commitment: The Issue For The 90's In Primary Care

BY PATTI ROBINSON & EVETTE TRETORN, *IP Reporters*

NORTH SEATTLE. Northland Primary Care Patients participating in the ICP are asked to make a commitment at the end of every program visit. Patients work collaboratively with the behavioral health consultants to develop plans and experiments that will improve quality of life. Then, the moment comes to assess the real potential of the carefully developed plan. The behavioral health consultant bravely pops the question, "*On a scale of 1 to 10, where 10 means 'you are totally committed to this plan' and 1 means 'you are not really behind this,' where are you?*" So far, Patti and Evette have not settled for less than a 7!!!

Commitment: *Pledge* Assurance
Promise GUARANTEE

****

Coming Soon:
**A Review of Problem Solving Skills*
**Coping with Holiday Blues*

THE ICP REVIEW

COPING WITH HOLIDAY BLUES

BY PATTI ROBINSON, *IP Reporter*

SEATTLE. Many patients experience mild depression during the holidays. In part, these low feelings derive from memories of past holidays that have not gone well. Patients may be apprehensive about the present holiday and may, inadvertently, bring about a "replay" of previous misfortunes by presenting their negative expectations.

For example, Jenny predicted that her aging parents would be irritable and that they would not express appreciation for her efforts to make the holidays pleasant for them. She focused her attention on the probable occurrence of her parents' irritability, and took any sign of dissatisfaction on their part as evidence for her perception of being a "not-good-enough-daughter."

In the Integrated Care Program (ICP), patients learn to use problem-solving skills to create enjoyable experiences and warm feelings during the holidays. Applying these problem-solving skills allows the patient to:

1. "Just notice" the negativity or irritability of loved ones--without taking on any responsibility for causing, changing, or even attending closely to that negativity,
2. Plan and do specific holiday activities that truly connote celebration for herself or himself as an individual.

****

Problem-Solving Skill Review

BY PATTI ROBINSON & EVETTE TRETORN, *IP Reporters*

NORTH SEATTLE. Northland Primary Care Patients participating in the ICP review problem-solving skills and plan skillful application to difficult life circumstances they currently face. Most of the patients have actually successfully solved numerous difficult problems during their lives. When overwhelmed, people have difficulty applying--and even recalling--the actual skills that have worked well for them in the past.

Problem solving skills involve:

- Defining the problem
- Brain storming
- Evaluating potential solutions
- Choosing a solution
- Implementing the solution and noting results carefully
- Making a new plan
- Celebrating success

These steps are difficult to implement. For example, defining the problem so that it can actually be solved is a very big first step. This is the step where most patients get "stuck" in the holiday blues.

Solve: *Answer* Explain *Fix*

WORK

Coming Soon:
A Technique for Achieving Balance in Life

Chapter 7

Behavioral Health Consultation in the Integrated Care Program

This chapter provides an overview of ICP educational materials and behavioral health consultation protocols. There are two basic protocols. The first is the Brief Treatment protocol. This protocol involves one to three contacts with the patient. The ICP Coping Plan, which is discussed in detail in Chapter 5, supports implementation of the Brief Treatment program. The second option is the Behavioral Treatment protocol. In this protocol, you and the patient negotiate the number of contacts, ranging from four to seven sessions. In this chapter, you learn the following.

- Key concepts underlying the two behavioral health treatment protocols
- Implementation strategies
- Implementation guidelines for all sessions in the Behavior Treatment protocol, including the following.
    - Planning use of time within the session
    - Identifying critical concepts for each session
    - Selecting optimal exercises for individual patients
    - Anticipating typical problems patients may have in using suggested strategies and ways to solve the problems
    - Discussing and resolving medication adherence issues
- Responsibilities of ICP Medication Specialists and External Providers

Instructions for Speed Readers: Allow 2 to 3 hours to read this chapter and related educational materials introduced in this chapter, including the self-management workbook that supports the Behavioral Treatment protocol. Take time to try some of the exercises suggested in *Living Life Well: New Strategies for Hard Times.*

Key Concepts

In the ICP model of depression treatment, the on-site behavioral health consultant implements one of two programmatic options. The first option is Brief Treatment and the second is Behavioral Treatment. Both programs are presented in this chapter. Mastery of the following key concepts underlying the behavioral health programs will help you proceed through later sections in this chapter on educational materials and implementation details.

Working with a Biopsychosocial Model

The ICP subscribes to and educates patients in a biopsychosocial model of depression. This model is described in detail in Chapter 4. The basic concepts of this framework are embodied in ICP educational materials. **The model empowers patients to choose behavioral treatment alone**

or in combination with antidepressant therapy. This model is a conceptual "skeleton" and behavioral health consultants "dress it up" during the course of treatment. This model should be referred to in virtually every personal contact with the patient. Following is one of several ways of presenting the biopsychosocial model to patients.

Draw a picture of *connecting neurons* on a piece of paper and discuss the following ideas with patients:

1. Stress may deplete certain neurotransmitter substances and limit the flow of energy between neurons.
2. Medications, *as well as strategic behavioral change*, may help improve the functioning of the nervous system.
3. After the nervous system returns to normal, strategic behavioral planning may help you maintain a healthy nervous system *and* prevent further episodes of depression.

Pictures are often very helpful to depressed patients, who may be experiencing significant difficulties with concentration and memory. In addition to a picture of several connecting neurons, you may draw the "mind-body-behavior circle" (see Chapter 4, Figure 4.1). On the outside of the circle, place a "m" for mind, a "b" for body, and a "b" for behavior. Explain that each area influences the others. Explain that treatment will address all three areas of human experience: mental activity (or thoughts), bodily sensations (including emotional experience) and behavioral action. Describe depressive behavior as behavior that generates dissatisfying outcomes. Alternatively, explain that non-depressed behavior enhances experience of pleasurable thoughts and sensations. Explain that negative thoughts are pessimistic and critical, while positive thoughts are self-valuing and self-encouraging. Explain how non-depressed behavior can create movement toward more positive thoughts and pleasant emotions. *Draw a spiral* (see Chapter 4, Figure 4.2). Use an example to demonstrate how depressive thoughts and behaviors impact mental and physical states of being.

As you explain the biopsychosocial model, attempt to *involve the patient.* Ask the patient to recall a time when he or she felt better during the previous week. Use the patient's experience to illustrate the biopsychosocial model. Introduce the concept of the behavioral health plan. Portray the plan as an *experiment* the patient conducts to assess the power of specific behavioral changes in moving her/him up or down the "mood spiral" and changing her/his biopsychosocial state of wellness.

Assessment

The ICP provides instruments for completing assessments efficiently. The majority of assessment data are collected from self-report measures. All forms are presented in Appendices. The ICP uses a two-tier approach. The Level 1 method applies to patients with mild depression who are likely to receive care exclusively from primary care providers. As a Behavioral Health Consultant, you will use the Level 2 method of assessment most often, as patients you treat are likely to suffer greater symptom severity. Assessment procedures are presented in detail in Chapter 3.

The ICP assessment method is compatible with the Patient Impairment Profile (PIP) (Goodman, Brown, & Deitz, 1992). The PIP has been well received by several large care management organizations as documentation for the clinical necessity of treatment. **Table 7.1 provides information to help you select an appropriate treatment that links with assessment findings. Use your clinical judgment to determine the *level of care* or intensity of treatment within the ICP treatment protocol selected.** For example, you could select the ICP Behavioral Treatment protocol for a patient with moderate symptoms and limitations. This option might also be your choice for a patient with more severe symptoms and limitations. However, you could specify a higher level of intensity for the more severely depressed patient. For example, you could schedule two contacts in the first week of treatment and include one or more supportive phone calls between standard weekly clinic visits for the more severely depressed patient.

As a rule, **implement the least intensive level of care needed to produce significant patient improvement.** After completing a functional assessment and discussing treatment options, you may send some patients back to the primary care provider for treatment. Other patients will demonstrate more severe symptoms and substantial impairment and hence will need the Behavioral Treatment protocol involving 4 to 7 contacts. A few patients will require services outside of the primary care clinic. **Record your treatment selection on the ICP Treatment Plan. Also, record your treatment start and review dates and notes about level of care.** The ICP Treatment Plan form provides a format for this important information. The Treatment Plan form is provided for you in Appendix C.

Table 7.1
ICP Treatment Selection Table

Assessment Results Suggest	Treatment Options
Mild to Moderate (2 to 4 symptoms, low coping use score)	Primary Care Team Clinical Management protocol
Moderate Symptoms (5 or more symptoms, low coping use score) *and* Moderate Difficulties with Functioning (scores 10-15 on functional assessment)	On-Site Behavioral Health Consultant Services, including: ☐ Brief Treatment protocol or ☐ Behavioral Treatment protocol
Severe Symptoms (6 or more symptoms, low coping use score) *and* Severe Difficulties with Functioning (scores 16+ on functional assessment, has 1+ areas rated imminently dangerous)	More intensive implementation of Behavioral Treatment protocol *Consider* Specialty Treatment Delivered Externally
Complex or Poor Response to Antidepressant Treatment (no improvement after 4 weeks of treatment)	Consultation with Medication Specialist *Consider* Specialty Treatment Delivered Externally

*Antidepressant Therapy may accompany any treatment option.

Time Management

In order to complete session agendas in the Integrated Care Program, you need to be comfortable working briefly, usually in a time frame of 30 minute appointments. Review the critical concepts for an agenda just prior to starting the session. Critical concepts, along with other implementation support materials, are located in a later section of this chapter. **The following guidelines will help you use time well.**

1. Start on time.
2. Explain to the patient that you need to structure use of time in every session in order to cover critical concepts and make skill-application plans with the patient.

3. Explain the agenda for the session and invite the patient to add any additional items to the agenda.
4. Review the patient's previous behavioral health plan and build the next plan with those results in mind.
5. Interrupt the patient when she/he talks in a non-productive fashion.
6. Always end on time.

Behavioral Health Plans

Behavioral health plans are the foundation of the Integrated Care Program. In every contact, you will help the patient develop a behavioral health plan designed to alter her/his biopsychosocial state of being. **Behavioral health plans need to be concrete, specific and limited in scope.** Patients need to have confidence in their ability to implement behavioral health plans. Assess patient confidence in implementing a plan by using *scaling* questions. For example, you might ask the following question.

> *"On a scale of 1 to 10, where 10 is 100% confidence that you will complete this plan as we have devised it, where would you put your confidence at this moment?"*

If a patient gives a confidence rating below 8, revise the plan. You might say, "I want to change this plan to make it more realistic for you. I was asking you to do too much this week." In general, the smaller and more specific the plan, the greater the patient's confidence level will be. Of course, the patient needs to view the plan as "large" enough to be "important."

Because depressed patients have significant problems with memory and concentration, it is best to summarize behavioral health plans in writing. The *Living Life Well* book includes a specific behavioral health plan form for each of the seven chapters. **Each of the behavioral health plans in the *Living Life Well* book asks the patient to (1) commit to practice of a specific skill *and* (2) to engage in an activity designed to further her/his expression of important values in one of seven critical areas of life.** Copies of the behavioral health plan formats from the *Living Life Well* book are available in Appendix F. Take a moment now to locate these forms and study the basic format. Placing a copy of the plan in the medical chart allows other providers to support the patient should they have contact with her/him.

At all follow-up contacts, ask the patient about her/his success with the previous behavioral health plan. Relate results to the biopsychosocial model, positive coping and movement on the mood spiral in the desired direction (i.e., less depressed). When a patient is not successful with a plan, accept some of the responsibility for the plan's failure. For example, you might say, "I'm sorry. I realize now that we made the plan too complex. We'll fix that this week. Don't be discouraged."

Medication Issues

When a patient expresses an interest in using an antidepressant medication, ask the patient to complete the Medication Assessment Questionnaire (MAQ). You will find a copy of this assessment in Appendix B. This will most likely occur in the initial visit with you, but may occur later in treatment with patients who are making slow progress in solo behavioral treatment. Use the MAQ to coordinate treatment planning between the prescribing primary care provider and the patient. The MAQ provides information concerning the patient's history of use of antidepressant medications, desired benefits from antidepressant therapy, skills for tolerating side effects, beliefs about medications for depression and anxiety, and knowledge about antidepressant therapy.

When you help a patient start antidepressant treatment during a behavioral health visit, provide the patient with a written plan regarding medication use. If the patient is returning to the primary provider's care after one or two behavioral health consultations, you will be using the ICP Coping Plan format. This format includes a form for providing the patient with written instructions regarding medication. For patients participating in the 4 to 7 session behavioral treatment protocol, you may want to have a tablet made with the following headings on it.

- Name of Medication
- Dose
- Time to Take
- Method of Administration (e.g., tablet, dissolved in water, with food)
- Target Symptom
- Anticipated Side Effects
- Plan for Coping with Side Effects

This format will help you be thorough and time-effective. Be certain that the patient understands the prescriber's instructions concerning titration and method of administration. Also, help the patient identify one or two "target" symptoms to monitor between sessions. Target symptoms are specific symptoms that are particularly troubling for the patient and that the patient hopes to see improved through the use of medications. Help the patient anticipate and plan for side effects. Always give the patient a copy of the booklet *Using Medications Successfully* at the time of initiation of antidepressant treatment. If you have not read this booklet, turn to Appendix D and read it now. The booklet will help you educate the patient so that treatment proceeds smoothly. Table 7.2 provides a summary of educational messages that are particularly important to patient medication compliance (Lin, et al., 1994; Lin, et al., 1995).

Table 7.2
Medication Information to Cover With Patient

1. It will take 2 to 4 weeks for you to begin to experience beneficial effects from the medication.
1. You will need to take the medicine every day.
1. Stop the medicine only when you decide with your provider that it is time to stop.
1. Call the clinic if you are concerned about any unpleasant sensations that you think might be related to your medication.

Special Sessions

Patients may elect to have an open-agenda session towards the end of treatment. Chapters 5 and 6 of the *Living Life Well* book address these optional sessions. Some patients will want to attend a session with you to work on these skill areas. Other patients will need a special session to practice other skills or work on a current life problem. **Special sessions may be used for couple or family meetings or for further study and application of a previously covered skill area.** As with all other sessions, structure is very important in special sessions. Set a clear agenda at the beginning of the session and be certain that it is an agenda that can be accomplished in 30 minutes.

Documenting and Coordinating Care

Chart immediately after every contact with patients in the ICP and place the chart note on the referring provider's desk before you leave the clinic. You will be able to complete charting during your allotted 30-minute contact if you use time wisely and use a structured charting form that includes the information suggested in Table 7.3.

You help to coordinate care when you strengthen the patient's relationship with her/his primary care providers. There are a number of ways of doing this. You may simply make a positive statement about the primary care provider. Alternatively, you may report that the primary care provider said something positive about the patient's participation in the ICP. In general, **try to make a favorable reference to the primary care provider in every contact you have with a patient.**

Table 7.3
Information to Chart After Every Contact With Client

ICP Chart Note Date:

Patient Name: Medical Number:

This patient was seen today for her/his:

☐ 1st, ☐ 2nd, ☐ 3rd, ☐ 4th, ☐ 5th, ☐ 6th, ☐ Last visit.

Patient assessment indicates depression in the:

☐ non-depressed, ☐ mild, ☐ moderate, ☐ severe range.

Treatment Plan

1. *Medication:*
   Dose:
   Beneficial Effects Reported:
   Target Symptom:
   Plans to Cope with Side Effects:
2. *Behavioral Health Plan:*
   Patient plans to practice the following skill(s):
   Patient plans to engage in the following activity to improve her/his mood:

How to Avoid Unnecessary Referrals to External Providers

After completing the Integrated Care Program, most patients will not need additional mental health treatment. The self management focus of the ICP is acceptable to most patients and is often preferred by patients who are reticent about seeking mental health care. Patients who lack specific skills may be candidates for externally located educational classes, such as parenting or couple communication classes. These classes may be available in the community or within the healthcare system's preventive care programs. **When a patient asks about additional mental health treatment, explain that you will continue to provide therapeutic support for six months after conclusion of in-clinic sessions in the ICP.** Explain that practicing relapse prevention skills in a "field experiment" may help the patient develop confidence in her/his ability to prevent depression and live life well. You may also tell the patient that you will be available to support the patient in the event of a crisis during the 6-month follow-up period. Explain to the patient that other members of the health care team are also available to support relapse prevention plans.

Relapse Prevention Plans

In the patient's last ICP clinic visit, help the patient develop a relapse prevention plan. The plan is called the "Progress Plan" and a format for this plan in provided in Appendix F. It is the last format included in the *Living Life Well* behavioral health plan section of the Appendices. **The relapse prevention plan asks the patient to engage in specific behavioral activities for the six month period following active treatment. The prevention plan also includes a list of the coping strategies that have been most useful to the patient and that will be strengthened through on-going practice and/or study.** Place a copy of completed relapse prevention forms in the medical chart for other providers to use in supporting the patient. In regular medical visits, primary care providers may ask the patient questions about progress in implementing the relapse prevention plan. Of course, the patient will have a copy of the written relapse prevention plan to review on a regular basis. You will initiate four calls to the patient over the course of the first six-month period following active treatment. In your calls, you inquire about the patient's success in implementing this plan.

Occasionally, a patient may need an in-clinic booster session with you during the follow-up phase of treatment. When a patient comes for a "booster" visit, structure the visit. Review the patient's use of strategies to address current problems. At the visit's conclusion, "update" the patient's existing relapse prevention plan.

After you have provided ICP behavioral services in a clinic for 6 months, you may be ready to start a booster treatment group. The content of the group could be a reoccurring sequence of seven topics, all of which are "repeats" of the original ICP in-clinic sessions. A "drop-in" format would provide maximal ease of access to patients and avoid the cost of scheduling patients. When the booster group census is down, the consultant can use the time to complete phone call follow-ups with patients.

Phone Therapy

You will support the patient's relapse prevention plan through a series of calls 2, 4, 12, and 24 weeks after the patient completes the in-clinic phase of treatment. Prior to initiating a phone call, review the patient's relapse prevention plan. You may start the call with a statement that encourages the patient to be brief. The following is an example.

> *"Hello. This is Dr. Strosahl. I am calling to check on you and your relapse prevention plan. Have you been following the plan?"*

If a patient begins a "long story," you may use some of the following questions to redirect the conversation.

- *Does that mean your plan is working to improve your mood (your enjoyment . . . your relationship . . .)?*
- *Does that mean that we need to make a change or "update" to your relapse prevention plan?*

Try to keep phone calls to 5 or 10 minutes. Complete a brief chart note on phone calls. Primary care providers need to be "up to date" on changes to the relapse prevention plan.

The ICP Report Card

There are three provider "report cards in the ICP." Formats for each of the three roles played by mental health professionals are located in Appendix G. The first report card concerns the on-site Behavioral Health Consultant. Patients who participate in the Behavioral Treatment protocol contribute to the ICP consultant's report card. The suggested format includes information about patient satisfaction with treatment and the ability of the consultant to retain referred patients in treatment. The format includes the number of patients who start treatment and the number who complete treatment, which estimates **the consultant's ability to *retain* patients.** This **is an important dimension because patients who complete treatment are much more likely to be clinically improved than those who drop out of treatment prematurely.** The behavioral health consultant's report card may be distributed to managed care professionals, clinic administrators and patients. Table 7.4 presents an example of an ICP provider report card.

Table 7.4
ICP Provider Profile

Provider: Leslie Thompson Date: May, 1996
I started providing ICP Behavioral Health Consultation services on: July, 1995.
During this time period, I have had: 72 referrals . Of the 64 who started the ICP treatment involving the 4 to 7 session protocol, I have completed 4 or more sessions and participated in the development of a relapse prevention plan with 59 patients.

Patients treated by me in this model reported mean satisfaction ratings of
7.2 at the time of treatment planning, and
8.4 at the end of treatment.
(The scale used for satisfaction ratings is 1 = not satisfied to 10 = very satisfied.)

There are two other provider evaluation formats in the ICP. The report card for the medication specialist includes the following criteria: accessibility, "thoroughness while being brief," provision of education and training (to the primary care provider and behavioral health consultant), and satisfaction with treatment by patients who have a face-to-face consultation. The report card for external providers of mental health services includes assessment of four areas: accessibility, use of ICP treatment strategies and materials, provision of efficacious treatment, and return of the patient with a strong relapse prevention plan.

Patient Education Materials

ICP educational materials include two booklets and a short patient workbook. The booklets are available in Appendix D. Educational materials are discussed extensively in Chapter 5. We provide only an overview here.

Seven Ways to Cope

Seven Ways to Cope is a 23-page booklet on how to use coping strategies. The format of the booklet encourages the patient to take an active role in treatment. Between appointments, the patient completes brief written exercises in the booklet. The patient brings the booklet to the follow-up appointment. The provider reviews the patient's work and provides additional instruction and assistance in planning as needed. *Seven Ways to Cope* gives practical pointers to the patient on how to use the same strategies that are covered in *Living Life Well: New Strategies for Hard Times. Seven Ways to Cope* is useful in the ICP Brief Treatment protocol, which is supported by the Coping Plan.

Using Medications Successfully

Using Medications Successfully is a 12-page booklet that explains use of medications in treating the syndrome of depression. The booklet answers questions commonly asked by patients starting antidepressant therapy. Also, the booklet identifies common problems patients have in adhering to prescribed medications and presents a variety of strategies for coping successfully. Use this booklet when a patient wants to start pharmacological treatment, regardless of whether the patient pursues the Brief Treatment protocol or the Behavioral Treatment protocol.

Living Life Well: New Strategies for Hard Times

We looked for a title for the ICP companion self-help book that would describe the purpose of the book in words that most primary care patients could understand and accept. Primary care patients vary in their willingness to recognize and label their struggles as "depression." In truth, many depressed patients face a wide array of problems in their lives that go beyond the troubling symptoms of depression. We hope that the title, *Living Life Well,* appeals to many of your discouraged patients, including those who do not identify "depression" as a chief complaint. Hopefully, the title will encourage patients to set treatment goals with you. Be sensitive to the patient's way of explaining his or her struggles, and adjust the treatment model to make it "user friendly."

Living Life Well: New Strategies for Hard Times is designed specifically for depressed primary care patients. It may be used as a "companion reader" to support the strategies suggested in the ICP Behavioral Treatment protocol or by patients participating in any other ICP protocol. The book is relatively brief and may be supported by phone calls from providers or clinic visits. Most patients will be able to read one or two chapters each week. The book may also be used to support patient participation in a group ICP model. Chapter 8 presents ideas concerning group formats.

When patients do not read *Living Life Well* or read it sporadically, you may want to stop assigning specific chapters. However, you may continue to use the book as a treatment support by presenting information and skill development exercises from the chapters in *Living Life Well* in your health care visits with patients who are not reading the book. This adaptation may prove particularly useful with more severely depressed patients, who lack adequate concentration for reading.

The ICP Brief Treatment Protocol

The Brief Treatment protocol for the Behavioral Health Consultant is quite simple. It utilizes the Coping Plan format that underlies the ICP Clinical Management protocol for primary care providers. Read Chapter 5 to learn more about the Coping Plan and the Clinical Management protocol.

The Initial Visit

After completing an assessment, explain the biopsychosocial model to the patient. If you believe the patient is a good candidate for the Brief Treatment protocol, explain the program to the patient. If you believe the patient to be a good candidate for either the Brief or Behavioral protocol, offer the patient a choice. If you believe the patient needs more intensive treatment, describe both protocols and recommend the Behavioral Treatment. On occasion, more severely depressed patients will prefer the Brief protocol. These patients may be more autonomous and prefer self-management strategies or have a close relationship with the primary care provider. Other patients face life circumstance problems that limit their availability for attending health care appointments (e.g., difficulties with obtaining leave time from the place of employment). **Remember, the basic guidelines are: (1) select the least intensive treatment needed to improve patient functioning and (2) allow the patient a choice.**

When you and the patient select brief treatment, use the Coping Plan to structure your interview. If medications are an issue, use the Medication Assessment Questionnaire in planning. Provide the patient with written instructions by using the last page of the Coping Plan to indicate the medication and behavioral health plans. If you see the patient for a single session, provide written suggestions to the primary care provider regarding on-going clinical management of the patient. For example, your chart note might indicate the following in the "Plan" section.

> *Plan: Patient will follow Coping Plan set up today. Patient has benefited from regular exercise and weekly social outings in the past. Needs support in restarting these as a regular part of lifestyle. Primary care follow-up needs to include weekly support calls to the patient. He prefers calls at end of day at home number. Leaving a message is fine.*

Follow-Up Visit(s)

For patients you see more than once in the Brief Treatment protocol, use the Coping Plan Follow-Up form. Provide the patient with written instructions by using the last page of this form. Often, you will be able to write a basic relapse prevention plan based upon your two or three contacts with the patient. Your chart note might provide the following instructions regarding primary care provider support of relapse prevention plans.

Plan: Patient plans to maintain and further treatment gains by continuing to

1. *use medication for 6 months*
2. *attend reading group weekly*
3. *take a painting class*
4. *take short walk on lunch hour and look at the fountain*

Patient will also monitor mood, using a 1 to 10 scale, when she goes out for breakfast on Sundays.

***Primary Care team needs to support** the patient with brief, supportive phone calls twice monthly for the next 2 months and then monthly for 3 months.*

The ICP Brief Treatment Protocol: An Example

Teresa had been living life "on the edge" for several years. She had survived a violent marriage, a difficult divorce, separation from her children, and a brief period of homelessness. She presented to her primary care provider with complaints of insomnia and headaches. During the interview, she indicated that she might lose her job due to her company's plans to lay off a large number of employees. Teresa cried and indicated periods of breathlessness and a fear that her heart would "burst from beating so hard." She reported fatigue throughout the day. When questioned regarding behavioral coping efforts, she reported that she had stopped exercising and socializing during the past month. While concentration was a concern, she indicated that she was able to perform job duties well. Teresa reported a positive response to brief pharmacological treatment of depression during her participation in a job training program for homeless people several years ago.

Teresa's primary care provider initiated antidepressant therapy and referred her to the on-site behavioral health consultant for further evaluation and planning. The primary care provider believed that Teresa would be a good candidate for the Brief Treatment protocol. Treatment selection was influenced by Teresa's history of positive response to pharmacological treatment and her current apprehension about missing time from work to attend medical appointments. Her primary care provider wanted consultation to assist with development of a strong clinical management plan for Teresa, given her symptoms of panic and history of trauma.

The behavioral health consultant saw Teresa six days after her visit with her primary care provider. At that visit, Teresa reported additional problems including intrusive images of being choked. She indicated terrifying dreams of being chased and attacked. Teresa had taken the medicine prescribed by her physician every morning, but noted no improvement. She reported having gone to a movie, as planned with her primary care provider. While she enjoyed the movie briefly, she felt "terribly alone" after the movie. She indicated increasing hopelessness and added, "I cannot even kill myself." The behavioral health consultant and patient discussed Teresa's problems and decided to focus treatment on depression and to see if the planned treatment would also alleviate other distressing symptoms.

At the first follow-up visit with the behavioral health consultant, Teresa indicated that she had complied with her medication and behavioral health plans. She noted that she felt more calm and able to concentrate at work. She was thankful for these improvements, but noted continued difficulties with sleeping. The consultant acknowledged her successes and encouraged her to continue with both plans, as they were yielding results. The consultant checked with the prescribing provider during the visit, and he decided to augment pharmacological treatment with use of a more sedative agent at a low dose in the evenings. The consultant and Teresa planned several additional lifestyle changes, including a structure for her evening routine. The program included completing two 10-minute small housecleaning tasks and engaging in one or more relaxing activities every evening prior to going to bed.

Three weeks later, Teresa returned for her third and last visit with the consultant. She was "75%" better at that visit. Both mood and sleep were improving. She reported more optimism about her job after having a talk with her supervisor about job security issues. The behavioral health consultant helped her to develop a relapse prevention plan that included a method of monitoring and regular participation in five activities Teresa identified as central to her sense of well-being. This plan was written for Teresa and charted for the primary care team. The consultant recommended that Teresa make monthly phone call "updates" on her continued improvement to a primary care nurse.

The ICP Behavioral Treatment Protocol

Table 7.5 provides an overview of possible patient visits during treatment in the ICP Behavioral Treatment protocol. Some patients will use medications in combination with the behavioral treatment, while others will use behavioral treatment as a solo treatment. Consultants and patients negotiate a specific number of contacts (i.e., 4, 5, 6 or 7) at the initial visit. The consultant also determines an appropriate level of treatment intensity. Less intensive treatment involves fewer sessions over a longer period of time. More intensive treatment entails more frequent visits over a shorter period of time. Phone calls to the patient between clinic visits are another way to increase treatment intensity.

For the average patient, the behavioral health consultant will provide 3 to 4 hours of behavioral treatment in direct contact with the patient at the primary care clinic (in-clinic phase) and 4 brief phone calls over the 6-month period following patient completion of in-clinic treatment. The tasks of the primary care provider in the ICP Behavioral Treatment protocol include: diagnosis and referral, medication treatment monitoring, and on-going support of the

Table 7.5
Contacts with Patient

Provider: BHC or PCP*	Week(s) after Diagnosis	Contact	Length of Contact	Topic
PCP	0	First-PCP	10-15 minutes	Diagnosis & Referral to BHC
BHC	1	First-BHC	30 minutes**	Hoping...Planning...Doing
BHC	2	Second-BHC	30 minutes	Building Acceptance and Making Value-Based Choices
PCP	2	Second-PCP *(optional)*	10-15 minutes	Medication Follow-Up
BHC	3	Third-BHC	30 minutes	Appreciating Your Mind and Body
BHC	4	Fourth-BHC	30 minutes	Solving Problems
BHC	5	Fifth-BHC *(optional)*	30 minutes	Responding to Interpersonal Conflict
BHC	6	Sixth-BHC *(optional)*	30 minutes	Expressing Yourself
BHC	7 (or 5 or 6)	Seventh-BHC	30 minutes	Continuing to Live Life Well
PCP	7, 8, or 9	Third-PCP *(optional)*	10-15 minutes	Medication Follow-Up Review Relapse Prevention Plan
BHC	7, 8, or 9	Phone Call-BHC	5 minutes	Relapse Prevention
BHC	9, 10, or 11	Phone Call-BHC	5 minutes	Relapse Prevention
BHC	17, 18, or 19	Phone Call-BHC	5 minutes	Relapse Prevention
BHC	29, 30, or 31	Phone Call-BHC	5 minutes	Relapse Prevention
PCP	on-going			Relapse Prevention

* BHC = Behavioral Health Consultant and PCP = Primary Care Prescriber
**The initial appointment will need to be 50 minutes in length if a patient is starting antidepressant therapy.

relapse prevention plan written at the conclusion of behavioral treatment. For patients using medications, treatment may involve coordination of visits to the primary care provider and the behavioral health consultant.

Some patients will start antidepressant therapy prior to their referral to you. Others may initiate antidepressant treatment later. On occasion, primary care providers do not have time to start a patient on an antidepressant at the time of diagnosis. Some patients are ambivalent about medications at the onset of treatment. **As a consultant, you need to be prepared to help patients make a decision concerning whether or not to include antidepressant therapy as a component of their treatment** in the Integrated Care Program. You will coordinate medication treatment through the primary care provider with prescriptive authority. You or the primary care provider may initiate a phone consultation or single brief patient visit with a Medication Specialist for the exceptionally complex patient. **No more than 5 to 10% of depressed primary care patients require direct contact with a mental health medication specialist.** The more critical role of the Medication Specialist in the ICP is that of supervising your work with patients who are receiving antidepressant treatment in conjunction with the behavioral intervention and advising primary care providers on medication issues. Medication specialists may also help you set up a system for monitoring prescription refills by patients who are taking antidepressant medication.

The following section is designed to help you implement the Behavioral Treatment protocol. It includes suggestions for using time effectively, individualizing treatment, and assisting with medication issues. Feel free to expand upon the material suggested in this section. Efficient use of your own strengths in treating patients may enrich your results.

Session 1: Hoping...Planning...Doing

Use of Time

Table 7.6 will help you plan your use of time during this session. Do explain to the patient at the beginning of treatment that this treatment program is educational in nature and that you will discuss key concepts related to behavioral strategies in each session. Explain that the initial contact may be a little longer than subsequent contacts, all of which will be 20 to 30 minutes in length. In the initial visit, you will need 30 to 45 minutes if a patient is planning to use medications as a part of their treatment for depression.

Table 7.6
How to Use Your Time with Patients: Hoping...Planning...Doing

Session Task	Minutes
Introductions, Establish Rapport	5
Explain Treatment Model	5
Present Critical Concepts	5
Discuss and Plan Medication Issues	5 to 20
Make a Behavioral Health Plan: "Hoping, Planning, Doing"	5
Total	25 to 45

Critical Concepts

There are four critical concepts to convey to the patient in this initial session.

1. On-going self-assessment helps you to live life well.

Use the depression spiral model to explain how assessment allows you to "stay in touch" with your mood during stressful times. Explain the role of thoughts, feelings and behaviors in living life well and in not living life well. Define "behavioral strategies" as tested techniques for helping you make upward movements on the depression spiral. Briefly review the three approaches to assessment presented in *Living Life Well* and ask the patient to complete one or more during the session, if they have not completed one before the session. The three approaches include the Quality of Life Scale (QL Scale), the Symptoms Checklist, and the Daily Wellness Check (DW Check). Copies of forms for most of these assessments are incorporated into the ICP Assessment and Treatment Plan, which is located in Appendix C. The QL Scale generates information about the patient's progress in applying behavioral strategies. The Symptoms Checklist is particularly useful for patients who choose to use medications. The Symptoms Checklist provides you with a symptom profile that is quite useful to busy physicians who assist with medication issues. The DW Check requires only a few minutes and has the advantage of requiring the patient to assess the extent to which she/he lived life well on a daily basis. Many patients prefer the DW Check. You may want to stock small pocket-sized spirals to give to patients who plan to apply the DW Check approach. You can write in the rating scale (1 = did not live life well, 10 = lived life well) on the inside cover for patients to use as a reference.

2. Depression is a biopsychosocial illness.

Explain that stress affects the biology of a person. In turn, biology affects a person's behavior. A person can "take charge" by changing her/his behavior (which will in turn change her/his biology back to a non-stressed state). Alternatively, a person can change her/his biology (which will facilitate the return of more functional behavior). Sometimes, a person will want to use behavioral and biological (medication) strategies in combination.

Allow the person to choose her/his treatment. If she/he wants to use medications, ask her/him to complete the *Medication Assessment Questionnaire* (Appendix B). Chapters 2 and 3 of this book present detailed information on helping patients use medications successfully. Complete the medication assessment and if you are not a prescriber, work closely with your prescribing colleague to keep care coordinated. When a patient is ambivalent about use of medications, indicate that you are willing to discuss it further in future meetings.

3. You can increase your hopefulness.

Explain that hope comes from believing that change is possible. Help the patient to revise self-critical explanations of their predicament, as these tend to inhibit experimentation with new behaviors. Discuss the concept of "just do it" (i.e., go to a movie, call a friend) and illustrate through an example how inspiration comes from doing.

4. You can make a plan to change your behavior.

Ask the patient if they have had times during the past week when they felt better. Ask what they were doing when they felt better. For example, a patient may say that he felt better when he saw an old friend at a restaurant. Use the patient's example to illustrate how behavior impacts mood. Explain that this fact underlies the "Behavioral Health Plan," and explain the steps in creating a Behavioral Health Plan.

Exercise Selection

Patients who are more chronically depressed are likely to need more help in revising explanations of their present dilemma. These patients have stronger beliefs about the impossibility of their situations. You may suggest that he or she develop a more self-affirming explanation of his or her current difficulty as a "hypothesis." Explain that they do not have to "believe" it right now--only that they consider it and plan accordingly.

Possible Problems

More severely depressed patients may have difficulties focusing their attention during the visit and reading material in the self-help book prior to or after the visit. Speak clearly. Check for understanding. As you develop the Behavioral Health Plan with the patient, record details on the Behavioral Health Plan Format. See Appendix F for the Behavioral Health Plan Formats for all seven treatment sessions.

Medication Issues

Unless patients are already taking a therapeutic dose of antidepressant medication, you may help the prescribing provider by completing the *Medication Assessment Questionnaire* with the patient. When patients have not started antidepressant therapy but have an interest in doing so, this exercise helps you evaluate her/his potential for successful medication treatment. In addition, your assessment may help the prescriber anticipate and plan for potential obstacles in antidepressant therapy. Help the patient thoughtfully consider beliefs she/he may have about psychotropic medications. Sometimes patients have limited and inaccurate information and you can be an educational resource for them.

Motivating Patients To Complete Behavioral Health Plans

The first "Behavioral Health Plan" needs to be extremely specific and simple. If the patient is not 100% confident in the plan, revise the plan in the direction of requiring less from the patient and/or more support from you. For example, you may want to offer a 5-minute phone follow-up on the Behavioral Health Plan to patients who are less confident.

Ask the patient if they believe in the model you are suggesting. Help patients identify someone who will support their efforts. Many will also need help in identifying and planning rewards or reinforcers. Help the patient generate a list of possibilities. Ask the patient to commit to participating in the planned activity to reward herself/himself for completing the Behavioral Health Plan. Find a way to acknowledge the effort the patient is making in seeking treatment. You may be the only person who compliments the patient that week.

Session 2: Building Acceptance and Making Value-Based Choices

Use Of Time

Table 7.7 will help you plan your use of time during this session.

Table 7.7
How to Use Your Time with Patients:
Building Acceptance and Making Value-Based Choices

Session Task	Minutes
Self-Assessment	5
Evaluate Behavioral Health Plan concerning "Stimulating Hope And Making Behavioral Health Plans"	5
Present Critical Concepts	5
Discuss and Plan Medication Issues	5
Make a Behavioral Health Plan concerning "Building Acceptance And Making Value-Based Choices"	5
Total	25

Critical Concepts

There are four critical concepts to cover in the second session. Three of these may be somewhat new and seem curious and even odd to patients who have participated in other forms of psychotherapy. To familiarize yourself with these ideas, read the second chapter of *Living Life Well* several times and experiment with using the recommended exercises in your own life. This will boost your skillfulness in this group of newer strategies. Additionally, you may want to read *Acceptance and Commitment Therapy: Understanding and Treating Human Suffering* (Hayes & Strosahl, 1996).

1. **We will always review your behavioral health plan from our previous session.**

   Always begin sessions with a weekly review that includes:

   - Patient self-assessment using the Quality of Life Scale, the Symptoms Checklist, and/or review of the patient's Daily Wellness Checks,
   - Thoughtful consideration of the patient's results from the Behavioral Health Plan made in the previous contact, and
   - Patient ratings on skillfulness in using the previous session's strategies (session 1: generating hope and making effective behavioral plans) on the Goal Attainment scale (where 1 = lower skillfulness and 10 = higher skillfulness).

2. **Psychological acceptance helps you stop avoiding uncomfortable thoughts, feelings, and images.**

   Briefly define psychological acceptance. Ask the patient to give examples of psychological experiences that she or he tends to resist, for example feeling sad or anxious. Then, help the patient explore the consequences of using avoidance strategies. When avoidance strategies prevail, a person may find herself/himself spending very little time being still or quiet, rarely going to parties, having few interactions with friends, or being less honest and open with loved ones.

Keep the tone of your discussion inquisitive and collegial. If the patient begins to speak critically of herself/himself, assure the patient that we all engage in avoidance strategies. Explain that you are working to use acceptance strategies more in your day-to-day life. Tell your patient that you believe that she/he can make progress in this area with concerted practice.

3. **Psychological acceptance allows you to choose a course of committed action.**

   Explain that psychological acceptance is an active process of embracing psychological experiences that are very difficult to tolerate. When you are able to "stop" momentarily to pay attention to more aspects of your life context (including unwanted thoughts, feelings, and actions), you disconnect from your "automatic cycle." You are empowered to respond to life in ways that differ significantly from long term patterns. Challenge the patient to recall a time in life when she/he chose a course of committed action; identify the types of suffering the patient "accepted" while pursuing the course of committed action.

4. **You feel most vitally alive when your behavior reflects what is most important to you.**

   Introduce the concept of vitality. Work with the patient to brainstorm synonyms for vitality (e.g., animation, energy, fervor, life, spirit, sprightliness, spunk, verve, vigor, vivacity, zest, zip). Ask the patient to identify an action that she/he takes on a regular basis that generates this feeling in this life. Connect this activity to the concepts of psychological acceptance and value-based living.

Exercise Selection

Patients who are more chronically depressed and/or anxious may need more assistance in working with their breath. Demonstrate a slow, deep breath. Place your hand on your stomach to show the patient how the "belly" moves in the full natural breath. Explain that the full natural breath helps one move into the "observation" or acceptance state of mind.

Possible Problems

Patients may have difficulties writing out more descriptive information about avoided psychological experiences. If you anticipate that a patient will struggle with this, you may ask the patient to quickly complete the checklist of psychological experiences that she/he wants to control or avoid in the session. Ask the patient to select a specific feeling, thought, or image. Then ask the patient to give you several phrases to describe the avoided feeling, thought, or image. You can write these descriptors on pieces of scrap paper and ask the patient to use these experiences in practice periods at home.

In addition, you may want to help more depressed or less psychologically sophisticated patients select a method of self-observation during the session. You might simply ask, "When you need to learn something new, do you prefer to watch a demonstration or read about it?" Most patients will be able to respond to this question in a straight-forward manner. You can then help to define a method of self-observation that reflects the individual patient's strength in experiencing life (i.e., visual or verbal/auditory).

Medication Issues

Patients who started antidepressant therapy in the first session may be suffering with side effects. Evaluate side effect severity and perceived self-efficacy in coping with side effects. Suggest behavioral strategies for minimizing the discomfort of side effects. Help the patient focus on beneficial medication effects, too. Patients who have not started antidepressant therapy may want to discuss use of medications with you further at this visit. Help the patient make a choice. Collaborate with prescribing professionals. Provide assessment information to prescribers so that they can work with you and the patient in a timely manner. Sometimes, a primary care prescriber is available to drop in and write a prescription at the time of the patient's visit with you.

Motivating Patients To Complete Behavioral Health Plans

Help the patient anticipate that this assignment will be difficult. Insist that she/he plan a significant self-reward and record this on the Behavioral Health Plan before the patient leaves the session. Set specific times and dates for practice of psychological acceptance. When a patient is less confident, you may ask the patient to call you in two days if she/he needs further information or support to follow the Behavioral Health Plan. Explain to the patient that this strategy requires her/him to be courageous and bold.

Session 3: Appreciating Your Mind and Body

Use Of Time

Table 7.8 will help you plan your use of time during this session.

Table 7.8
How to Use Your Time with Patients: Appreciating Your Mind and Body

Session Task	Minutes
Self-Assessment	5
Evaluate Behavioral Health Plan Made Last Session: "Building Acceptance and Making Value-Based Choices"	5
Present Critical Concepts	5
Discuss and Plan Medication Issues	5
Make a Behavioral Health Plan: "Increasing Mind-Body Awareness and Relaxation Skills"	5
Total	25

Critical Concepts

There are three concepts to cover in the third session. Again, the concepts are complex and you need to focus on keeping your patient actively involved in your explanation of concepts. Providing some in-session practice helps the patient feel more confident in using new strategies later at home.

1. **Your ability to concentrate or focus your awareness on your mind-body develops through practice.**

   Concentration is difficult and pivotal to your success in work and leisure activities. Explain that sustained concentration on the body is a skill which many people lack. Describe the benefits of a close relationship with your mind and body, e.g., early identification of and effective response to tension.

2. **You can create sensations of well-being in the body through skillfully working with your mind-body.**

   Emphasize that the amount of practice time required to generate sensations of well-being decreases with practice. You can use a metaphor to make your point. For example, you might talk about the lengthy process of self-instruction and experimentation involved in learning to ride a bicycle. After the basic skill is learned, it requires only seconds of preparation to ride again. With a patient who appears to present with a high level of tension, take time to ask her/him to make a tense fist, hold it 20 seconds and then to relax the hand. Ask the patient to close her/his eyes to "tune in" to the sensations of "*letting go*" and to describe these sensations of well-being to you.

3. **Consider developing more neotenous qualities during the next year.**

   Most people who are vulnerable to depression are unnecessarily serious. Often, they struggle with perfectionist tendencies and worry about offending or displeasing others. Explain to the patient that he or she once "just knew how" to play, make a mess, do exactly what he or she wanted, laugh whenever something seemed funny. Elucidate on this point by suggesting that development of more neotenous qualities in day-to-day life is really a matter of *remembering.*

Exercise Selection

Patients who suffer from a great deal of general motor tension may benefit from on-going practice of the Jacobson (1974) tension and relaxation exercise. Patients who are more facile in relaxation skills may want to focus on improving their concentration abilities in exercises that focus on the body. Encourage patients with panic attacks to practice both the systematic relaxation and the breathing exercises. Patients will probably be able to select an exercise to help further develop skills for positively influencing mind-body experience. Once a patient selects an exercise to practice, spend a minute discussing the importance of "chaining" a cue to the exercise practice. A cue is a special word or phrase or specific image or sound rehearsed just prior to the exercise. You may want to help some patients develop their cue in session.

Possible Problems

Patients with chronic excessive tension may need an additional session with you, where you can talk them through the tension relaxation exercises and help them check for tension in troublesome muscle groups. Additionally, some patients will need your help in developing specific tensing procedures for muscles they have difficulty relaxing.

Patients who attempt to engage in neotenous activities may report success in creating moments of greater vitality in their life *and* report sadness that much of life had passed without this vitality. Be prepared to accept their sadness and explain that sadness is also a part of vital living. Encourage patients to continue experimenting in this area in order to create a more stable presence of playfulness and spontaneity in life.

Medication Issues

Continue medication discussions with patients who are using antidepressant medications. If you have concerns, work closely with the patient and prescriber to address problems. Help patients to notice small improvements that may be related to adherence to prescribed medications. Some patients may want to stop antidepressant therapy early and some patients may just now be willing to start antidepressant therapy. Help the patient to work collaboratively with the prescriber.

Motivating Patients To Complete Behavioral Health Plans

In the "Awareness and Mind-Body Integration Strategies" section of the Behavioral Health Plan, write specific practice times and any important adaptations beside the endorsed skill. This provides important structure for the patient. In the section on living according to values, remember to be specific and simple. There is a tendency to become more general in behavioral planning as treatment continues and the patient makes improvements. There is also a tendency to assign multiple behavioral plans as treatment progresses. Counter or at least temper these tendencies so that your patient continues to successfully adhere to behavioral plans.

Session 4: Solving Problems

Use Of Time

Table 7.9 will help you plan your use of time during this session.

Critical Concepts

There are four important concepts to cover in this session, which may be the next to last active treatment phase contact for patients electing to complete only the basic program of 4 or 5 sessions.

Table 7.9
How to Use Your Time with Patients: Solving Problems

Session Task	Minutes
Self-Assessment	5
Evaluate Behavioral Health Plan Made Last Session: "Increasing Mind-Body Awareness and Relaxation Skills"	5
Present Critical Concepts	5
Discuss and Plan Medication Issues	5
Make a Behavioral Health Plan: "Building Self-Efficacy and Problem-Solving Skills"	5
Total	25

In beginning this session, clarify treatment plans with the patient. Some patients will want to change any previously-made treatment plan in the direction of lengthening or shortening treatment. Ask a patient who plans to "graduate" or complete treatment in the next visit to read the seventh chapter in *Living Life Well.* Ask the patient to complete the written exercises and to bring them to your last visit. Present the following concepts briefly.

1. There are four necessary elements in making personal changes.

Review the four steps with your patient:

- identifying that something is a problem,
- accepting the possibility that something can be done about the problem,
- expressing a desire to change, and
- being willing to work and to make an effort to change.

Acceptance strategies help patients succeed in the first step toward making an intentional change in life. Self-efficacy helps patients succeed with the second step in making a personal change. Strategies in this session will help your patient plan change in more difficult and sensitive areas of their life.

2. Self-efficacy is your belief in your ability to cope with what life brings you.

Explain that when self-efficacy about a problem is high, you tend to see the problem as a challenge. You are able to bring positivity and creativity to your efforts to handle difficult situations. When you lack self-efficacy, you are more likely to use avoidance strategies and *less* likely to get the results you want. Another word for self-efficacy is self-confidence. Self-confidence grows by experiencing success in solving problems, one small problem at a time.

3. A solution to a problem may not have a direct relationship to the problem.

Explain that a person may overlook a viable solution at times because he or she assumes a direct relationship between the problem and solution. For example, a person may assume that the only solution to the problem of living with an alcoholic spouse is the spouse's cessation of alcohol. You may help your patient to disconnect the solution and problem link by asking questions. For example, you might inquire, "What could you do that would help you feel better while living with your spouse, even if he did not stop drinking?" This type of question helps the patient explore potential solutions that are unrelated to the solution of eliminating the problem.

4. Skillful problem-solving includes carefully evaluating results of a problem-solving plan.

Excellent problem-solving plans may go unevaluated. Unfortunately, one misses out on important information when this happens, even when the plan has gone well. Thoughtful evaluation of problem-solving plans brings greater awareness. Expanded awareness will benefit subsequent problem-solving efforts.

Exercise Selection

You may ask a patient about her/his strengths and weaknesses in the area of problem-solving. Is she/he able to:

1. Define problems so that they can be solved?
2. Creatively brain storm solutions?
3. Evaluate potential solutions?
4. Identify "first steps?"
5. Plan for obstacles?
6. Engage in committed action or "*do it*?"

7. Evaluate the results?

You will want to help the patient anticipate and plan details in weak areas of problem-solving.

Possible Problems

More chronically depressed patients may have difficulties with brainstorming solutions. When thinking patterns are predominately negative, patients may filter out solutions prior to carefully evaluating their potential effectiveness. When working with a patient who is suffering with more firmly established negative thinking patterns, encourage her or him to brainstorm with you and just "blurt out" potential solutions without evaluating them at all. Invite the patient to "take turns" with you in generating even "wild and crazy" solutions.

Patients with a tendency to think in more global terms will need your help in defining specific solvable problems *and* in specifying precise practical solutions. Some patients might tolerate your drive toward explicit definitions better if you use humor and explain, "Just a minute. I'm not sure I see what you mean. Can you paint me a little more of the picture?"

Medication Issues

Most patients will require little support with medication issues at this point in treatment. Patients who are not using medications will be noting considerable improvement in mood and functioning. Patients using medication will be past the break-in period when side effects are more troubling. As patients sustain treatment at a therapeutic level, treatment benefits will be more significant. If new side effects appear (e.g., a change in libido), work collaboratively with the patient and physician to address them.

Motivating Patients To Complete Behavioral Health Plans

Patients are more likely to complete the Behavioral Health Plan about using problem-solving strategies if they have a friend or loved one who will support them. If the patient has no one, you may write out an encouraging phrase on their Behavioral Health Plan or simply write your name on the line beside question 3, "Who is a resource for me in solving this problem?" Remember to have the patient plan a specific self-reward and to ask the patient the extent to which he or she is committed to the plan. The problem-solving strategy plan is complex and involves more steps than previous plans. Remember to keep the steps small and specific. In ending this session, you may want to compliment the patient on progress she/he has made in recent weeks.

Optional Session: Responding to Interpersonal Conflict

Use Of Time

Table 7.10 will help you plan your use of time during this session.

Critical Concepts

There are three critical concepts to cover in this session. Most of the patients who elect to attend this session are currently struggling with interpersonal conflicts. Interpersonal problems are the single most common stress reported by depressed primary care patients. Further, on-going marital dissatisfaction is highly predictive of recurrent episodes of depression. Begin your presentation of concepts this week by praising the patient for taking time to become more skillful in this important area.

Table 7.10
How to Use Your Time with Patients: Responding to Interpersonal Conflict

Session Task	Minutes
Self-Assessment	5
Evaluate Behavioral Health Plan Made Last Session: "Building Self Efficacy And Problem-Solving Skills"	5
Present Critical Concepts	5
Discuss and Plan Medication Issues	5
Make a Behavioral Health Plan: "Working On Relationship Conflicts"	5
Total	25

1. **The only way to successfully avoid conflict with other human beings is to avoid *contact* with human beings.**

Explain to the patient that conflict can be a healthy part of life. There is no need to avoid conflict when one learns to work skillfully with it. In fact, a good conflict can be invigorating.

2. **You can learn to "stay in touch" with your mind-body, even during a moment of conflict with another.**

Learning to "stay in touch" with yourself *during* conflict is the first and most important step in improving your effectiveness in this area. When you lose touch with yourself, you can easily resort to older less effective strategies, such as passivity, unproductive reciprocal grousing, or aggression. When you "stay in touch," you can take time to care for yourself as you work with the other person.

3. **When you are "in touch" with your mind-body, you can choose more productive responses to conflict.**

Explain that many people want to avoid conflict. A person who wants to avoid conflict may "simmer" internally and this may cause physical damage to vital organs. Alternatively, a person who wants to avoid conflict may choose to dampen the flames with alcohol, which of course, may backfire. Other people do not mind conflict and seek to "win" at any cost. These people may win a battle, but lose the war, as they usually have few friends.

Some people are able to see conflict as a necessary part of a healthy life. In conflict situations, their intention is to express themselves, to listen and to learn through a lively exchange. The experience of conflict is vital because:

- There is no intention to harm the other person.
- There is no unresolved anger or pain after the conflict ends.

Exercise Selection

Patients who are excessively dependent may benefit from concerted practice with "beginning exercises" (i.e., daily caring moment exercise, awareness of personal feelings exercise, and respectful expression of feelings exercise). Patients who are now less depressed and in a relationship with a partner who is not depressed may want to use the "connecting exercises" (i.e., the caring days exercise, Aikido blending exercise) and the "dancing exercises" (i.e., use of the 5 steps in solving interpersonal conflicts skillfully).

Possible Problems

As a patient becomes less depressed, she/he behaves differently in significant relationships. While a loved one will welcome some changes, other changes will result in interpersonal conflicts. Use of exercises from this session will help the patient assess the possible need for mental health services for couples. Often, participation in a couples communication class will be helpful. Sometimes, a couple may want to consult with you for a single appointment to resolve a specific and isolated problem. Occasionally, a couple will pursue couples counseling.

Medication Issues

Most patients will not require education and planning services regarding use of medication at this point in treatment. Patients who are not using medications will be much improved and no longer interested in considering medications. Patients using medications will be maintaining treatment at a therapeutic level. You can now devote all of your time to behavioral treatment.

Motivating Patients To Complete Behavioral Health Plans

Encourage the patient to focus on one or two exercises from this chapter. He or she can always spend more time on these exercises after completing the treatment program. Patients are most likely to succeed when Behavioral Health Plans specify clear practice of limited exercises with an explicit intention of improving quality of life in a specific area. Again, compliment your patient for choosing to improve use of effective strategies in this challenging area of life.

Optional Session: Expressing Yourself...Assertively and Creatively

Use Of Time

Table 7.11 will help you plan your use of time during this session.

Critical Concepts

Patients who want to attend this session are probably feeling much better. They are likely to be ready to further develop strategies of effective personal assertion and/or restorative creative expression. Both of these strategies will increase the patient's resilience to stress in the future and will reduce the risk of a future episode of clinical depression. There are four concepts to cover in this session.

1. **"Driven doing" is an avoidance strategy that uses up one's time and energy and returns little in the way of restoration.**

Table 7.11
How to Use Your Time with Patients: Expressing Yourself

Session Task	Minutes
Self-Assessment	5
Evaluate Behavioral Health Plan Made Last Session: "Working on Relationship Conflicts"	5
Present Critical Concepts	5
Discuss and Plan Medication Issues	5
Make a Behavioral Health Plan: "Personal Assertion and Creative Expression"	5
Total	25

"Driven doing" is a way of distancing oneself from the pain of not accepting oneself as one is. Explain to the patient that all humans are many things--good and bad, helpful and hateful, generous and stingy, kind and cruel. If you are unwilling to accept your less positive thoughts, images and feelings, you are vulnerable to the development of "automatic" driven patterns. These patterns help you momentarily hide from the parts of yourself that you see as the enemy. Driven doing takes many forms (e.g., drinking, compulsive shopping, remote control channel surfing) and fails to restore us emotionally, mentally, or physically.

2. **Acceptance is a form of validation.**

Explain to the patient that self-acceptance is a strong affirmation of basic worth, unconditioned upon acceptance or validation by others. Acceptance of another person is likewise a validation of that person and her/his human right to be as she/he is--separate from you *and* responsible for herself/himself. This concept is particularly important for patients who are prone to excessive guilt and have an exaggerated sense of personal responsibility.

3. **"Not doing" allows you time to choose personal assertion and creative expression, which help restore energy and balance.**

A very good point-blank question to ask your patient is, "When is the last time you just did nothing?" High achieving patients will have difficulty identifying a time when they "just sat." It is good to commiserate with the patient by saying, "Well, I guess the saying we heard more often in growing up was, 'don't just sit there, do something.'" Continue to help the patient explore the potential value of "not doing" and suggest a new saying to the patient, such as "*Don't just do something, sit there.*" Challenge the patient to spend 5 minutes alone in a room later in the day. The space of "not doing" allows your awareness to grow bigger and your acceptance of yourself and others, more authentic.

4. **When you accept yourself, you are able to validate your need to have opinions and preferences, as well as creative abilities and avenues for expression.**

Help the patient evaluate the strength of belief she or he has in basic assertive rights and the extent to which she or he "lives" these rights in day-to-day life. Explain that we may be able to subscribe to numerous basic rights when we are in a psychological state of self-acceptance. However, endorsement of these rights at the level of committed behavioral action requires repeated practice and perseverance.

Help the patient investigate time she/he has spent in creative activity in the past week. If the patient perceives this area to be out of balance, help her/him explore resources for creative expression.

Exercise Selection

Patients who are lacking effective assertion skills need to explore assertion exercises, and patients who have little opportunities for creative expression in their present lifestyle need to explore creative expression. Patients with continuing symptoms of depression and/or exceedingly difficult life circumstances will benefit from both of these exercises.

Possible Problems

Personal assertion skills require time to master and most patients who have deficits in these areas will need on-going support and training. Many community centers and community colleges have 6-week Assertiveness Training classes. You may encourage patients to continue practice by giving them phone numbers for community resources. Also, a patient may be more likely to follow through on your recommendation of a class if you provide a schedule of available classes or workshops.

Classes may also be a resource for patients who are unsure of their creative talents and/or interests. You may want to maintain a list of community resources for patients to use in locating potential creative activities. Emphasize the importance of trying new and different activities and explain that interests change over time.

Medication Issues

Most patients will not require education and planning services regarding use of medication at this point in treatment. Patients who are not using medications will be much improved and no longer interested in considering medications. Patients using medications will be maintaining treatment at a therapeutic level. You can now devote all of your time to behavioral treatment.

Motivating Patients To Complete Behavioral Health Plans

When a patient plans to implement a difficult assertiveness plan, you may want to help her/him develop an "assertive chant" within the session and to practice it briefly with you. Be positive. Compliment the patient on his or her efforts. Unless the patient is functioning very well, you may want to suggest that she/he choose only one area--assertive expression or creative expression--as a target in their behavioral health plan. Remember to target a specific area of life concerning behavioral expression of values and write out who will support the patient in her/his efforts. Congratulate the patient on having completed six (or five) weeks of treatment.

Last Session: Continuing to Live Life Well...Planning Your Lifestyle

Use Of Time

Table 7.12 will help you plan your use of time during this session.

Table 7.12
How to Use Your Time with Patients: Continuing to Live Life Well

Session Task	Minutes
Self-Assessment	5
Evaluate Behavioral Health Plan Made Last Session: "Personal Assertion and Creative Expression"	5
Present Critical Concepts	5
Discuss and Plan Medication Issues	5
Make a Relapse Prevention Plan: "The Progress Plan"	5
Total	25

Critical Concepts

There are six important concepts to present in the last in-clinic visit. Before presenting the concepts, ask the patient to complete the Symptoms Checklist and compare present responses with the pre-treatment results. Share areas of change with the patient. Compliment the patient for staying with the program.

The purpose of the last visit is to identify key strategies, including an approach to self-assessment, and to collaboratively develop a written relapse prevention plan. The relapse prevention plan is the final Behavioral Health Plan. It is referred to as the "Progress Plan." A copy is included in Appendix F. You need to make multiple copies of this plan at the end of your last visit. Copies need to go to the patient, the patient's medical chart, and to a record-tracking system that will be easy for you to access at the time of phone call follow-ups. Reviewing the "Progress Plan" is the primary focus in all four phone call follow-ups.

1. **Evaluate what has helped you the most in this approach.**

   Use the Strategy Review Exercise to help the patient evaluate the usefulness of this treatment model to her/him. In this exercise, the patient identifies strategies that need to be continued during the critical follow-up phase, which continues for the six months after active treatment. Discuss ways that she/he can incorporate use of these key strategies into her/his lifestyle.

2. **Stay in touch with your body/mind.**

   Help the patient decide upon a method of self assessment. The patient may select from the Quality of Life Scale, the Symptoms Checklist, or the Daily Wellness Check. Some patients will prefer a less intense approach to self-monitoring. An option that requires little time is to have the patient rate her/his sense of having lived according to her/his values once each week on a specific day of the week. For example, a patient might plan to make her rating on Sunday morning before reading the paper. The patient might use a 1 to 10 scale, where 1 = did not live according to my values that week and 10 = lived life according to my values that week. You can instruct the patient to adjust her/his attention to use of behavioral coping strategies according to the results of their weekly monitoring. For example, a patient might want to review her/his Progress Plan when her/his weekly rating is below 6. **Simplify the method of planned self-assessment to the point where the patient feels committed to doing it on a**

weekly basis. Most patients need to use a formal self-assessment technique weekly for at least the first month after in-clinic treatment and on a monthly basis for five additional months.

3. **Anticipate and plan for stressful times in life.**

Ask the patient to anticipate upcoming changes (e.g., a child leaving home, a friend's move, retirement, a change in income). Ask the patient to select one anticipated change and work with the patient to plan ways to manage the stress of this change. Challenge the patient to plan for the other changes she/he is anticipating.

4. **Associate with others you trust.**

Life can be fairly grim at times and having someone you trust and see often provides protection to your mental and physical health. Sometimes the people you trust most do not live near you. When this is the case, you may consider getting a pet, as our affiliation with animals appears to boost our mental and physical health in the same ways that our affiliation with humans does.

5. **Know your values and live them.**

Ask your patient to share her/his work on the values exercise in Chapter 7. Commend your patient for demonstrating important values in day-to-day life.

6. **Make a written plan and review it monthly for the next six months.**

Work collaboratively with the patient to help her/him develop a Progress Plan. Discuss where the patient will keep her/his copy of the plan and when she/he will review it. Explain that you will telephone the patient 2, 4, 12 and 24 weeks later to see how able she/he is to follow the plan and to assist with making updates.

Exercise Selection

All of your patients should complete all of the exercises. Hopefully, patients will complete some of the exercises before the appointment. If not, complete the Progress Plan during the visit.

Possible Problems

A few patients may struggle with ending treatment. You may acknowledge that you enjoyed working with them. If a patient's daily functioning has improved, emphasize the improvements and encourage the patient to "test out" new strategies by using them more independently for the next six months. Assure patients that you will be calling them on a regular basis. Explain that you will support continued use of strategies and that you will be available by phone should there be a need to check-in prior to a scheduled phone call. In fact, you may want to ask the patient is to call you if self-assessment results indicate a problem.

Occasionally, you will have a patient who is progressing slowly in this model of treatment. You may discuss treatment options, including the patient's use of more intensive mental health services. When patients elect to start an episode of counseling immediately after the program, you may ask the patient to give a copy of her/his Progress Plan to the subsequent provider. This will maximize continuity of care.

Medication Issues

Check to see that patients taking antidepressants have a clear plan regarding continuation of the medication after their last in-clinic visit with you. Also, ask the patient what they know about stopping antidepressant medications. The following three educational messages are useful at this visit.

1. Do not stop your antidepressant medication without making a plan with your prescriber.
2. Most often, stopping antidepressant therapy involves a "tapering" plan.
3. Most depressed primary care patients take antidepressants for 3 to 6 months after reaching a therapeutic dose.

Ask the patient to schedule a visit with their primary care physician in the next month to discuss the relapse prevention plan and use of medications.

Motivating Patients To Complete Behavioral Health Plans

Tell your patient you know that she/he might like to forget her/his recent difficulties. Explain that this would be a mistake because life will send them a golden, engraved invitation to become stressed out or depressed again in the near future. The patient needs to be ready to respond strategically to this invitation. Challenge the patient to review her/his Progress Plan on a regular basis. Ask patients to identify a "helper" in their social network with whom they are willing to share their plans. That person might be a primary care physician or nurse, a neighbor, friend, relative or spouse. Write down the name of the person they believe will be able to support them in fulfilling their plan to continue to live life well. If they have no one to support the plan, suggest yourself or a primary care provider. End the meeting by complimenting the patient for making so much progress and developing a strong relapse prevention plan.

Phone Call Follow-Ups

Use Of Time

Table 7.13 will help you plan your use of time during phone calls to patients.

Table 7.13
How to Use Your Time with Patients: Phone Call Follow-Ups

Session Task	Minutes
Evaluate patient adherence to the "Progress Plan"	5
Present Critical Concepts	5*
Discuss and Plan Medication Issues	5*
Update Progress Plan	5*
Total	5 to 20

* Devote additional time to these tasks when a patient is not adhering to her/his plan, when a new stress requires an update to the plan, or patient is experiencing problems with medication.

Critical Concepts

Review the patient's Progress Plan prior to initiating the phone call. Then you are ready to ask key questions and support use of important strategies in a time-effective manner. You can help the patient understand what to expect by starting with the statement, "I need about five minutes of your time to review the plan we made X weeks ago. Is now a good time?" There are three concepts to cover in the four phone call follow-ups.

1. **You are still vulnerable. Stay aware.**

   Explain to the patient that they continue to be vulnerable. New skills are vulnerable for 6 to 12 months. Encourage the patient to use her/his planned self-assessment approach on a regular basis. Compliment the patient for any and all attempts she or he reports concerning "staying in touch" with herself/himself.

2. **Behavioral Health Plans can help you develop the lifestyle you choose.**

   Briefly review with the patient the types of strategies she/he planned to continue to use. If needed, help the patient see the connection between the planned use of a strategy and a sense of living life well.

3. **Change your Progress Plan when you need to change it.**

   If a portion of the Progress Plan is out-of-date at the time of your phone call, review potential changes with the patient. Support her/him in making necessary updates. Explain that we can not anticipate and plan for all difficulties in life. Encourage the patient to continue to make planned changes to the relapse prevention plan as needed.

Exercise Selection

During the period of phone call follow-ups, you may notice that a patient is not using and did not intend to use a potentially powerful strategy. Sometimes, you may simply ask the patient to reread a section of *Living Life Well* to see if she/he sees any potential value of a specific exercise at this point in her/his life. You may suggest use of this strategy. If the patient agrees, you can simply make a note on your copy of the Progress Plan. This will remind you to ask the patient about the results of this update in your next phone call follow-up.

Possible Problems

During the six month period of phone call follow-ups, patients may experience numerous problems. There may be new dramatic stresses, such as deaths of loved ones or diagnosis of serious health problems. When a patient reports a recent crisis, express concern and support and stay with the structure of the phone call follow-up.

Patients may discontinue and, then, restart antidepressant treatment during the follow-up period. Always encourage the patient to monitor symptoms and, if you are not a prescriber, request that the patient work closely with the prescriber, or coordinate medication treatment through the primary care provider.

Motivating Patients To Complete Behavioral Health Plans

During the phone call follow-up phase of treatment, patients may have contact with other health care providers. Placing the patient's Progress Plan in the medical chart enables other providers to support the patient's on-going efforts. When you have contact with other members of the patient's health care team, you may want to acknowledge the patient's progress. In phone call follow-ups, you may mention a positive comment about the patient that another health care provider made. Your patients are often living in difficult circumstances and your nourishment helps them to live life well.

The ICP Behavioral Treatment Protocol: An Example

Annalise retired from her job as a school secretary in her early 60's in order to spend time with her spouse. Bill, her 66-year-old husband, was retiring from a busy real estate office. They were both interested in traveling during their retirement years. Shortly after their retirement, Bill developed a cardiac problem that required him to be near a medical facility. Bill worried about his health and avoided travel. The relationship between Annalise and Bill deteriorated. Bill missed his work and struggled with ways to structure his free time. Bill became overly focused on Annalise. He followed her around the house and questioned her frequently about her plans. Annalise was a quiet person who lacked effective assertion skills. In an effort to enrich her life, she became involved in church work. Unfortunately, the church work proved to be highly stressful, as it required her to request contributions from church members. Annalise felt more and more annoyed with her spouse, worried about her lack of success in the volunteer position with her church, and dissatisfied with the overall quality of her life.

Annalise sought help for insomnia from her primary care physician, who diagnosed depression. Her physician prescribed Nortriptyline and referred her to the on-site behavioral health consultant for further evaluation and treatment planning. Assessment by the behavioral health consultant indicated limited use of coping strategies and multiple symptoms of depression with significant social, family, psychobiological, and productivity or work limitations.

Annalise was willing to participate in the ICP model of treatment. In an early ICP session, her behavioral experiments centered on creating more enjoyment in her daily life. She began to listen to Spanish tapes on a daily basis. Next, she attempted to engage in enjoyable activities outside of her home and without her husband. Her trips to the donut shop and the library gave her a sense of satisfaction about being alone and free from the watchful eyes of her spouse. Towards the end of the program, Annalise made a behavioral health plan to make a trip to see a friend in another state. One of her last plans included notifying her church leaders that she would be leaving her volunteer position at the end of her term. Annalise decided to involve her spouse in a single special session. The two worked in the session to resolve their on-going struggle with finding "alone" time during their retirement years. Annalise's relapse prevention plan included scheduling pleasurable and relaxing activities, practicing assertion skills, and exploring avenues for creative expression.

Medication Consultation with Specialists

Psychiatrists, pharmopsychologists, clinical pharmacists or prescribing psychiatric nurses may serve your needs for consultation regarding medication issues. In the ICP, the medication specialist provides consultation, supervision, and training to the primary care provider and the behavioral health consultant. Your medication specialist may work in an externally located clinic or provide on-site service in the primary care setting. Medication consultation may occur by phone or in multi-disciplinary staff meetings. A small minority of depressed primary care patients may need a single direct consultation with a medication specialist. If you have a medication specialist on-site in your clinic, you will be able to have on-site multi-disciplinary team meetings and patients will not have to go to an external facility for these services. An on-site medication specialist can enrich the ICP program by providing brief summaries of new medications, innovative strategies for dosing and combining medications, the latest information on drug interactions, etc. If you do not have an on-site medication specialist, use medication specialist services by phone and arrange quarterly team meetings.

Medication specialists will need to be familiar with all aspects of the ICP, including assessment materials. When you contact the medication specialist for a consultation, have the following information available on your patient:

1. ICP Assessment Information
2. Current medical status
3. Current medications
4. Alcohol and drug use information
5. Your question

Formulate a specific question prior to the consultation. Relate pertinent information briefly. Over time, your consultations with the medication specialist will become more efficient.

In addition to consultation and training, the medication specialist may help develop a tracking service for patients receiving antidepressant treatment in the ICP model. The tracking service needs to identify patients taking antidepressants and details concerning their treatment (including the date the medication was started, the type of medication, the therapeutic dosage, and the planned length of treatment). An ICP provider needs to evaluate refills of prescriptions on a monthly basis and to notify a prescriber when a patient fails to request a planned refill of an antidepressant medication. This type of communication can be accomplished quickly in systems with clinical computing work stations.

In summary, the medication specialist role includes the following.

1. Availability for phone consultations
2. On-going supervision and training of behavioral health consultants concerning medication issues
3. Monitoring of antidepressant prescription refills on selected patients and relating refill information to primary care prescribers

Less than 5 to 10% of depressed primary care patients will need direct consultation with a medication specialist. Reserve direct consultation services for medically complex patients and the small minority of patients who fail to respond well to other treatments.

Medication specialists need to be evaluated by primary care providers and behavioral health consultants who use their services. Table 7.14 presents a format for evaluating medication specialists. Providers might complete this scale every 3 to 6 months on medication specialists involved with their clinic. Try completing the performance evaluation (Table 7.14) on the ICP medication specialist who serves your clinic. Rate each of the 4 criteria on a scale ranging from 1 to 25. Assume that **1 is the least positive evaluation and 25 is the most positive evaluation**.

Intensive Treatment by External Mental Health Providers

The most severely impaired depressed patients may need intensive treatment in an external location. External services may be provided by any single discipline or a mix of providers, including psychologists, psychiatrists, psychiatric nurses, nurse practitioners, and master's level therapists. Their treatment needs to be consistent with the ICP model and to incorporate ICP assessment methods and treatment materials. Patients benefit most when care is continuous and consistent. External providers may use group and family or couples sessions in addition to the individual treatment format to help a more seriously depressed patient.

Table 7.14
Performance Evaluation for the ICP Medication Specialist

Please complete the following performance evaluation concerning the ICP Medication specialist who treats more seriously depressed patients identified in primary care. Rate each of the four criteria on a scale ranging from 1 to 25. Assume that 1 is the least positive evaluation and 25 is the most positive evaluation.

Rating	Performance Criteria
1.	Medication specialist is easy to access.
2.	Medication specialist is thorough yet brief.
3.	Medication specialist provides education and training to me as part of the consultation.
4.	Patients are satisfied when they have a direct consultation with medication specialist.
	Total Score

External providers need to complete an ICP assessment at the beginning and end of an episode of external treatment and to send copies of assessment results to the ICP primary care team. Ideally, the external specialist will initiate a brief phone contact with the on-site behavioral health consultant when the patient is completing an episode of specialty treatment. In this call, the external specialist needs to explain the patient's need for a follow-up treatment plan. The primary care team and the on-site behavioral health consultant are responsible for follow-up, including support of a relapse prevention plan.

Primary care and on-site behavioral health consultants may evaluate the work of external providers every 3 to 6 months. Table 7.15 presents a scale for providing feedback to mental health professionals who provide external services for ICP patients.

Summary and Helpful Hints

This large chapter presents all information needed for you to start providing on-site behavioral health services according to the ICP model. Your initial efforts will pay off most if you are also very familiar with the information, examples, and exercises in *Living Life Well: New Strategies for Hard Times*. As you begin to provide on-site behavioral health services to depressed patients, remember the following critical concepts.

1. The Brief Treatment protocol involves 1 to 3 sessions with the patient.
2. The Behavioral Treatment protocol involves 4 to 7 sessions with the patient. Encourage patients to complete sessions 1, 2, 3, 4, and 7 at minimum. If an additional session needs to be omitted to better meet the time limitations of a patient, omit the third session (Body/Mind Strategies). Encourage the patient to study omitted strategies between sessions.
3. In both protocols, you are a *consultant*. Your relationship with the patient is limited and temporary.

Table 7.15
Performance Evaluation of the ICP External Provider of Mental Health Services

Please complete the following performance evaluation on the ICP external provider of mental health services who treats more seriously depressed patients identified in primary care. Rate each of the 4 criteria on a scale ranging from 1 to 25. Assume that 1 is the least positive evaluation and 25 is the most positive evaluation.

Rating	Performance Criteria
1.	External provider was easy to access.
2.	External provider used ICP materials.
3.	External provider provided efficacious treatment.
4.	External provider returned patient with a strong relapse prevention plan.
	Total Score

4. In both protocols, you provide specific recommendations to the patient and the primary care team.
5. Review Critical Concepts and Tables summarizing session tasks and timelines prior to each visit with the first 10 patients you treat in the Behavioral Treatment protocol.
6. Be accountable for keeping patients involved the Behavioral Treatment protocol. If a patient fails to show for an appointment, call that patient within 24 hours of the missed appointment.
7. Ask clinic staff to obtain patient satisfaction information for you, so that patients are more able to be honest in their feedback.
8. Hold medication specialists and external mental health providers accountable for incorporating elements of the ICP model into their treatment and doing their part to assure that treatment is "seamless" for the patient.

References

Goodman, M., Brown, J., & Deitz, P. (1992). *Managing managed care: A mental health practitioner's survival guide.* Washington, DC: American Psychiatric Press, Inc. 1.

Hayes, S., Strosahl, K., & Wilson, K. (1999). *Acceptance and commitment therapy: An experiential approach to behavior change.* New York, NY: Guilford.

Jacobson, E. (1974). *Progressive relaxation.* Chicago, IL: The University of Chicago Press, Midway Reprint.

Lin, E., Von Korff, M., Katon, W., Bush, T., Simon, G., Walker, E., & Robinson, P. (1995). *Achieving Guidelines for the Treatment of Depression in Primary Care: Training Model vs. Reorganization of Service Delivery.* Presented at the Eighth Annual NIMH International Research Conference on Mental Health Problems in the General Health Care Sector, McLean, Virginia, September 7-9, 1994.

Lin, E., Von Korff, M., Katon, W., Bush, T., Simon, G., Walker, E., & Robinson, P. (1995). The role of the primary care physician in patient's adherence to antidepressant therapy. *Medical Care, 33*(1), 67-74.

Chapter 8

The Integrated Care Program: Group Models

The purpose of this chapter is to present possible group formats in the ICP model. The context of care created by group approaches is particularly useful after the ICP Brief Treatment and Behavioral Treatment protocols are "up and running" in a clinic. In this chapter, you will learn the following.

- Advantages and disadvantages of using groups
- Adaptations that enhance success in an ICP Behavioral Treatment Group
- How to provide an ICP Medication Group
- How to provide an ICP Relapse Prevention or "Progress" Group

---

Instructions for Speed Readers: Allow 5 minutes to read this chapter. Critical information is printed in bold.

ICP Groups: Advantages and Disadvantages

For the most part, individual treatment advantages outweigh group treatment advantages in the ICP model. **However, some mental health providers may prefer to treat depression in the group format. Group cognitive therapy and group behavior therapy have repeatedly been shown to result in statistically significant changes in depressive symptomatology** (Nezu & Perri, 1989; Fleming & Thornton, 1980; Nezu, 1986). Group treatments may play an important role in prevention of more severe forms of depression (Muñoz, et al., 1995). Also, group cognitive therapy demonstrated significantly statistically better results than usual care as provided by general practitioners (Ross & Scott, 1985; Scott & Stradling, 1990). **Finally, group models may help behavioral health consultants meet challenges to access in a clinic with a well-developed ICP.** Review the following advantages and disadvantages for using the ICP Behavioral Treatment model in groups. This will help you decide how and when to use groups in your setting.

Advantages of an ICP Group

1. May help diminish social isolation.
2. Provides patients with a setting for practice of interpersonal strategies and skills recommended in the ICP.
3. May help with specific aspects of the treatment (for example, start of antidepressant therapy).
4. May help with management of patients who start to relapse and need "booster" treatment.
5. Serves multiple patients with a minimum of resources.

Disadvantages of an ICP Group

1. Is not an acceptable treatment format for a significant group of patients.

2. May present an access barrier to patients, as multiple groups at multiple times of the day and week are unrealistic.
3. May not allow for patients to have adequate individualization of ICP treatment materials and plans.
4. Is a challenging context for close monitoring of important treatment outcomes.
5. Often has a higher drop-out rate than individual treatment.

ICP Behavioral Treatment Groups: Important Adaptations

You may adapt the ICP model of individual care described in earlier chapters to a group format. Patients may read assigned chapters in the book *Living Life Well: New Strategies for Hard Times*, and you may use the session-by-session agenda suggested for the individual treatment program. The following adaptation strategies will help you succeed in implementing treatment in the group setting.

1. **Prescreen referrals for the group.** Require patients to complete ICP assessment materials prior to the prescreen appointment. Evaluate the patient's interest in a group format in the prescreen appointment. Explain the advantages of the group approach to the patient. The group program may not be an adequately intensive treatment for more severely depressed patients. For these patients, you will need to supplement the group treatment or proceed with a plan that does not include group. Prescreens may be completed in brief clinic visits or in phone consultations.
2. **Require patients to monitor** their own functioning and response to treatment on an on-going basis. Ask patients to come prior to the start of each group in order to complete weekly assessments. Keep assessments brief. The ICP Level 1 assessment form is usually an adequate approach to weekly assessment. You may ask patients to report improvements in key areas of functioning (family, work, leisure) in a brief "going around the circle" check-ins at the beginning of each group session.
3. **Require patients to read the book,** *Living Life Well: New Strategies for Hard Times.* Assign one chapter each week. Have copies of exercises and behavioral health plans for each chapter available in each class. Center weekly group meetings around strategies and exercises from the assigned chapter.
4. **Introduce critical messages** in a "lecture" format. Be prepared to present relevant examples to portray key concepts. Encourage patients to suggest a current, personal problem for you to use in illustrating concepts.
5. **Create a group value for adherence to behavioral health plans.** Begin group sessions with a brief report from each patient concerning (a) results of self-monitoring and (b) adherence to behavioral health plans. Compliment patients for small successes in implementing plans. Encourage patients to commend and support each other for small, consistent efforts to improve quality of life on a daily basis.
6. **Schedule the group for the middle or the end of the work day.** Saturday mornings are also a good time for groups. Plan a 1-hour group. Start and end on time.
7. **Plan to arrive 15 minutes early and stay 15 minutes late** to consult individually with patients. Let patients know that you will be available at these times. Use consultations to help patients develop behavioral health plans that they can implement with confidence.
8. **Circulate information about groups to primary care providers several times in the 3 weeks just prior** to the start of a group. Prepare one-page handouts about the group for providers to give to potential candidates. Handouts need to include the start date and time, the number of

planned sessions, and the goals of the group program. Additionally, you may include a phone number for patients to call to schedule prescreen appointments and/or to obtain more information about the group.

9. **Start groups on a regular basis.** A workable schedule may be to start groups on even-numbered (or odd-numbered) months. A seven-session format allows for one holiday every eight-week cycle.
10. **Allow relapsing patients to enter Behavioral Treatment groups at any session.** Give relapsing patients praise for "seeking" support on their relapse prevention plan. Work with them to add needed "updates" to their relapse prevention plans.
11. **Consider using the group format for a target patient population.** For example, groups for older patients may fill quickly in clinics who serve a large number of older patients. You are most likely to realize economic benefits from a group approach when you target patients who are (1) more available for group treatments (e.g., retired patients) and (2) whose risk status (e.g., for social isolation) is reduced by the treatment.
12. **Use examples that are age appropriate.** Examples need to address the experiences of members of the group. Have examples from all age groups ready.
13. **Give ample time to explaining acceptance strategies.** Avoid giving the impression that your patients just need to "buck up."
14. **Suggest that each person in the group have a partner** in the class *or* outside of the class. Responsibilities of the partner might include discussing the assigned chapter and exercises in a contact between group meetings and being available to support the partner's behavioral health plan.

ICP Medication Groups

Group formats may also help patients start antidepressant therapy successfully. Medication groups require that the leader have expertise in antidepressant therapy. Medication specialists may lead these groups. However, non-prescribing mental health providers may also be leaders in medication groups. When a non-prescribing provider is the leader, she or he will need to work closely with a supervising prescriber. Following is a list of guidelines to help you succeed in providing medication group services.

1. Require patients to attend a prescreen prior to starting the group. If the patient has not completed an **ICP Medication Assessment Questionnaire** (MAQ), complete the MAQ at the prescreen. Work with the referring provider regarding start of a medication.
2. **If you do not have prescreen appointments, include completion of the MAQ as a referral requirement.** The group leader or a nurse colleague may complete MAQ assessments by phone and coordinate any needed changes with physicians, physician assistants, or nurse clinicians prior to the patient's start in the group.
3. **Require patients to read** *Living Life Well: New Strategies for Hard Times.* Explain that treatment is more likely to be successful when it includes education about behavioral health issues.
4. **Devote half of the group meeting time to medication issues and half to behavioral health planning.**
5. Start each class with self-monitoring of symptoms of depression.
6. **Ask participants to "go around the circle"** and briefly summarize any desired changes in symptoms or troublesome side effects in the prior week and results of behavioral health experiments from *Living Life Well: New Strategies for Hard Times* during the first 15 minutes of each meeting.

7. **Provide patients with small, pocket spirals** to use in recording medication and behavioral health plans week to week.
8. **Review common side effects and suggested coping strategies. Compliment patients** for discovery of creative strategies for coping with use of medications.
9. **Create a group value for adherence to medication *and* behavioral health plans.** Be positive with patients and encourage them to support each other for small, consistent efforts to use medications and to improve quality of life through behavioral change.
10. Schedule the group for the middle of the day or the end of the work day. Plan a one-hour group. Start and end on time.
11. **Plan to arrive 15 minutes early and stay 15 minutes late to consult** individually with patients. Tell patients that you plan to be available at these times. Use pre- and post-group consults to help patients address problems with medication plans and/or develop strong behavioral health plans.
12. **Determine treatment completion criteria,** for example, that the patient reaches a therapeutic treatment dose and reports 2 or fewer symptoms of depression.
13. **Allow patients to determine the number of sessions they attend.**
14. **Allow new patients to enter the Medication Group program at any session.**

ICP Relapse Prevention Groups

Symptoms of depression will reappear for the majority of depressed primary care patients, and the presence of an on-going relapse prevention group may help the healthcare system provide timely and accessible treatment. Patients may be more likely to seek early intervention if it is easily available. You may avoid the high cost of having a group with few patients by waiting to start a Relapse Prevention group. You are probably ready to start a Relapse Prevention group after you see thirty to fifty patients in the ICP Behavioral Treatment program. Additionally, you may **conduct this group as a 30-minute service.** Schedule the ICP relapse prevention group into an end-of-the-day appointment opening. When no patients attend the group, the leader may use the time for therapeutic phone call follow-ups to patients in the Behavioral Treatment relapse prevention phase. The following guidelines will help you succeed in offering ICP Relapse Prevention groups.

1. Announce Relapse Prevention groups to patients when they complete treatment and at phone-call contacts during the relapse prevention phase.
2. Ask patients to bring relapse prevention plans to group meetings.
3. **Focus your intervention on making "updates" to the relapse prevention plan.**
4. Attempt to **build other interpersonal supports** into the patient's relapse prevention plan.
5. Be patient and upbeat in your response to relapsing patients. Congratulate them for noticing symptoms of depression "before things got worse."

Summary and Helpful Hints

Groups can add variety to your practice, whether you work as a behavioral health consultant or a primary care provider. Consider the following suggestions.

1. Groups provide a social setting for isolated patients and a resource for emotional support for patients demoralized by substantial medical co-morbidity.
2. To ease scheduling problems, allow patients to "sign up" for groups.

3. Develop charting formats that help you save time. Consider a form that includes patient assessment results and a two-sentence summary from the leader.
4. When on-site consultants are not available in a clinic, a group of external providers may provide an ICP Behavioral Treatment group in an out-patient mental health clinic.
5. ICP groups may be most useful to you *after* you implement other aspects of the ICP model in your healthcare system.

References

Fleming, B.M., & Thornton, D.W. (1980). Coping skills training as a component in the short-term treatment of depression. *Journal of Consulting and Clinical Psychology, 48*, 652-654.

Muñoz, R.F., Ying, Y.W., Bernal, G., Pérez-Stable, E.J., Sorenson, J.L., Hargreaues, W.A., Miranda, J., & Miller, L.S. (1995). Prevention of depression with primary care patients: A randomized controlled trial. *American Journal of Community Psychology, 23*, 199-222.

Nezu, A.M. (1986). Efficacy of a social problem-solving therapy approach for unipolar depression. *Journal of Consulting and Clinical Psychology*, *54*, 196-202.

Nezu, A.M., & Perri, M.G. (1989). Social problem-solving therapy for unipolar depression: An initial dismantling investigation. *Journal of Consulting and Clinical Psychology*, *57*, 408-413.

Ross, M., & Scott, M. (1985). An evaluation of the effectiveness of individual and group cognitive therapy in the treatment of depressed patients in an inner city health centre. *Journal of General Practice*, *35*, 239-242.

Scott, M.J., & Stradling, S.G. (1990). Group cognitive therapy for depression produces clinically significant reliable change in community-based settings. *Behavioral Psychotherapy*, *18*, 1-19.

Chapter 9

Working with Managed Care Using the Integrated Care Program

The crisis in health care is bringing many changes to the work lives of health care providers. As providers, we are empowered when we face the dilemma of change with a spirit of creativity. Innovative models of care must fit within the culture of "reform" that permeates health care as we approach the turn of the century. This chapter introduces the following.

- A review of significant changes in health care systems during the past 25 years
- The "ingredients" of the ICP managed care package
- How to use the ICP managed care package to save time

Instructions for Speed Readers: Allow 10-15 minutes to read and study this chapter. Critical information is printed in bold. The last section, "The Challenge of Accountability: The Integrated Care Program," is particularly important.

The health care system in America is in dire straits. American doctors perform more procedures than physicians in any other country in the world. However, Americans do not appear to have better health status than citizens of other developed countries (Hilts, 1991). Thirty to 50% of all medical procedures have little or no documented benefit (Brook & Lohr, 1986). **Almost half of controllable health costs reside in provider practice style.**

Health care expenditures are increasing. In 1965, health care costs were 6% of the national product. By 1990, this figure jumped to 12%. By the year 2000, health care will consume at least 15% of the nation's total output of goods and services (Gray, 1991).

In the past two decades, providers have made a transition from working in a fee-for-service "private" sector to working in a "public" sector, under the auspices of managed care. Our **survival depends upon continuous development of skills for answering questions posed by the newest members of the health care team–health care managers and informed consumers.** An understanding of the historical context adds depth to problem-solving efforts.

The Way It Was

Until 1972, health care providers diagnosed and treated patients with little external oversight. Treatments were selected based upon the provider's professional knowledge, personal practice style, and ethical and moral standards. The first federally mandated professional standards review organization (PSRO) was formed in 1972 and health care began to change. **The Peer Review Improvement Act of 1982 mandated both utilization and quality review** for government funded health services. For the first time, private payers also initiated review prior to payment. External review organizations proliferated. Their questions and requests for information needed to certify care plans were new to medical and mental health providers.

The Way It Is

"Managed care" is any care review process that is not determined by the provider alone. Who, other than providers, may determine care? First, utilization review (UR) experts bring their expertise in defining necessity and quality of care. These new experts may work for external companies or for the same company as the health care provider. Other professionals who help to determine care plans are those who develop systems of incentives for providers. System incentives involve shifting profit from the fee-for-service model to a capitated or prepaid health care arrangement. In the older fee-for-service model, providers profit from providing more treatment. In capitated systems, providers profit from providing fewer services. Capitated systems encourage providers to work efficiently and effectively. **In capitated systems, unnecessary or needlessly expensive treatment reduces the profit margin.**

Managed care is not a fad. **Our country is turning a corner, and, on the new street, medical knowledge and provider activities belong to the community.** This shift in ownership has far-reaching implications. One of the newer aspects of care-management involves development of a roster that captures questionable practices of providers of all types of health care. The United States Public Health Service recently started a computerized data bank of all disciplinary actions concerning health care providers. In addition, the Joint Commission is developing specialty-specific "clinical indicators." These include definitions of treatment acceptability based on patient outcome. The American Health Care Policy and Research department is busy developing treatment guidelines, including one for treatment of depression in the primary care setting.

More and more emphasis is placed on approaches that reduce variation among providers and produce high quality outcomes. "Best Practice" models are structured, evidence-based models. Increased structure supports optimal clinical decision-making by busy providers. **The ICP grew from a "best practice" approach.**

The Way It Will Be: Service and Outcomes Accountability

In the future, heath care executives will apply principles of business to make decisions about the use of limited health care resources. For-profit and non-profit health care companies will continue to consolidate diverse groups of providers under uniform corporate structures. Managed care companies will provide corporate connections for providers. Delivery systems will become more integrated. Dr. Russ Newman, Executive Director of the American Psychological Association Practice Directorate, predicts that "one-stop health care shopping" will be a major theme in the near future (1995).

Health care will evolve toward creation of "mega" organizations. Models of care will be multidisciplinary and integrated. Capitation will be the dominant financing model. External utilization review is an expensive process and likely will give way to other management strategies for assuring quality. Case management, practice guidelines and clinical outcome management will replace utilization review. Mental health and primary care providers need to become involved in the marketplace of health care. Business acumen will help providers discover (1) ways to assume the risk inherent in a capitated system and (2) methods to market integrated health care services to an informed public.

Addressing the Challenges of the New Era: The Issues

We can manage the health care resources we use to treat depressed patients. Optimal systems of management use a descriptive language; link assessment, treatment and outcomes; support time management, and facilitate a positive attitude on the part of providers. In designing the ICP, we attempted to address these basic issues, as well as other care-management issues. After discussing the four basic challenges, we will discuss care-management requirements and explain how the ICP addresses these.

1. Language

The function of language is to communicate with others. **As we work in multidisciplinary health care teams more, we see the problems with discipline-specific language.** A language for health care products needs to transcend different theories of treatment. A descriptive language helps us avoid the nuances of specialty-specific jargons. In the book, *Managing Managed Care* (1994), Goodman and colleagues suggest a language based on functional impairments to justify treatment outcome. The ICP draws heavily from their approach. The ICP model assesses multiple areas of role functioning including family, work, social, and other areas. All areas of assessment are descriptive.

2. Integrating Assessment, Treatment, and Outcomes

We can only manage something we can measure. **Effective strategies for measuring treatment outcome begin with initial assessment of the patient and relate closely to both the type and intensity of the treatment.** A method of linking assessment and treatment needs to be simple and clear, yet flexible. Guidelines help providers match assessment results to treatment selection. However, providers need to use clinical judgment to plan implementation details, including *intensity* of care issues. Treatment outcomes warrant on-going assessment. Well-timed assessment enables providers to make needed and timely changes in type or intensity of treatment. Outcomes at the conclusion of treatment need to link with relapse prevention and provider monitoring plans.

3. Time

Time is a critical issue in health care because **time is money and money is scarce**. Indeed, the daily challenge of providers in most areas of health care is to "do more, with less." The ICP requires the patient to complete much of the assessment battery independently and prior to the visit. In the treatment and planning encounter, the provider briefly clarifies patient responses to assessment instruments, assesses patient limitations, and collaboratively plans to implement a treatment protocol. Use of ICP assessment forms and protocols may free the provider to spend more time in developing "healing relationships" with patients (Delbanco, 1993).

4. Attitude

Loss of autonomy in selecting and implementing treatment can be a jarring experience and defensiveness is an understandable response. **However, an attitude of collaboration and a spirit of enthusiasm and initiative help you envision creative management strategies.** Perhaps with tongue-in-cheek, an anonymous writer (Anonymous, 1995) recently suggested the following "hidden benefits" of managed care:

- Technical Assistance and Education
- Opportunities for Socializing
- Promotion of Interdisciplinary Collaboration
- Free Supervision

A sense of humor and a willingness to experiment and be bold are the "teaspoons of sugar" that will help the "medicine of accountability" work miracles.

The Challenge of Demonstrating Accountability: The Integrated Care Program

In designing the ICP, we attempted to develop materials to help providers address accountability issues in time-effective *and* clinically meaningful formats. Table 9.1 lists nine care-management requirements and ICP materials that address these requirements. The ICP Managed Care Package helps you meet documentation requirements with ease. In this section, we describe the interface of ICP protocols with managed care requirements. In the following section, we present directions for using the ICP Managed Care Package. All forms associated with that package are provided at the end of this chapter. An index proceeds the forms and helps you locate them easily.

Table 9.1
ICP Materials for Managed Care

Care-Management Requirements	ICP Materials
Assessment and Treatment Plan	ICP Assessment and Treatment Plan
Appropriateness of Care	ICP Assessment and Treatment Selection Table
Cost Efficiency	ICP Assessment and Treatment Selection Table
Treatment Goals	Summary of ICP Treatment Plans and Goals
Treatment Effectiveness	ICP Treatment Efficacy Reference List
Provider Competence	ICP Provider Profile Format
Patient Satisfaction	ICP Treatment Plan
Safety	ICP Form Letter for Managed Care
Accessibility	ICP Form Letter for Managed Care

1. Assessment and Treatment Plan

You may copy ICP assessment materials and submit them to managed care professionals. Copies of all assessment forms and treatment support materials are provided in the Appendices. Chapter 2 provides detailed information on conducting assessments. The two-tier approach involves patient self-report materials and provider assessment of functional limitations. The "Treatment Plan" format allows you to indicate the selected treatment by check mark and to specify review and completion dates. Additionally, the treatment plan page includes a place for documenting relapse prevention services to the patient.

2. Appropriate Care: The Right Treatment and the Right Intensity

ICP assessment results are formally linked to treatment. ICP treatment options include the following three protocols: (1) Clinical Management by Primary Care Providers, (2) *Brief* Treatment by the Behavioral Health Consultant, (3) *Behavioral* Treatment by the Behavioral Health Consultant. Patients may use antidepressant therapy as an adjunct to treatment in any of the three protocols. Providers adjust "levels of care" to provide adequate intensity of treatment within each of the three treatment protocols. For example, a behavioral health consultant may decide to treat a more severely depressed patient in the 4 to 7 session Behavioral Treatment protocol and to use a maximum level of care within that treatment option. The maximum level of care might involve two clinic visits in the first week of treatment and several phone calls to the patient as supplements to weekly visits suggested by the protocol. Occasionally, initial or on-going assessment results will indicate the need to intensify treatment by involving the expertise of externally located specialists for medication consultation or intensive outpatient treatment. Table 9.2 summarizes guidelines for ICP treatment selection.

Table 9.2
ICP Assessment and Treatment Selection Table*

Assessment Results Suggest	Consider Treatment
Mild to Moderate (2 to 4 symptoms, low coping use score)	Primary Care Team Clinical Management protocol
Moderate Symptoms (5 or more symptoms, low coping use score) *and* Moderate Difficulties with Functioning (scores 10-15 on functional assessment)	On-Site Behavioral Health Consultant Services, including ☐ Brief Treatment protocol or ☐ Behavioral Treatment protocol
Severe Symptoms (6 or more symptoms, low coping use score) *and* Severe Difficulties with Functioning (scores 16+ on functional assessment, has 1+ areas rated imminently dangerous)	Behavioral Health Consultant provides more intensive implementation of Behavioral Treatment protocol *Consider* Specialty Treatment Delivered Externally
Complex or Poor Response to Antidepressant Treatment (no improvement after 4 weeks of treatment)	Consultation with Medication Specialist *Consider* Specialty Treatment Delivered Externally

*Antidepressant Therapy may accompany any treatment option.

3. Cost Efficiency

The ICP Assessment and Treatment Selection Table provides guidelines for selecting a specific treatment option. The philosophy of the ICP is to select the most cost-efficient treatment. As a rule, treatments implemented in primary care are less expensive than treatments provided in mental health outpatient or inpatient settings. Also, **the ICP model encourages the use of the least expensive provider who is competent to render the selected ICP treatment protocol.** For example, medical receptionists may assist patients in completing self-report components of the ICP, while nurses evaluate the nature and severity of patient impairment in functioning. More expensive medical providers attend to more medically complex and severely impaired patients. With less complex patients, master's level therapists provide Behavioral Health Consultation services. After assigning providers to treatment options that are viable in your setting, we encourage you to cost model your program and make additional adjustments as necessary.

4. Treatment Goals

Goals of treatment in the ICP extend beyond a reduction in symptoms of depression. Specific goals are associated with each of the ICP treatment options. Each goal is quantifiable. Progress toward the goals is measured by comparing initial assessment information with completion assessment information. Table 9.3 summarizes ICP treatments and goals.

Table 9.3
ICP Treatments and Goals

ICP Treatment	ICP Treatment Goals
Clinical Management (Primary Care Team)	Decrease symptoms of depression. Increase frequency of use of coping strategies.
Brief Treatment (On-Site BHC*)	Decrease symptoms of depression. Increase frequency of use of coping strategies.
Antidepressant Treatment	Adherence to prescription plan. Skillful coping with medication side effects. Decrease symptoms of depression.
Behavioral Treatment (On-Site BHC)	Decrease symptoms of depression. Increase frequency of use of coping strategies. Increase ability to accept negative emotions. Decrease intensity of negative emotions. Improve quality of life in 1+ areas. Decrease number and severity of limitations in functioning.
Mental Health Treatment Delivered Externally	Same goals as Behavioral Health Treatment.

5. Treatment Effectiveness

Care-management efforts can only improve care to the extent that the treatments used are efficacious. The ICP model is evidence-based. Pertinent research information is discussed in detail in Chapter 10. Additionally, the ICP Managed Care Package includes a list of reference citations that support the efficacy of ICP assessment and treatment protocols, as well as ICP educational materials.

6. Provider Competence / Profiling

Mental health providers need feedback from primary care patients and providers in order to improve services and maintain integrity to programmatic treatments. Appendix G includes an ICP format for evaluating the On-Site Behavioral Health Consultant. Additionally, we present formats for estimating the effectiveness of Medication Specialists and External Mental Health Providers who serve the On-Site Behavioral Health Consultant, primary care staff and depressed patients. The format for on-site mental health providers may be used for primary care providers who want to assess patient satisfaction and retention.

7. Patient Satisfaction

Patients are more likely to complete treatments they perceive to be helpful and gratifying. Also, providers take more pleasure from treatment of depression when their patients are contented with the results. In the ICP model, patients rate their satisfaction level regarding (1) the initial treatment plan and (2) their overall satisfaction at the conclusion of treatment, whether the end occurs at completion of the planned course or sooner. Patients use a scale of 1 to 10 in their ratings, where 1 = "not satisfied" and 10 = "very satisfied." Satisfaction ratings are recorded on the ICP Treatment Plan form.

8. Safety

Safety is an issue in treatment of depression. While completed suicides are rare, suicidal ideation is more common. Certain types of antidepressant medications may potentially create a fatal method for implementing a suicidal plan. The ICP Managed Care Package includes a form letter that addresses patient safety. The letter gives providers an opportunity to indicate whether medication overdose is or is not a safety issue and whether or not a patient is suicidal at the beginning of treatment. The letter encourages providers to specify procedures that will be used to address suicidal risk (Chiles & Strosahl, 1995). Potential procedures include the following.

1. Assure that the available means have been removed from the patient's home
2. Form a 24 hour crisis plan with the patient
3. Reduce the amount of anti-depressant prescription to a 7-day supply
4. Plan brief follow-up phone contacts scheduled with the patient every other day

9. Accessibility Factors

While a health care system may offer effective treatment from qualified staff, patients still have to find their way to the facility where services are delivered. The barrier of geographical location is effectively addressed in the ICP model. Most patients will receive care in the primary care clinic, which is usually located in the patient's neighborhood. The ICP Managed Care form letter includes a fill-in-the-blank section for providing information about treatment accessibility. The format includes distance and travel time from the patient's home or job to the site of treatment and type of transportation available to the patient.

ICP Managed Care Package

The ICP Managed Care Package includes the documents listed in Table 9.4. Each document is presented at the end of this chapter. When you submit information to managed care professionals, send the "Basic Package" for all patients. This package includes ICP Assessment results, ICP Treatment Plan, ICP Form Letter for Managed Care and the ICP Care-Management Information sheet. When you are making an *initial* contact with a managed care organization regarding a patient treated in the ICP model, send additional materials (including: the Assessment and Treatment Selection Table, the Summary of ICP Treatment Plans and Goals and the ICP Treatment Efficacy Reference List). After you have had a patient approved for treatment in the ICP model, many managed care organizations will prefer to receive only the "Basic Package" on subsequent ICP patients. If a managed care organization requests information on provider effectiveness, use ICP provider profile formats and send biannual or annual "report cards" to them.

Table 9.4
Documents in the ICP Managed Care Package*

Basic Package	1.	The Patient's ICP Assessment
	2.	The Patient's ICP Treatment Plan
	3.	ICP Form Letter for Managed Care
	4.	ICP Care-Management Information
Additional Documents	*5.*	ICP Assessment and Treatment Selection Table
	6.	Summary of ICP Treatment Plans and Goals
	7.	ICP Treatment Efficacy Reference List
	8.	ICP Provider Profile Formats

*All documents are provided at the end of this chapter.

Summary and Helpful Hints

The ICP approach includes a Managed Care Package to help you meet the requirements of accountability in a clinically meaningful and time-effective manner. The following suggestions will help you use these materials.

1. Set up a simple computer program to help you track assessment and treatment planning information.
2. Use a "tickler file."
3. Schedule phone call follow-up time on provider templates.
4. Allow flex-time so that phone call follow-ups can be made from home one evening each week or month.
5. Delegate responsibility for assessing patient satisfaction.
6. Make a file for each of the documents in the Managed Care Package, so you have copies available when you need them.
7. Scan copies of Managed Care Documents into your computer.
8. After you "plod through" five cases using this system, you will be close to "earning your wings."

References

Anonymous. (1995). Hidden benefits of managed care. *Professional Psychology: Research and Practice, 26*(3), 235-237.

Belar, C.D. (1995). Collaboration in capitated care: Challenges for psychology. *Professional Psychology: Research and Practice, 26*(2), 139-146.

Brook, R.H., & Lohr, K.N. (1986). Will we need to ration effective health care? *Issues in Science and Technology, 3*, 68-77.

Chiles, J., & Strosahl, K. (1995). *The suicidal patient: Principles of assessment, treatment and case management.* Washington, DC: American Psychiatric Press.

Delbanco, T. (1993). The healing roles of doctor and patient. In B. Moyers, B.S. Flowers, & D. Grubin (Eds.), *Healing and the mind.* New York, NY: Doubleday.

Fox, R.E. (1995). The rape of psychotherapy. *Professional Psychology: Research and Practice, 26*(2), 147-155.

Galbraith, J.K. (1958). *The affluent society*. Boston: Houghton Mifflin.

Goodman, M., Brown, J., & Deitz, P. (1992). *Managing managed care: A mental health practitioner's guide.* Washington, DC: American Psychiatric Press, Inc.

Gray, B. (1991). The profit motive and patient care. Cambridge, MA: Harvard University Press.

Hilts, P. (1991). Demands to fix U.S. health care reach a crescendo. *New York Times*, May 19, 1991, sec 4, pages 1, 5.

Johnstone, B., Frank, R.G., Belar, C., Berk, S., Bieliauskas, L.A., Bigler, E.D., Caplan, B., Elliott, T. R., Glueckauf, R.L., Kaplan, R.M., Kreutzer, J.S., Mateer, C.A., Patterson, D., Puente, A.E., Richards, S., Rosenthal, M., Sherer, M., Shewchuk, R., Siegel, L.J., & Sweet, J.J. (1995). Psychology in health care: Future directions. *Professional Psychology: Research and Practice, 26*(4), 341-365.

McDaniel, S.H. (1995). Collaboration between psychologist and family physicians: Implementing the biopsychosocial model. *Professional Psychology: Research and Practice, 26*(2), 117-122.

Nickelson, D.W. (1995). The future of professional psychology in a changing health care marketplace: A conversation with Russ Newman. *Professional Psychology: Research and Practice, 26*(4), 366-370.

Sullivan, M.J. (1995). Medicaid's quiet revolution: Merging the public and private sectors of care. *Professional Psychology: Research and Practice, 26*(3), 229-234.

Wasson, J., Gaudette, C., Whaley, F., Sauvigne, A., Baribeau, P., & Welch, G. (1992). Telephone care as a substitute for routine clinic follow-up. *Journal of the American Medical Association, 267*(13), 1788-1793.

ICP Managed Care Package Index*

***Use this index to locate specific documents supporting the interface of the ICP with managed care requirements.**

Level 1 Assessment Form

Level 1 ICP Assessment (Patient Completes)			
Patient:	**Provider(s):**		
Dear Patient: Please respond to the following questions. If you need help with any of the questions, ask your doctor or nurse.			
Mark an "X" by any symptom that has troubled you *more days than not* during the past ☐ one or ☐ two (*check one*) week(s).		Today's Date	Return Visit Date
1. Anger or Irritability – often during the day		☐	☐
2. Sadness – often during the day		☐	☐
3. Sleep Problems: ☐ too much; ☐ slow to go to sleep; ☐ waking in middle of night; ☐ early morning waking		☐	☐
4. Interest Problems – a lack of interest in others and in activities you usually enjoy		☐	☐
5. Guilt, self critical thoughts, feeling inadequate or worthless		☐	☐
6. Energy Problems – tired most of the time		☐	☐
7. Concentration Problems		☐	☐
8. Appetite Changes: ☐ significantly greater; ☐ significantly less; ☐ weight gain; ☐ weight loss		☐	☐
9. Psychomotor Problems: ☐ very "slowed down" or ☐ very "speeded up"		☐	☐
10. Pain Problems – more aches and more pain		☐	☐
11. Suicidal Thoughts		☐	☐
How often have you used the following coping strategies in the past ☐ one or ☐ two (*check one*) week(s).			
0 = Not at all; 1 = Once; 2 = Several times; 3 = Almost Daily; 4 = Daily			
1. Participating in pleasurable activities		______	______
2. Participating in activities that boost your confidence		______	______
3. Simply being aware of an uncomfortable thought, feeling, or emotion without struggling with it.		______	______
4. Participating in activities that help you relax		______	______
5. Using problem-solving techniques for problems you're having in life such as problems with your job or relationships		______	______
6. Noticing negative thoughts and replacing them with more realistic thoughts		______	______
7. Participating in creative activities		______	______

Level 2 Assessment Forms

Level 2 ICP Assessment – Page 1 (Patient Completes)		
Patient:	**Provider(s):**	
Dear Patient: Please respond to the following questions. If you need help with any of the questions, ask your doctor or nurse.		
Mark an "X" by any symptom that has troubled you *more days than not* during the past ☐ one or ☐ two (*check one*) week(s).	Today's Date	Return Visit Date
1. Anger or Irritability – often during the day	☐	☐
2. Sadness – often during the day	☐	☐
3. Sleep Problems: ☐ too much; ☐ slow to go to sleep; ☐ waking in middle of night; ☐ early morning waking	☐	☐
4. Interest Problems – a lack of interest in others and in activities you usually enjoy	☐	☐
5. Guilt, self critical thoughts, feeling inadequate or worthless	☐	☐
6. Energy Problems – tired most of the time	☐	☐
7. Concentration Problems	☐	☐
8. Appetite Changes: ☐ significantly greater; ☐ significantly less; ☐ weight gain; ☐ weight loss	☐	☐
9. Psychomotor Problems: ☐ very "slowed down" or ☐ very "speeded up"	☐	☐
10. Pain Problems – more aches and more pain	☐	☐
11. Suicidal Thoughts	☐	☐
How often have you used the following coping strategies in the past ☐ one or ☐ two (*check one*) week(s). **0 = Not at all; 1 = Once; 2 = Several times; 3 = Almost Daily; 4 = Daily**		
1. Participating in pleasurable activities	______	______
2. Participating in activities that boost your confidence	______	______
3. Simply being aware of an uncomfortable thought, feeling, or emotion without struggling with it.	______	______
4. Participating in activities that help you relax	______	______
5. Using problem-solving techniques for problems you're having in life such as problems with your job or relationships	______	______
6. Noticing negative thoughts and replacing them with more realistic thoughts	______	______
7. Participating in creative activities	______	______

Level 2 ICP Assessment – Page 2 (Patient Completes)

Which of these emotions have you experienced on a daily basis during the past week and with how much intensity (1 = "not intense" to 10 = "very intense") and willingness (1= "I cannot tolerate this feeling" to 10 = "I accept this feeling completely")?

Today's Date:			Return Visit Date:		
	Intensity of Feeling	Willingness to Feel		Intensity of Feeling	Willingness to Feel
1. Sadness	1.	1.	1. Sadness	1.	1.
2. Anger	2.	2.	2. Anger	2.	2.
3. Fear	3.	3.	3. Fear	3.	3.

Please record a number beside each activity to indicate how much you "lived your values" in that area *during the past week.* Use this rating scale:

1 2 3 4 5 6 7 8 9 10

Did not live what I value — *Lived according to my values*

	Today's Date:	Return Visit Date:
1. Enjoying Things Alone	1.	1.
2. Accomplishing Things Alone	2.	2.
3. Talking with Others	3.	3.
4. Contentment with Work	4.	4.
5. Sensual Experience	5.	5.
6. Fun with Others	6.	6.
7. Images of a Better Future	7.	7.

For Health Care Provider's Use

If additional measurement used, indicate whether:

☐ *Beck Inventory – Short Form or* ☐ *Geriatric Scale*

☐ *Other:* ______________________________

The Beck Inventory – Short Form has the following norms:

0 - 4 = None or minimal; 5 - 7 = Mild; 8 - 15 = Moderate; 16+ = Severe

Today's Date	Score	Return Visit Date	Score

Level 2 ICP Assessment – Page 3 (Provider Completes)

Note: After reviewing the patient's responses on pages 1 and 2, complete the following assessment to determine the impact of a patient's symptoms on her/his functioning. Interview the patient to clarify the extent of limitation. The format allows you to rate each area today and again at treatment completion. **Critical areas of functioning are in bold font** and need greater weighting in planning treatment intensity.

Today's Date	Return Visit Date	Functional Limitations / Severity Ratings: 0 = Absent/Nonpathological; 1 = Moderate; 2 = Debilitating; 3 = Incapacitating; 4 = Imminently dangerous*

*Severity Rating (0 - 4)		*Family Limitations* (Check if limitation is present)
1. ____	1. ____	1. ☐ Family dysfunction
2. ____	2. ____	2. ☐ Family dysfunction with substance abuse
3. ____	3. ____	3. ☐ Marital/relationship dysfunction
4. ____	4. ____	4. ☐ **Marital/relationship dysfunction with violent behavior**

*Severity Rating (0 - 4)		*Work and Productivity Limitations* (Check if limitation is present
1. ____	1. ____	1. ☐ Work dissatisfaction
2. ____	2. ____	2. ☐ Work performance problems
3. ____	3. ____	3. ☐ Educational performance deficits
4. ____	4. ____	4. ☐ **Inadequate survival skills**

*Severity Rating (0 - 4)		*Social Limitations* (Check if limitation is present)
1. ____	1. ____	1. ☐ **Assaultiveness**
2. ____	2. ____	2. ☐ Manipulativeness
3. ____	3. ____	3. ☐ Social withdrawal
4. ____	4. ____	4. ☐ Oppositionalism
5. ____	5. ____	5. ☐ Uncommunicativeness
6. ____	6. ____	6. ☐ Verbal aggressiveness

*Severity Rating (0 - 4)		*Emotional Experiencing Limitations* (Check if limitation is present)
1. ____	**1.** ____	**1.** ☐ **Self-mutilation**
2. ____	**2.** ____	**2.** ☐ **Substance abuse history**
3. ____	3. ____	3. ☐ Hopelessness
4. ____	**4.** ____	**4.** ☐ **Suicidal thoughts/behavior**

*Severity Rating (0 - 4)		*Psychobiological Limitations* (Check if limitation is present)
1. ____	1. ____	1. ☐ Altered sleep
2. ____	2. ____	2. ☐ Decreased concentration
3. ____	3. ____	3. ☐ Decreased frustration tolerance
4. ____	4. ____	4. ☐ Dysphoric mood
5. ____	**5.** ____	**5.** ☐ **Mood lability**
6. ____	**6.** ____	**6.** ☐ **Psychomotor agitation**
7. ____	**7.** ____	**7.** ☐ **Psychomotor retardation**
8. ____	**8.** ____	**8.** ☐ **Concomitant medical condition**
9. ____	9. ____	9. ☐ Medical treatment noncompliance
10. ____	**10.** ____	10. ☐ **Inadequate health care skills**

Treatment Plan Form

Treatment Plan (Provider Completes)			
Mark an "X" by treatment(s) selected.	Today's Date:	Review Date	Completion Date
1. ☐ Clinical Management by Primary Care Team			
☐ Antidepressant Treatment by Primary Care Team Medication: Target Dose:			
2. ☐ Behavioral Health Treatment by Primary Care Mental Health Consultant ☐ Brief ☐ Behavioral			
3. ☐ Consultation with Medication Specialist			
Medication: Target Dose:			
4. ☐ Intensive Treatment Delivered Externally			

Relapse Prevention Support

We developed a relapse prevention plan with the patient on __________. The relapse prevention plan pertains to the following 6-month period: __________ to __________.

We will contact the patient by phone to evaluate the on-going helpfulness of this plan according to the following schedule.

Dates to Call Patient to Support Relapse Prevention Plan*	Results of Call
1.	1.
2.	2.
3.	3.
4.	4.

*2, 4, 12, and 24 weeks after active treatment

Indicate the patient's level of satisfaction with the initial treatment plan and satisfaction at the time of withdrawal or completion of treatment.

1 2 3 4 5 6 7 8 9 10

Not Satisfied *Very Satisfied*

Patient describes her/his satisfaction with our **initial** treatment plan as: __________________

Patient describes her/his satisfaction with this program of care at the time of :

☐ **withdrawal** as: ______________________________

☐ **completion** as: ______________________________

Form Letter for Managed Care

To Whom It May Concern: Regarding Patient:_______________________

Assessment Date: _______________________

This patient completed assessment with me today. She/he will receive treatment in the **Integrated Care Program (ICP).**

The ICP model involves evidence-based, integrated programmatic treatment of depression by a multidisciplinary team involving primary care physicians, physician assistants, nurse practitioners, pharmacists, nurses, psychologists, psychiatrists and master's level therapists. Research indicates this type of approach significantly improves patient use of coping strategies that lessen depression. Also, patients receiving care in models like the ICP report higher levels of satisfaction with care than patients who receive usual treatment. Participation in this type of treatment results in improved clinical outcomes for patients with major depression. Clinical outcomes for patients with less severe symptoms of depression improve, to a more limited extent, but at a rate consistent with other treatments.

I am attaching copies of:

1.____ Assessment results: ☐ Level 1 ☐ Level 2
2.____ Treatment Plan
3.____ Care-Management Information
4.____ Assessment and Treatment Selection Table
5.____ Summary of Treatments and Treatment Goals
6.____ Treatment Efficacy Reference List
7.____ Provider Profile Data

ICP Care-Management Information

A summary of care-management information follows:

Assessment

Patient's depression level is: ☐ mild, ☐ moderate, ☐ severe, ☐ very severe (check one)

Patient's limitations in functioning are: ☐ minimal, ☐ significant, ☐ moderate, ☐ severe (check one)

Appropriateness of Care

Patient's treatment is appropriate to depression severity and limitations measured in the initial assessment. The patient's treatment is indicated on the ICP Treatment Plan. All treatments and associated goals are described in the attached document titled, "Summary of ICP Treatments and Treatment Goals."

Cost Efficiency

The ICP is a cost-effective model. The most effective and least costly treatment is selected and implemented by the least costly, adequately competent professional.

Treatment Goals

Please see attached document titled, "Summary of ICP Treatments Plans and Treatment Goals" for a list of treatment goals for each ICP treatment. Patient attainment of goals is measured by comparing today's scores with scores at the time of treatment termination.

Provider Competence

Data concerning my experience in treating and retaining patients for treatment completion in the ICP are available upon request. Additionally, competence information is available on my colleagues who provide medication specialist services and external mental health provider services. Available information includes patient satisfaction ratings.

Patient Satisfaction

Patient satisfaction ratings are included on the ICP Treatment Plan form.

Safety

The planned behavioral treatment is safe. Medication overdose ☐ is or ☐ is not (check one) a safety issue for this patient. The patient ☐ is or ☐ is not (check one) currently suicidal. To address suicidal risk, we have:

- ☐ assured that the available means have been removed from the patient's home.
- ☐ formed a 24 hour crisis plan with the patient.
- ☐ reduced the amount of antidepressant prescription to a 7-day supply.
- ☐ planned brief follow-up phone contacts scheduled with the patient every other day.

Accessibility

The planned treatment will be delivered to the patient ____ miles from his/her home or job. This site is accessible to the patient in ____ minutes by way of __________ as a form of transportation.

ICP Assessment and Treatment Selection Table

Assessment* Results Suggest	Treatment Selected	Treatments**
Mild to Moderate (2 to 4 symptoms, low coping use score)		Primary Care Team
	☐ Yes ☐ No	Clinical Management Protocol
	☐ Yes ☐ No	Antidepressant Treatment
Moderate Symptoms (5 or more symptoms, low coping use score) *and* Moderate Difficulties with Functioning (scores 10-15 on functional assessment)		On-Site BHC***
	☐ Yes ☐ No	Brief Treatment
	☐ Yes ☐ No	Behavioral Treatment
	☐ Yes ☐ No	Antidepressant Treatment
Severe Symptoms (6 or more symptoms, low coping) *and* Severe Difficulties with Functioning (scores 16+ on functional assessment has inadequate social support, has 1+ areas rated imminently dangerous)	☐ Yes ☐ No	On-Site BHC Intensive Behavioral Treatment
	☐ Yes ☐ No	Antidepressant Treatment
	☐ Yes ☐ No	Referral for Specialty Treatment Delivered Externally
Complex or Poor Response to Treatment (no significant improvement after 4 weeks of antidepressant treatment)	☐ Yes ☐ No	Medication Consultation with Specialist

*Symptoms are calculated using the depression symptom checklist included in the ICP Assessment protocol. Scores on functional assessment derive from limitation ratings on 28 areas using a 0 to 4 scale, where 0 = Absent/Nonpathological; 1 = Moderate; 2 = Debilitating; 3 = Incapacitating; 4: Imminently dangerous. Assessed areas include: family dysfunction with substance abuse, marital/relationship dysfunction, **marital/relationship dysfunction with violent behavior**, work dissatisfaction, work performance problems, educational performance deficits, **inadequate survival skills**, **assaultiveness**, manipulativeness, oppositionalism, social withdrawal, uncommunicativeness, verbal aggressiveness, **self-mutilation, substance abuse,** hopelessness, **suicidal thoughts/behavior,** altered sleep, decreased concentration, decreased frustration tolerance, dysphoric mood, **mood lability,** pathological grief, **psychomotor agitation, psychomotor retardation, concomitant medical condition,** medical treatment noncompliance, **inadequate health care skills.** Areas that are particularly crucial are printed in bold. These are weighted more heavily when determining intensity of care.

**Definitions of treatment and treatment goals are summarized on the attached handout titled, "Summary of ICP Treatment Plans and Goals." Within each ICP treatment, the provider specifies the intensity of care, which may range from very frequent in-clinic visits to infrequent phone contacts with the patient.

***BHC: Behavioral Health Consultant

Summary of ICP Treatment Plans and Goals

Table 1 summarizes ICP treatments and goals associated with each treatment. Brief descriptions of ICP treatments follow.

Table 1
ICP Treatments and Goals

ICP Treatment	Planned?	ICP Treatment Goals
Clinical Management (Primary Care Team)	☐ Yes ☐ No	Decrease symptoms of depression. Increase frequency of use of coping strategies.
Brief Treatment (On-Site BHC*)	☐ Yes ☐ No	Decrease symptoms of depression. Increase frequency of use of coping strategies.
Antidepressant Treatment	☐ Yes ☐ No	Adherence to prescription plan. Skillful coping with medication side effects. Decrease symptoms of depression.
Behavioral Treatment (On-Site BHC)	☐ Yes ☐ No	Decrease symptoms of depression. Increase frequency of use of coping strategies. Increase ability to accept negative emotions. Decrease intensity of negative emotions. Increase quality of life in 1+ areas. Decrease number and severity of limitations in functioning.
Mental Health Treatment Delivered Externally	☐ Yes ☐ No	Same goals as Behavioral Health Treatment.

*BHC: Behavioral Health Consultant

Clinical Management

This treatment is based upon patient and primary care provider use of an educational booklet titled, *Seven Ways to Cope*. The booklet introduces the patient to the following seven coping strategies.

1. Generating hope and making effective behavioral change plans
2. Psychologically accepting painful emotions and making value-based choices about behavioral actions
3. Increasing awareness of the body and increasing skills in creating physiological states of well-being
4. Actively and effectively solving difficult problems of living
5. Resolving interpersonal conflicts with respect for self and others

6. Effective personal assertion and creative expression
7. Balancing negative and positive thoughts

In this treatment, the patient goes through an initial assessment, reads the educational booklets and completes the "ICP Coping Plan" with the provider. Appointments where the provider and patient develop and evaluate the ICP Coping Plan are 15 minutes in length. The total treatment involves 30 to 45 minutes of provider time over the course of each month of clinical management. Follow-up contacts may be phone rather than clinic appointments. The ICP provider evaluates treatment gains in a second assessment 4 weeks after the initial assessment. At the time of the second assessment, some patients will require no further treatment while others will need a second month of clinical management or additional treatment, such as addition of medications or referral to the ICP Behavioral Health Consultant.

Antidepressant Treatment

Patients who are candidates for antidepressant treatment receive a booklet to read prior to the start of antidepressant treatment. The booklet is titled "Using Medications Successfully." It addresses the following four important areas.

1. Patient previous experience with medications for depression and anxiety
2. Patient beliefs about medications for depression and anxiety
3. Patient knowledge of basic information about medications for depression and anxiety
4. Patient ability to anticipate and plan for problems in using medications

Prior to the medication prescription visit, the patient completes the ICP Medication Assessment Questionnaire. In the visit, the provider reviews the patient's responses, discusses the patient's beliefs about medications, selects an initial medication and an initial dosage, educates the patient regarding use of the medication, and helps the patient anticipate and plan for potential side effects.

The primary care team will often check with the patient by phone several times during the first two weeks of treatment. Providers adjust subsequent follow-up to meet individual patient needs. Follow-up may include monthly phone check-ins or monthly clinic visits during the course of treatment. The average course of medication treatment for a primary care patient ranges from 4 to 9 months. Providers follow guidelines for medication selection, dosing, continuation, switching, augmentation, and cessation suggested in the Clinical Practice Guideline for Treatment of Depression in Primary Care (1993).

Behavioral Health Treatment

This treatment involves coordinated visits to the primary care provider and the behavioral health consultant who works with the primary care team. The tasks of the primary care provider are medication treatment monitoring (for patients who are using antidepressant medications), management of medical problems, and on-going support of the relapse prevention plan written when the patient completes the active phase of working with the consultant. The behavioral health consultant has an option of two treatment protocols in the ICP. The Brief Treatment protocol involves one to three contacts with the patient. Several patient educational materials may be used to support this treatment (including booklets *Seven Ways to Cope* and *Using Medications Successfully* and a self-management workbook *Living Life Well: New Strategies for Hard Times*). This protocol uses the Coping Plan format used in the Primary Care Clinical Management protocol. The behavioral health consultant may also help the patient start anti-depressant treatment in the Brief Treatment protocol by consulting with the primary care physician, and providing medication assessment, patient education and treatment planning services to the patient. The purpose of the Brief

Treatment protocol is to assist the patient and primary care team in developing a strong clinical management program.

Table 2
Integration and Course of Treatment When a Behavioral Health Consultant Becomes Involved in Treatment

Time	Provider		Treatment	
Weeks after Diagnosis	Primary Care	Behavioral Health	Length of Visit	Visit Focus
1		First	30 minutes	Hoping, Planning, Doing
2		Second	30 minutes	Building Acceptance and Making Value-Based Choices
2	Second (optional)		10-15 minutes	Medication Follow-up
3		Third*	30 minutes	Appreciating Your Mind and Body
4		Fourth	30 minutes	Solving Problems
5		Fifth (optional)	30 minutes	Responding to Interpersonal Conflict
6		Sixth (optional)	30 minutes	Expressing Yourself
7 (or 5 or 6)		Seventh	30 minutes	Continuing to Live Life Well
7, 8, or 9	Third (optional)		10-15 minutes	Medication Follow-up Review Relapse Prevention Plan
7, 8, or 9		Phone Call	5 minutes	Relapse Prevention
9, 10, or 11		Phone Call	5 minutes	Relapse Prevention
17, 18, or 19		Phone Call	5 minutes	Relapse Prevention
29, 30, or 31		Phone Call	5 minutes	Relapse Prevention
	on-going			Relapse Prevention
Total	3+ visits	5-7 visits, 4 phone calls		

* Some patients may omit this contact due to time constraints or a lack of interest.

In the Behavioral Treatment protocol, the behavioral health consultant provides 3 to 4 hours of behavioral treatment to the patient (in-clinic phase) and 4 brief phone calls over the 6-month period following patient completion of active treatment (follow-up phase). Most patients treated in this protocol will read *Living Life Well: New Strategies for Hard Times* and complete suggested exercises between sessions. Table 2 summarizes visits in this protocol. Optional contacts are indicated by shading in Table 2. The primary care provider's initial appointment is the appointment when depression is diagnosed. If the primary care provider wants the patient to use medications, she/he may complete the Medication Assessment Questionnaire and start medications in the diagnosis visit. If the primary care provider does not have time to start medication or the patient wants to discuss medication treatment further, the behavioral health consultant completes the Medication Assessment Questionnaire in the initial visit. Additionally, the behavioral health consultant confers with the primary care provider about the start of medication and provides educational information about medications to the patient in the initial behavioral health appointment. This requires an additional 15-20 minutes, so that the original contact with the behavioral health consultant may approach 45 to 50 minutes rather than 30.

Post-Treatment Follow-Up

All patients participate in post-treatment follow-up. The intensity of post-treatment follow-up varies based upon the patient's initial severity level and response to treatment. Providers complete written relapse prevention plans for patients and these plans are supported in all post-treatment follow-up contacts. Table 3 provides guidelines for follow-up of patients treated in the ICP.

Table 3
ICP Post-Treatment Follow-Up

Patients Who	Follow-Up Plan
Had mild symptoms and responded well to one month of clinical management	Phone call to patient 3 months later
Had moderate symptoms and responded well to two months of clinical management	Phone call to patient 3, 6, and 9 months later
Had moderate symptoms and responded well to medication treatment and clinical management	Coping Plan Visits 2, 4, and 6 months after patient reaches therapeutic dose Phone call to patient 9 and 12 months later
Had moderate to severe symptoms and responded well to behavioral health consultation, with or without medication treatment	Phone call from Behavioral Health Consultant 2, 4, 12, and 24 weeks after completion of active treatment Phone call from primary care 9 and 12 months after completion of active treatment
Had moderate to severe symptoms and responded well to specialty treatment	Phone call from Behavioral Health Consultant 2, 4, 12, and 24 weeks after completion of specialty treatment Phone call from primary care 9 and 12 months later

Consultation with Medication Specialists

The Behavioral Health Consultant needs on-going supervision by a medication expert in order to assist primary care providers with medication issues. Supervision may occur by phone or in person. Consultation improves the expertise of the behavioral health consultant without increasing costs significantly. Usually, 15+ cases can be briefly reviewed in 30 minutes. Both the primary care provider and Behavioral Health Consultant need access to a Medication Specialist when patients fail to respond positively to medication treatment or experience severe or unusual side effects. Additionally, the expertise of a Medication Specialist is important when patients have on-going health problems that require the use of multiple medications. Only about 5 to 10% of depressed primary care patients require direct consultation with a Medication Specialist. When a direct consultation is needed, a single 15- to 30-minute visit is usually adequate.

Specialty Treatment Delivered Externally

Specialty treatment may include cognitive behavioral therapy in individual and/or group formats, cognitive therapy or interpersonal therapy in an individual format, or problem solving therapy. ICP patient education materials are supported in specialty treatment. At completion of treatment, the external mental health provider completes ICP assessment materials and returns the patient to primary care providers with a relapse prevention plan similar in format to the relapse prevention plan formulated at completion of behavioral health treatment in the primary care setting.

ICP Treatment Efficacy Reference List

Chiles, J., & Strosahl, K. (1995). *The suicidal patient: Principles of assessment, treatment and case management.* Washington, DC: American Psychiatric Press.

Depression Guideline Panel. (1993). *Depression in primary care: Vol. 2.* Treatment of major depression (Clinical Practice Guideline, No. 5, AHCPR Pub. No. 93-0551). Rockville, MD: U.S. Department of Health and Human Services, Public Health Service, Agency for Health Care Policy and Research.

Hayes, S.C., Strosahl, K., & Wilson, K.G. (1999). *Acceptance and commitment therapy: An experiential approach to behavior change.* New York, NY: Guilford.

Katon, W., Von Korff, M., Lin, E., Walker, E., Simon, G., Bush, T, Robinson, P., & Russo, J. (1994). Collaborative management to achieve treatment guidelines: Impact on depression in primary care. *Journal of the American Medical Association, 273,* 1026-1031.

Katon, W., Robinson, P., Von Korff, M., Lin, E., Bush, T., Ludman, E., Simon, G., & Walker, E. (1996). A multifaceted intervention to improve treatment of depression in primary care. *Archives of General Psychiatry, 53*(10), 924-932.

Lin, E.H.B., Von Korff, M., Katon, W., Bush, T., Simon, G.E., Walker, E., & Robinson, P. (1995). The role of the primary care physician in patient's adherence to antidepressant therapy. *Medical Care, 33*(1), 67-74.

Lin, E., Katon, W.J., Simon, G., Von Korff, M., Bush, T., Rutter, C.M., Saunders, K.W., & Walker, E. (1997). Achieving guidelines for the treatment of depression in primary care: Is physician education enough? *Medical Care, 35*(8), 831-842.

Mynors-Wallace, L., Gath, D.H., Lloyd-Thomas, A.R., & Tomlinson, D. (1995). Randomized controlled trial comparing problem solving treatment with amitriptyline and placebo for major depression in primary care. *British Medical Journal, 310,* 441-446.

Robinson, P. (1995). New territory for the behavior therapist . . . hello, depressed patients in primary care. *The Behavior Therapist,* September.

Robinson, P., Bush, T., Von Korff, M., Katon, W., Lin, E., Simon, G.E., & Walker, E. (1995). Primary care physician use of cognitive behavioral techniques with depressed patients. *Journal of Family Practice, 40*(4), 352-357.

Robinson, P., Afari, N., & Ludman, E. (1994). Depressed men in primary care. *Group Health Cooperative Medical Forum,* Spring.

Robinson, P., Bush, T., Katon, W., Von Korff, M., Lin, E., Walker, E., & Simon, G. (1996). The education of depressed primary care patients: What do patients think of interactive pamphlets and a video? *Group Health Cooperative Medical Forum,* Fall.

Robinson, P., Katon, W., Von Korff, M., Bush, T., Ludman, E., Simon, G., Lin, E., & Walker, E. (1996). Use of coping strategies by depressed primary care patients: Results of a randomized controlled trial. Submitted for publication.

Strosahl, K., & Goepfert, R. (1992). A collaborative model for the management of depression in the Group Health Cooperative setting. *Group Health Cooperative Medical Forum,* Winter.

*ICP Provider Profile Formats**

Behavioral Health Consultant	
Provider	Date
I started providing ICP Behavioral Health Consultation services on: ___________ During this time period, I have had _____ referrals. Of the _____ patients who started the ICP treatment involving the 4 to 7 session protocol, I have completed 4 or more sessions and participated in the development of a relapse prevention plan with _____ patients.	
Patients treated by me in this model reported mean satisfaction ratings of: _____ at the time of treatment planning, and _____ at the end of treatment. (The scale used in satisfaction ratings is 1 = not satisfied to 10 = very satisfied.)	

Medication Specialist	
Provider	Date
Behavioral Health Consultants and Primary Care Providers rated my work on each of the following 4 criteria on a scale ranging from 1 to 25. On this scale, **1 = the least positive evaluation and 25 = the most positive evaluation**. As of this report, ______ providers have contributed to the mean or average ratings below. I started providing ICP External Mental Health Provider services on ___________.	
Rating	**Performance Criteria**
1.	Medication specialist is easy to access.
2.	Medication specialist is thorough yet brief.
3.	Medication specialist provides education and training to me as part of the consultation.
4.	Patients are satisfied when they have a direct consultation with medication specialist.
	Total Score

*Formats for collecting provider profile data are presented in Chapter 7

External Mental Health Provider	
Provider	Date
Behavioral Health Consultants and Primary Care Providers rated my work on each of the following 4 criteria on a scale ranging from 1 to 25. On this scale, **1 = the least positive evaluation and 25 = the most positive evaluation**. As of this report, ______ providers have contributed to the mean or average ratings below. I started providing ICP External Mental Health Provider services on ____________.	
Rating	**Performance Criteria**
1.	External provider was easy to access.
2.	External provider used ICP materials.
3.	External provider provided efficacious treatment.
4.	External provider returned patient with a strong relapse prevention plan.
	Total Score

Chapter 10

Research Supporting the Integrated Care Program

The Integrated Care Program (ICP) has a strong empirical basis. Dozens of research investigations have contributed to its development. At the end of this chapter, we provide a list of 40 relevant citations for investigations conducted in the past 25 years. This list is titled "The Empirical Basis of the ICP." Each of these earlier studies made a contribution to our work. Review this list to select authors for additional reading.

In this chapter, we present research findings from two randomized clinical trials conducted in a health maintenance organization in the early 1990's. Both trials evaluated interventions for improving depression treatment outcomes in the primary care setting. In this chapter, you will learn the following.

- The results of pioneer investigations concerning treatment of depression in primary care
- Results of recent clinical trials evaluating innovative treatments for depression
- How innovative educational materials and treatments are received by primary care patients
- How innovative treatments like the ICP are received by primary care providers

---

Instructions for Speed Readers: Allow 10-15 minutes for this chapter. Critical information is printed in bold. Scan the first two sections. Slow your pace for the last two sections, as they summarize the results and condense findings into a practical question and answer format.

Pioneer Investigations in Primary Care

A number of pioneer efforts paved the way for design and implementation of the most recent investigations of innovative treatments for depressed primary care patients. Brown and Schulberg (1995) provide an excellent review of randomized clinical trials assessing the efficacy of psychosocial treatments in primary care. Eight of the 18 studies reviewed focused on treatment of depressed patients. Findings generally support the efficacy of psychosocial treatments for primary care patients with psychiatric disorders.

In a large clinical trial, **Schulberg and his colleagues (1996) established that standardized pharmacotherapy and psychotherapy are significantly more effective than a primary care physician's usual care in resolving episodes of major depression.** Their treatments were designed to be consistent with AHCPR guidelines.

Several other findings from Schulberg's pioneer efforts are important to the design of implementation models. First, they found that 14% of patients who accepted randomization to either pharmacotherapy or psychotherapy failed to keep their initial treatment appointment. Schulberg points out that this finding underscores the AHCPR Depression Guideline Panel recommendation that *patient preference* be considered when selecting a treatment. Second, only 33% of the pharmacotherapy and 42% of the psychotherapy patients completed both the active treatment and continuation treatment phases. The continuation phase of pharmacotherapy started at the point when the patient achieved a steady therapeutic blood level. It included 6 monthly follow-up appointments. The continuation phase of psychotherapy involved four monthly appointments. It followed the acute phase of treatment, which consisted of 16 weekly sessions of interpersonal therapy at the clinic. A high drop-out rate warrants attention to the length of treatment in primary care protocols and methods for tracking patients in the primary care delivery system.

Other researchers have also contributed important findings. Mynors-Wallace and Gath (1994) found that primary care providers could learn to use psychotherapeutic techniques with depressed patients. They compared a brief problem-solving treatment delivered by primary care providers to a combined clinical management and antidepressant treatment protocol. Both approaches were superior to usual care, and both involved less than 4 hours of provider time over a 6-week period. Katon and his colleagues (1992) tried giving primary care physicians written suggestions concerning diagnosis and treatment and found no improvement in clinical outcomes. Miranda (1994) and her colleagues used cognitive behavioral group treatment in a primary care setting and found that outcomes improved further when case management services were added. Brown and Lewinsohn (1984) found that psychoeducational treatment of depression (under conditions of individual treatment, a minimal contact protocol, and a group format) resulted in clinical improvement of depressed patients recruited by community announcements.

From results of these pioneer efforts, two models of treatment were created and evaluated in the early 1990's. Both models required primary care and mental health providers to change their usual approach to care and to work collaboratively. Both involved use of a biopsychosocial model by all providers. Both introduced cognitive behavioral techniques to depressed primary care patients. In the second model, providers attempted to complete active treatment with patients in less than 4 hours over a 6-week time period and to avoid use of mental health specialty services. Both studies used patient education materials to support treatment, and, in study two, patients received new educational materials at every contact. These models stimulated the development of the Integrated Care Program. This chapter provides detailed information on these research models and the studies that evaluated them.

Index Studies for Design of the ICP

Description of Studies

Setting. The setting for both studies was a large primary care clinic in a health maintenance organization serving over 380,00 persons in western Washington state. Twenty-two primary care physicians provided care to 22,000 adult patients at the clinic at the time of the study. All participating physicians were board-certified family physicians.

Sample. Physicians identified patients with probable major depression who were willing to initiate antidepressant therapy. Physicians invited patients to participate in a study designed to "investigate a new method of care for depression." Exclusion criteria included current alcohol abuse, psychotic symptoms or serious suicidal ideation or plan, dementia, pregnancy, terminal illness, or limited command of English.

Study One Procedure. After diagnosis by the primary care physician, patients were screened by a research assistant working in the clinic. Consenting patients were randomly assigned to either intervention or "usual care" after completing a baseline interview. The research assistant gave intervention patients educational materials, scheduled patients for two follow-up appointments with their primary care physician (one 30-minute visit where educational materials were discussed and one 15-minute treatment plan follow-up) and a scheduled medication consultative visit with an on-site psychiatrist. Intervention patients completed a brief phone interview regarding the educational materials one week after receiving the materials. Usual care patients received treatment as usual from their primary care physician. **Patients in the new method of care and the usual care groups had access to individual and group cognitive behavioral treatment and psychiatric consultation regarding antidepressant use in the HMO staff model mental health service, which was located seven miles away from the primary care clinic.**

Study One Educational Materials. The educational materials used in the study included two booklets on medication and self-help strategies and a video summarizing information in the booklets. All educational materials presented a biopsychosocial model and linked closely to a structured treatment planning format used by the physician.

Study One Training and Support of the Primary Care Physician. The multifaceted intervention included training primary care physicians in (1) using educational materials to support patient use of effective coping strategies and (2) prescribing antidepressant medications according to AHCPR Guidelines. Also, on-site psychiatrists (1) saw most intervention patients at least one time for medication consultation and (2) monitored automated pharmacy data regarding patient refills of prescribed antidepressants. When a patient failed to refill a prescribed medication at the predicted time, the psychiatrist contacted the primary care physician, who in turn contacted the non-adhering patient.

Study One Measures. Patients completed follow-up phone interviews 1, 4, and 7 months after the baseline. Areas of assessment included evaluation of educational materials, adherence to medications, depression severity, use of coping strategies, patient satisfaction, neuroticism, and chronic disease.

Evaluation of Educational Materials. Patients were asked to evaluate the educational materials in a phone interview one week after receiving the materials. Evaluation measures included these questions: (1) "Did you read or view the materials?" and (2) "How helpful were the educational materials?" Patients described their use of the educational materials by indicating that they read/viewed all, part or none of the material. Patients described the helpfulness of the educational material on a 1 to 10 scale with 1 = not helpful and 10 = very helpful.

Patient Adherence to Medications. Adherence to medications was assessed at all follow-ups. Adequacy of dosage and duration of antidepressant medication was measured using the HMO computerized records of prescriptions filled and refilled. Refill records were processed to determine which patients continued antidepressant use for at least 30 days and used medication at a rate that was within 10% of that recommended by AHCPR guidelines. A similar analysis estimated adequacy of treatment over a 90-day period.

Depression Severity. The Symptom Checklist 90 (SCL) items that measure depression include 20 questions scored on a 0-4 measure of severity (Derogatis, Rickels, Uhlenhuth, & Covi, 1974). The average item score of the 20 SCL items is reported (range 0 to 4.0). The SCL has been used in numerous studies of medical patients and has been found to have high reliability and validity. The Inventory of Depressive Symptomatology (IDS) (Clinician Rated) served as a second measure of depressive symptoms. This 28-item scale measures symptoms on a 0-3 severity index (range 0 to 84). It has been demonstrated to have high reliability and validity. The IDS was modified for administration by telephone and a computer program was written by the study team to allow structured rating of DSM-III-R criteria for major and minor depression.

Coping Strategy Use Scale. The Coping Strategy Use Scale (CSUS) measures patient frequency of use of six specific cognitive behavioral strategies that improve mood.

Patient Satisfaction. Satisfaction with management of depression was measured on a 5-point ordinal scale that rated treatment from "poor" to "excellent." Perceived helpfulness of antidepressant medications was rated on a 4-point ordinal scale from helping "not at all" to helping a "great deal."

Neuroticism. The NEO Personality Inventory is a 5-factor inventory consisting of 60 items (12 items for each factor) (Costa & McCrae, 1985). The individual items are scored on a 0 to 4 scale, ranging from strongly disagree to strongly agree. Seven items from the neuroticism scale were used in this study (range: 0-28).

Chronic Disease. The Chronic Disease Score is a measure of chronic medical illness derived from the patient's use of prescription medications over a 6-month period (Von Korff, Wagner, & Saunders, 1992). The Chronic Disease Score has been found to have high stability over a one-year period and to have a high correlation with physician ratings of severity of medical illness. It has also been found to predict hospitalization and mortality in the year following assessment after controlling for age, gender and health care visits.

Study Two Procedure. As in Study One, patients were screened by a research assistant after diagnosis by the primary care physician. Consenting patients were randomly assigned to either intervention or "usual care" after completing a baseline interview. Intervention patients were given educational materials and scheduled for an initial visit with the psychologist who was responsible for implementing the intervention. Usual care patients received treatment as usual from their primary care physician. Patients in both the intervention treatment and the usual care groups had access to individual and group cognitive behavioral treatment and psychiatric consultation regarding antidepressant treatment in the HMO staff model mental health service, which was located seven miles away from the primary care clinic.

Study Two Materials. Patients were given educational materials at every contact to support knowledge and application of coping strategies to lessen symptoms of depression and improve quality of life. Additionally, patients who were interested in reading a self-help book were given a copy of *You Can If You Want To* by Arnold Lazarus and Leslie Faye (1979).

Study Two Intervention. Patients in the intervention group received a behavioral treatment based on multimodal therapy (Lazarus, 1992), social learning theory (Lewinsohn, Antonuccio, Breckenridge, & Teri, 1984), cognitive theory (e.g., Rush, Beck, Kovacs, & Hollon, 1977), and psychological acceptance theory (Hayes, 1987). Additionally, development of skill work exercises in the intervention treatment was influenced by the works of Gath (unpublished), Jacubowski & Lange (1978), Jacobson (Unpublished), and Kabat-Zinn (1990).

A 125-page manual supported implementation of the intervention treatment. Patients selected among 4, 5, or 6 contacts with a psychologist working in the primary care setting as an extended member of the primary care treatment team. The lead psychologist had 10 years of experience in cognitive behavioral treatment. She provided supervision to the second mental health provider, who was a Ph.D. participating in a post-doctoral internship. **Total direct treatment time between the patient and behavioral consultant ranged from 2.5 to 3.5 hours of contact. Active treatment ended within 4 to 6 weeks of referral and patients received telephone calls from the behavioral consultant 2, 4, 12, and 24 weeks after completion of active treatment.**

The main components of Behavioral Health Consultation in the intervention treatment were (1) provision of written and verbal instruction in use of coping skills; (2) assessment, education and planning about benefits and side effects of medication, and (3) collaborative development of weekly behavioral experiments tailored to patient psychosocial needs. Patients used self-assessment techniques, including a symptom checklist and the Beck Depression Inventory-Short Form (Beck and Beck, 1972), and actively participated in behavioral and medication planning. During and between intervention treatment visits, the behavioral consultant worked with both the primary care physician and the consulting psychiatrist to assist with medication starts, switches, dose changes, augmentations and stops. The behavioral consultants conferred with the psychiatrist consultant regarding medications in brief weekly staff meetings conducted by phone or in the clinic. The behavioral consultants or primary care physician could refer patients with complex problems for a direct medication consultation with the psychiatrist consultant.

In the initial session, the behavioral consultant helped the patient develop a conceptual model for understanding her/his particular symptoms of depression and introduced basic components of behavioral health experimenting and intentional application of effective coping strategies to improve quality of life. Additionally, the behavioral consultant conducted a 5-step medication risk adherence evaluation. When patients were at higher risk, more attention was given to medication planning, including application of cognitive re-structuring techniques to exaggerated attitudes about use of medications (Wright, 1994). **When patients held strong beliefs against use of medications and had not yet started antidepressant therapy, the behavioral consultant implemented the intervention treatment without patient use of medications.**

In visits 2 and 3, the behavioral consultants coached patients in use of coping strategies, including planning and engaging in daily pleasurable activities and use of problem-solving techniques with current difficulties. In the first optional session, the behavioral consultant introduced cognitive change strategies. In the second optional session, the behavioral consultant and patient collaboratively decided upon learning a skill relevant to the individual patient at that particular time in her/his life. Examples of strategies for the optional session included psychological acceptance strategies, personal assertion, relaxation and further practice of cognitive strategies. Patients were allowed to bring a significant other to the second optional session. Patients received educational handouts and written treatment plans concerning behavioral health and medications at all intervention treatment visits.

In all intervention treatment visits, the behavioral consultant and patient worked together to plan behavioral experiments to improve quality of life in one or more areas of daily living. A written relapse prevention plan, called the "Progress Plan," was developed in the final contact and served as the basis for telephone checks during the follow-up phase of treatment. Brief chart notations regarding behavioral and medication treatment plans and the patient's Progress Plan were given to the primary care physician on the same day of the visit and then placed in the medical chart. Primary care providers were encouraged to reinforce intervention treatment materials in medical contacts with the patient.

Study Two Measures. Measures for Study Two were the same as for Study One with the following substitutions or additions: patient report of improvement in problems which prompted them to initially seek treatment, patient *self-report* of adherence to antidepressant medications, patient satisfaction with care *specifically for depression*, patient use of a relapse prevention plan, and patient discussion of relapse prevention with the primary care physician. Patients were assessed at baseline and again 1 month, 4 months and 7 months after baseline on most measures.

Perceived Improvement in Problems Prompting Episode of Care. Patients used a Likert scale (1 = not at all, 2 = a little, 3 = somewhat, 4 = a great deal) to indicate the extent to which the problems that prompted their originally seeking care when depression was initially diagnosed had improved during the time period between phone interviews. At the 1-month interview, the question referred to the previous month. In the 4- and 7-month follow-ups, the question referred to the previous 3-month period.

Use of medications. Patients were asked if they had taken an antidepressant medication **at all during the month prior** to the follow-up interview. If they said "yes," they were asked **to estimate the number of days in the past 30 days** that they had taken antidepressant medication **at any dose.**

Satisfaction with care. At all follow-ups, patient satisfaction "with care for depression" was measured by a single question that referred to care received during the time intervals between interviews. Patients rated quality of care received on a Likert scale (5 = poor, 4 = fair, 3 = good, 2 = very good, 1 = excellent).

Relapse prevention. At the 4-month follow-up, we asked patients if they were following a relapse prevention plan. Additionally, we asked patients if they had talked with their primary care physician in the previous 2 months about using coping strategies to prevent relapse into depression.

Results Of Studies

Study One Patient Characteristics. Of the 281 patients referred over a 15 month period, 217 (77.2%) were successfully randomized to the study. Ninety-one (42%) of the randomized patients met DSM-IIIR criteria for major depression at the baseline interview. While the remaining patients reported 4 or less symptoms of major depression, over three-quarters of this group reported previous episodes of major depression. Within the Intervention group (N = 108), 49 (45%) met criteria for major depression. Patients were usually started on a tricyclic antidepressant rather than a serotonin reuptake inhibitor in accord with HMO guidelines that recommend use of tricyclic antidepressants as initial therapy. Only 14 of 108 Intervention and 11 of 109 Usual Care patients started a serotonin reuptake inhibitor as an initial medication. Table 10.1 summarizes demographic and clinical characteristics of intervention patients in study one.

Table 10.1
Study One: Demographic and Clinical Characteristics of Intervention Patients

	Major Depression (n = 49)	Minor Depression (n = 59)
Mean Age (SD)	43.2 (15.4)	52.2 (14.3)
% Female	77.5	76.3
% with 1+ years of college	67.4	81.0
% Married or cohabiting	46.9	52.5
% Employed full or part-time	71.4	57.6
Chronic Disease Score Mean (SD)*	1.3 (1.9)	2.3 (3.2)
NEO Neuroticism Mean (SD)	16.8 (5.2)	14.9 (5.1)
SCL Depression Mean (SD)	2.35 (0.49)	1.67 (0.40)
% with recurrent major depression (2+ prior episodes)	68.1	76.5

* Median scores on chronic disease are not useful because over half of the patients did not have chronic medical illness and scored 0. Possible ranges: Chronic Disease 0-35; NEO 0-28; SCL 0.75-4.0 (0-0.74 were ineligible scores)

Study One Patient Evaluation of Educational Materials. The number and percentage of patients who read/viewed educational materials are presented in Table 10.2. The majority of patients read/viewed all or part of the materials. **The majority of patients found the booklets to be significantly helpful (ratings of 7 to 10), while only 46% found the video to be significantly helpful.** Graph 10.1 summarizes patient ratings of helpfulness on the booklets and the video. Several additional analyses were completed withdata concerning the booklet on behavioral strategies. For these analyses, patients were divided into negative (ratings of 1 to 5) and positive (ratings of 6 to 10) evaluators. Significant findings are summarized in Table 10.3. Being young

Table 10.2

Study One: Number And Percentage of Patients Who Read or Viewed Materials			
Educational Product	**All**	**Part**	**None**
Medication Booklet	83 (80%)	13 (13%)	8 (8%)
Behavioral Self-Help Booklet	82 (80%)	15 (14%)	7 (7%)
Video summarizing booklets	79 (76%)	6 (6%)	19 (18%)

(aged 18 to 54 versus 55+ years), identification of relationship problems as a cause of the present depression, higher levels of neuroticism on the NEO and greater depression severity on the SCL were significantly related to more positive evaluation of the behavioral booklet. Sex of patient was of borderline significance in evaluation of the behavioral booklet, with 60% of the males and 82% of the females giving the booklet more positive helpfulness ratings. Evaluation of the behavioral booklet was not significantly related to patient education level, chronic disease level, satisfaction with primary care physician, or number of previous episodes of depression. Patients also gave narrative information about the booklets. Table 10.4 summarizes patient comments about the booklets.

Graph 10.1
Patient Ratings of ICP Booklets and Video

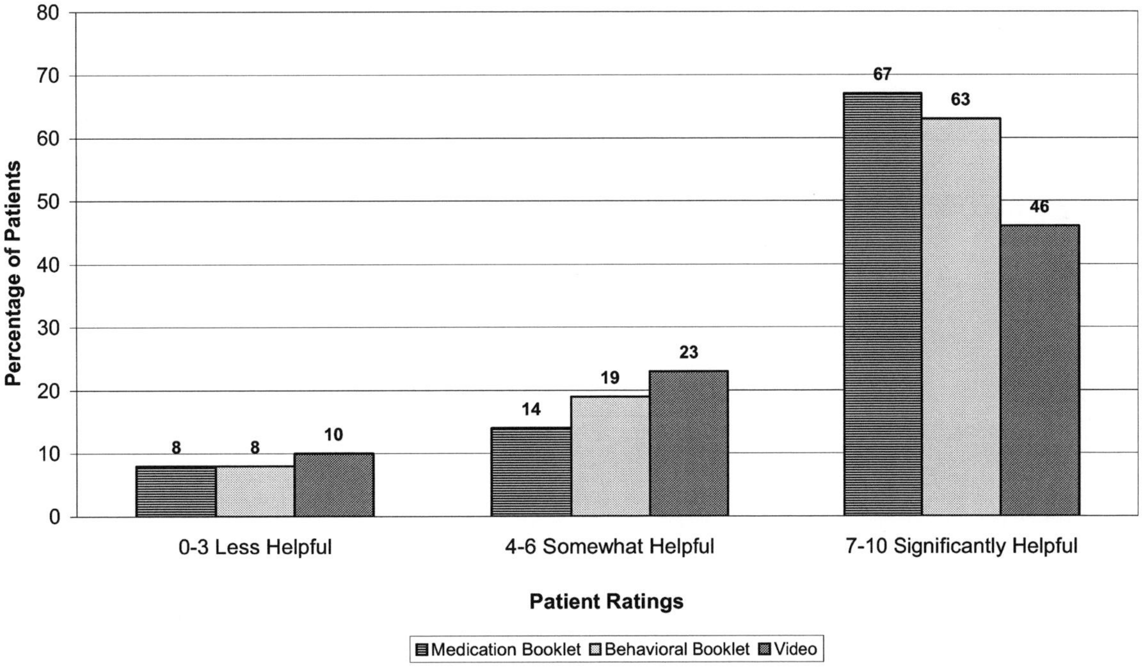

In summary, most depressed primary care patients will read booklets on use of medications and behavioral coping strategies *and* evaluate the booklets as helpful. **While most patients also viewed the video used in the present study, they did not evaluate the video to be as helpful as the booklets. Patients who are younger, having relationship problems, and**

Table 10.3

Study One: Summary of Significant Findings Concerning Evaluation of Behavioral Booklet

Variable	Positive Evaluators (Rated 6-10)	Negative Evaluators (Rated 1-5)	N	*df*	Test	*p*
Aged 18-54	85.71%	12.50%	82	2	chi-square = 6.26	0.044
Aged 55+	61.54%	30.77%				
Relationship problem yes	84.62%	15.38	78	1	chi-square = 3.761	0.052
Relationship problem no	65.38%	34.62				
NEO Mean Score (SD)	16.42 (5.47)	12.83 (5.02)	82	29.4	t-test = -2.63	0.01
SCL Mean (SD)	40.44 (11.53)	34.02 (11.45)	82	27.5	t-test = -2.0982	0.05

reporting greater severity of neurotic and depressive symptoms tend to evaluate a behavioral self-help booklet as more helpful. The educational materials were one part of a multifaceted treatment program, and the design of the larger study did not allow for isolation of the impact of educational materials on patient outcomes.

Study One Patient Adherence to Antidepressant Medications. Intervention patients were significantly more likely to receive an adequate dosage of antidepressant medication for at least 30 days compared with usual care patients. Among patients with major depression, 87.8% of the intervention patients versus 57.1% of the usual care patients received an adequate dosage of antidepressant medication for at least 30 days ($p<.001$). Concerning the more stringent criteria of 90 days of treatment at an adequate dosage of antidepressant medication, 75.5% of the intervention patients with major depression versus 50.0% of the usual care patients with major depression received an adequate treatment ($p<.01$). For patients with minor depression, 88.1% of the intervention patients versus 47.8% of the usual care patients received an adequate dosage of antidepressant medication for at least 30 days ($p<.001$) and 79.7% of the intervention patients versus 40.3% of the usual care patients received an adequate dosage of an antidepressant medication for at least 90 days ($p<.001$).

Study One Depression Severity. Both intervention and usual care patients tended to report substantial improvement from baseline to 1-, 4- and 7-month follow-ups. There were no significant differences in the percentage of intervention and usual care patients with minor depression who improved 50% or more at 4 months on either the SCL (60.0% versus 67.9%) or the IDS (48.0% versus 55.4%). **Among patients with major depression, intervention patients showed significantly greater improvement than patients in usual care.** Among patients with major depression, 74.4% of the intervention versus 43.8% of usual care patients improved by at least 50% on the SCL ($p<.01$). On the IDS, 61.5% of the intervention versus 40.6% of the usual care patients with major depression showed 50% or more improvement ($p<.08$).

Study One Use of Coping Strategies. Age was a significant factor in predicting change in use of coping strategies among patients with less severe symptoms of depression. Older patients tended to remain at a constant level in CSUS scores while younger minors increased in use of strategies, particularly between baseline and the 1-month follow-up. For patients with major depression, a time by randomization group effect was significant ($p<.003$) in a multivariate

Table 10.4
Study One: Patient Comments in Response to the Question, "What ideas from this booklet have you actually used since reading it?"

"How Medications Can Help"	"Planning to Feel Better"
Helped me cope with side effects.	Have started setting smaller goals rather than larger ones.
How depression is related to stress.	Taking time for pleasure.
The way stress affects the brain and causes depression.	Focusing on finishing projects.
When my back hurts now, I try to remove myself from the situation to reduce the stress.	Allowed myself to feel angry with my son when he was rude rather than blaming myself and worrying.
The relationship between stress and pain.	Scheduled to meet someone and didn't feel like it but forced myself to do it.
Take medicine at dinner rather than later on so that I'm not so tired in the morning.	Started getting out of the house more.
Helped me decide on questions to ask my physician.	Called friends I have not called in a long time.
Helped me not worry that I would get addicted.	Started being with people who make me feel better.
Helped me know that I would get over feeling tired.	More aware when I do things I enjoy.
Drinking more liquids.	Using positive suggestions.
Took advice to call MD when medication wasn't working.	Exercise.
Stop under MD's direction.	Balancing Thoughts.
Understanding the upward spiral.	Looked for those books mentioned in the booklet at the library.
Follow directions of MD.	Replaced stressful situation with a pleasant activity–playing organ.
Realizing that what I have is common.	Identified things I used to do when I felt better, then made a list of things to actually do. Also listed names of people who could help me carry out list of things to do.
Persevere.	I'm not as bad off as my mind tries to tell me-- some people who've had strokes are a lot worse off than me–I *can* do things.
Changed how I was taking the medicine.	Finding someone to talk to everyday.
Walking.	Went to see a funny movie.
Took 2 weeks off work to give myself time to get through the adjustment to medication.	Shifting from negative to positive thoughts.
Be patient about getting to the point where I sleep better.	Identifying problem causing depression/sadness and working on it.
Started taking stool softeners.	Went to see a counselor.
Lessened amount of coffee and substituted tea.	Learning to recognize symptoms so I can catch start of depression earlier in the future and nip it in the bud.
Getting out of bed slowly.	
Allowed myself to take a nap when drowsy from the medication.	
Going to bed earlier.	

repeated measures analysis controlling for age, gender, neuroticism and chronic disease. **Intervention patients with major depression reported greater use of coping strategies at the 4-**

month follow-up than usual care patients with major depression. Use of coping strategies by patients with minor depression was not significantly improved by the intervention.

Study One Patient Satisfaction. At the 4-month follow-up, significantly more intervention patients with major depression rated the quality of care they received for depression as good to excellent compared with the controls (93.0% for intervention versus 75.0% for usual care, p<.03). In addition, at the 4-month follow-up, significantly more intervention patients with major depression than usual care patients rated antidepressant medications as helping "somewhat to a great deal" (88.1% for intervention versus 63.3% for controls, p<.01). At the 4-month follow-up, intervention patients with minor depression did not differ from controls in rating the quality of care they received for depression as good to excellent (94.4% for intervention versus 89.3% for usual controls). At the 4 month follow-up, intervention patients with minor depression rated antidepressant medication as helping somewhat to a great deal significantly more often than the usual care patients (81.8% for intervention versus 61.4% for usual care, p<.02).

Study One Conclusions. A multifaceted intervention providing increased patient education, longer and more frequent visits in the first 6 weeks of treatment, surveillance of adherence to medication regimens, primary care physician training in the treatment of depression, and an integrated role for the psychiatrist in primary care significantly improved the process of care for depression. **Among patients with major and minor depression, this treatment program led to significant improvement in patient adherence to an adequate dosage of antidepressant medication** as established by the AHCPR guidelines for treatment of depression in primary care. **The intervention program also improved satisfaction with care and clinical outcomes in patients with major, but not minor depression.**

Study One Impact on Primary Care System. Innovations evaluated in the present investigation were well accepted by primary care providers. In a post-study survey, **over 80% of the primary care physicians stated that the multifaceted intervention greatly increased their satisfaction in treating depression**. However, Lin et al. (1995) conducted a post-study investigation of the prescribing practices of participating physicians, and found that **providers tended to return to previous prescribing patterns after the study ended** and all aspects of the intervention were removed from the clinic. Improvements to treatment outcomes associated with the present intervention appear to be dependent upon continued presence of "intervention pieces" in the primary care system.

Study Two Patient Characteristics. Physicians referred 217 patients over a 10-month period. Seventy percent were successfully randomized to the study. Thirty patients (13.8%) refused enrollment (seven were not interested in involvement, seven did not show for baseline interview, nine were too busy, three preferred treatment by the primary care physician alone, two felt better or no longer depressed, one was too medically ill, and one could not be contacted after referral). Patients ranged in age from 21 to 82 years of age. Almost 75% of the study group were female. The group was somewhat highly educated, with most reporting one or more years of college. Patients were more likely to be single than married or cohabiting. Over 75% of the patients were employed part or full-time. While over half of the group had no chronic medical illness, **older patients in the sample had considerable illness burden** and two patients died of cancer during the course of the study. More than 60% of the sample reported 2+ previous episodes of depression. No patients attempted or completed suicide during the course of the study. Findings are based on randomized patients who completed one or more follow-up assessments.

Study Two Patient Use of Behavioral Health Consultant Treatment. Of the 77 referred patients, 68 (88.3%) completed the Integrated Program. Of the 72 patients who attended at least the first intervention treatment visit, 68 (94.4%) completed the program. Patients starting the intervention treatment attended a mean of 5.2 behavioral health visits (SD = 1.7). Of the 72 patients who started the Integrated Program, 57 (79.2%) completed 6 sessions, 7 (9.7%) completed 5 sessions, 4 (5.6%) completed 4 sessions, 2 (2.8%) completed 3 sessions, 1 (1.4%) completed 2 sessions, and 1 (1.4%) completed 1 session. Ninety percent elected to attend 1 or more of the 2 optional sessions. Among the 88% of intervention treatment patients who attended an optional

Graph 10.2
Study Two: Mean CSUS Scores for Intervention Treatment (IT) and Usual Care (UC) Patients

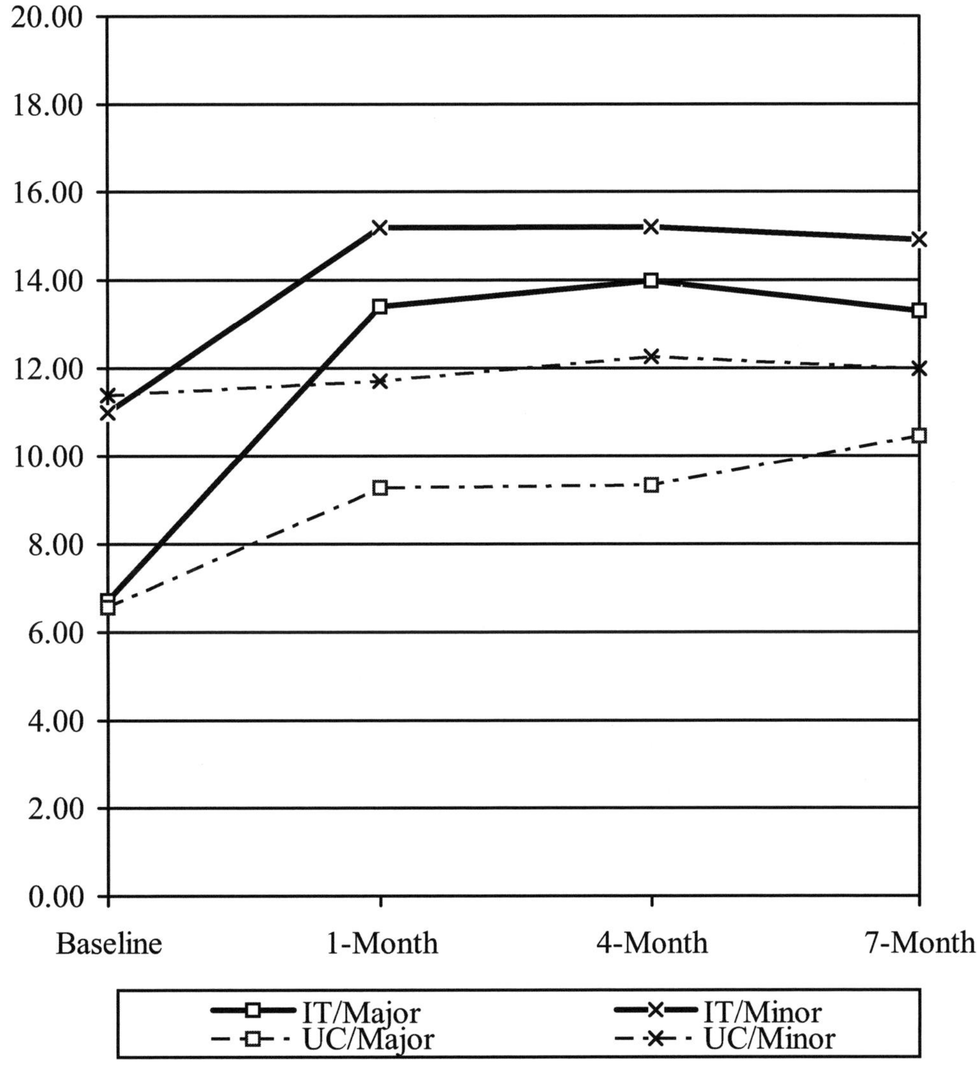

special session, the topic most frequently selected was additional coaching in use of cognitive and acceptance strategies, as 32% of the patients chose this as their focus. Other strategies selected for optional sessions included: personal assertion/expression (17%); additional problem-solving skill application (11%); mind body/relaxation training (9%); breathing skills (9%); couple's consultation (6%), and additional instruction in behavioral planning (3%). A psychiatrist who supervised behavioral health consultants regarding medication treatment issues saw 5 of the 77 patients referred (6.5%) directly due to medication complications. The psychiatrist saw one other patient directly because she lost her medical coverage temporarily and needed to see a prescriber to help continue her medication. Behavioral health consultants made an average of 4.1 telephone calls (SD = 1.09) to the 68 patients who completed the Integrated Program. These calls included an optional supportive call between the first and second appointments (which was requested by 44% of the patients), and a mean of 3.68 follow-up calls (SD = 0.95) after completion of in-clinic treatment.

Study Two Patient Adherence to Antidepressant Medications. Patients estimated the number of days they used medication at any dose during the 30-day period just prior to the interview. Intervention and usual care patients did not differ significantly at the 1-month follow-up. However, intervention patients reported significantly more days of use of medications at the 4-month follow-up. This finding held for patients with major and minor depression. Significantly greater medication use continued at the 7-month follow-up for minor depressives, but not for major depressives.

Study Two Depression Severity. At the four-month follow-up, intervention treatment patients tended to show 50% or more improvement on the SCL more often than patients who received usual care (Major Depression: 70.4% of Intervention versus 42.3% of Usual Care, p = .04; Minor Depression: 66.7% for Intervention versus 52.8% for Usual Care, p = .22). In repeated measures analyses, **both patients with major and minor depression who received the intervention package demonstrated significantly better outcomes on the SCL than patients who received usual care.** Proc Mixed analyses for patients with minor depression found a significant group by time interaction on the SCL depression score (p = .03). On the IDS, 74.1% of the intervention treatment patients with major depression showed 50% or more improvement compared to 42.3% of Usual Care patients. **Analyses of patients with major depression found a significant group by time interaction on the SCL depression score (p =.001). Proc Mixed analyses for patients with major depression also found a significant group-by-time interaction on the IDS (p = .03).**

Study Two Use of Coping Strategies. As can be seen in Graph 10.2, intervention patients with major and minor depression demonstrated higher rates of use of coping strategies at all follow-ups. Planned comparisons for minor depressives indicated significant treatment differences at the 1-month (F = 10.66; df = 1; p = 0.002), 4-month (F = 5.34; df = 1; p = 0.024), and 7-month (F = 6.68; df = 1; p = 0.012) follow-ups. For major depressives, planned comparisons indicated statistically significant treatment differences in use of coping strategies at the 1-month follow-up (F =6.35; df = 1; p = 016) but not significant differences at the 4-month (F = 7.12; df = 1; p = 0.11) and 7-month follow-ups (F = 3.16; df = 1; p = 0.083).

Study Two Patient Satisfaction. Intervention patients were consistently more satisfied with treatment than usual care controls. T-tests were conducted to evaluate patient satisfaction with treatment. As can be seen in Table 10.6, intervention and usual care groups with major and minor depression were similar at baseline and significantly different at all follow-ups.

Table 10.6
Study Two: Satisfaction with Treatment for Depression*

	Major Depression (n = 43)				Minor Depression (n = 59)			
	CC Mean	UC Mean	t-test	p value	CC Mean	UC Mean	t-test	p value
Baseline	2.75 (n=12)	2.70 (n=10)	0.09	0.931	2.64 (n=14)	2.56 (n=16)	0.19	0.852
1-Month	1.54 (n=24)	2.61 (n=21)	-3.33	0.002	1.60 (n=35)	2.46 (n=28)	-3.43	0.001
4-Month	1.83 (n=24)	2.76 (n=21)	-2.58	0.014	1.91 (n=33)	2.63 (n=30)	-2.63	0.012
7-Month	1.83 (n=24)	2.72 (n=18)	-2.21	0.035	1.78 (n=32)	2.84 (n=25)	-3.63	0.000

*Measured on a 1-5 Likert scale, where 1=Excellent, 2=Very Good, 3=Good, 4=Fair, 5=Poor

Study Two Conclusions about Outcomes. In summary, findings from this study suggest that a combined primary care treatment for depression which emphasized a behavioral health intervention significantly improved clinical outcomes for patients with major and minor depression and positively influenced patient self-management skills. Coping strategies targeted by the intervention significantly increased for patients with minor depression at all follow-ups. This finding is noteworthy in that recent research has documented an association between use of active coping strategies and severity of depression (Burns & Nolen-Hoeksema, 1991). Minors, as well as majors, reported significant increases in frequency of use of effective strategies for improving mood at the 1-month follow-up. Both minors and majors also reported significantly greater perceived improvement at the 1-month follow-up than controls in the problems that prompted them to seek care, with similar but non-significant trends at 4 and 7 months. Furthermore, the intervention was significantly more satisfying to both minor and major depressives than the usual standard of care was to control patients. Intervention patients with major and minor depression were much more likely than control patients to be following a relapse prevention plan at the 4-month follow-up. Finally, both major and minor depressives who received the intervention were more likely to report use of medications during the third month of treatment.

Study Two Impact on Primary Care System. All physicians preferred the intervention treatment to specialty mental health treatment for their depressed patients. Additionally, 88% of the physicians surveyed indicated that intervention treatment materials were easy to use with patients. At the end of the study, participating physicians rated the usefulness of 7 components of the intervention program. Table 10.7 summarizes the ratings given by physicians.

Questions and Answers

1. Were study interventions acceptable to patients?

Only 8.9% of referred patients refused enrollment in Study 1. Study 2 treatment completion criterion was attendance of 4 planned sessions of active treatment. Of the 77 referred patients, 68

Table 10.7
Study Two: Physician Ratings of the Usefulness of the 7 Components of the Model

7 Components of the Integrated Program	Not Useful	Possibly Useful	Definitely Useful	Essential
1. Behavioral Treatment Program	0%	0%	37%	62%
2. Medication Assessment Questionnaire	4%	0%	80%	14%
3. Medication Monitoring	0%	6%	68%	25%
4. Medication Education	0%	6%	56%	38%
5. Relapse Prevention Plan Development	0%	6%	56%	38%
6. Same-Day Charting	0%	6%	88%	6%
7. Educational Newsletter on Depression	0%	44%	50%	6%

(88.3%) completed the Integrated Program. **Of the 72 patients who attended at least the first intervention treatment visit, 68 (94.4%) completed the program.** Patients starting the intervention treatment attended a mean of 5.2 visits (SD = 1.7). **Psychologists wrote relapse prevention plans for 96% of the patients who started the program.**

> **Lesson:** *Most patients find primary care mental health interventions acceptable. Further, most patients will complete behavioral health treatment packages offering four to six visits.*

2. Did interventions improve depression treatment outcomes?

In both studies, significantly more of the intervention patients with major depression showed 50% or more improvement on the SCL compared to patients who received usual care. Repeated measures analyses of **Study 1** data indicated that **patients with major, but not patients with minor depression, who received the intervention treatment demonstrated significantly better outcomes on the SCL** than patients who received usual care. Repeated measures analyses of **Study 2** data indicated that **patients with major *and* with minor depression who received the intervention treatment demonstrated significantly better outcomes on the SCL** than patients who received usual care._

On the IDS statistically significant improvement of 50% or more was achieved by patients with major depression, in comparison with controls, by Study 2 patients but not by Study 1 patients. In Study 2, 74.1% of intervention patients showed 50%+ improvement on the IDS while 61.5% showed such improvement in Study 1.

> **Lesson:** *The integrated behavioral intervention in Study 2 appears to have had a slightly stronger impact on depression outcomes. Further, this model of care had more impact on patients with milder symptoms of depression, who constitute about half of the depressed patients in primary care. The ICP incorporates most aspects of the intervention model used in Study 2._*

3. Did interventions improve coping outcomes?

The impact of the intervention in Study 1 on patient use of coping strategies was relatively weak and limited to patients with major depression. However, **the Study 2 intervention resulted in significant increases in use of coping strategies by both major and minor depressives at the 1-month follow-up** relative to the usual care control patients. Further, this difference continued to be significant at the 4- and 7-month follow-ups for patients with minor depression.

Lesson: *Patients who receive behavioral treatment emphasizing use of coping strategies report higher coping strategy use rates. Use of coping strategies most likely provides a buffer against stress and (1) may prevent patients with minor depression from developing major depression and (2) reduce the probability of future episodes of major depression among treated patients who have suffered previous episodes of major depression. Additionally, use of coping strategies may help patients work more successfully with on-going medical problems, such as chronic pain or diabetes, and, therefore support better overall health.*

4. Did interventions improve medication adherence?

In Study 1, intervention patients in both the major and minor depression groups were significantly more likely to receive an adequate dosage of antidepressant medication (according to AHCPR Guidelines) for 30 and 90 days compared with control patients. In Study 2, intervention patients with major depression did not differ significantly from usual care patients in use of medications at Guideline levels for 30 or 90 days. Study 2 intervention patients with minor depression were more likely than usual care minors to receive an antidepressant medication (at or above the lowest level recommended by AHCPR) for at least 30 days, but this did not hold true for the 90 day evaluation. When self-report data were used, Study 2 major and minor patients did not differ from usual care patients in days of use of medications at the 1-month follow-up. However, both major and minor groups reported use of medications more days than usual care patients at the 4-month follow-up.

Lesson: ***There does not appear to be a one-to-one relationship between adherence to medications and depression outcome.*** *In Study 1, significantly improved rates of medication adherence were associated with improvement in outcomes for patients with major depression, but not for patients with minor depression. Patients with major depression who received the Study 2 intervention demonstrated significantly greater improvement in depression outcomes without demonstrating significantly greater adherence to medications at guideline levels. This was also true for minors in Study 2 at the 90 day adherence evaluation, when one would be more likely to attribute improvement to medication treatment. Therefore, the ICP gives patients the option of behavioral treatment with or without antidepressant therapy and encourages more severely depressed patients to use a combination approach. Additionally, the ICP encourages providers to use behavioral treatment for the first month after diagnosis with patients with minor depression, and then to evaluate the potential need for antidepressant medications. The intervention in Study 2 appears to be effective in helping patients start medications and/or use them more consistently after the first month of treatment.*

5. Did the intervention effect patient beliefs about medication?

Study 2 involved assessing and modifying patient beliefs about medications. **At the 4-month follow-up, minor depressives in the intervention indicated more positive beliefs about medication than usual care patients.**

Lesson: *A beliefs-about-medication checklist is an acceptable, time-effective approach to eliciting beliefs that could obstruct a patient's successful use of antidepressant medications. Using Socratic questioning techniques appears to help change problematic beliefs endorsed by minor depressives. A medication adherence package is included in the Integrated Care Program. Questions are included for providers to use to help patients thoughtfully reconsider beliefs that could impede antidepressant treatment.*

6. Did the intervention result in improvement in problems that prompted patients to seek medical care?

At the one-month follow-up, Study 2 patients with major and minor depression in the intervention group reported significantly greater improvement in the problems that prompted them to seek care at the time when the episode of depression was diagnosed.

Lesson: *Depressed primary care patients seek treatment for many different reasons. A behavioral health intervention appears to have a significantly positive impact on reasons for seeking medical care, and this may translate to a medical cost offset from a long-term perspective.*

7. Did the intervention improve rates of patient use of relapse prevention plans?

In Study 2, **both major and minor depressives who received the intervention treatment were significantly more likely to be following a relapse prevention plan at the 4-month follow-up** (Major depression: 74.1% versus 26.9%; Minor depression: 89.5% vs. 33.3 %).

Lesson: *A behavioral health intervention that included development of a written relapse prevention plan significantly improved patient adherence to relapse prevention plans after active treatment. The ICP includes development of a written relapse prevention plan that is supported by the on-site mental health provider and the primary care team.*

8. Did the intervention improve rates of patient interaction with the primary care physician about use of behavioral coping strategies to prevent depression?

In Study 2, **intervention patients with minor depression were more likely than usual care patients with minor depression to report having talked with their primary care physician in the past 2 months about use of coping strategies to prevent depression** at the 4-month follow-up (50% versus 27.8%). The rates of patient-physician interaction about relapse prevention were less dramatic between intervention and usual care patients with major depression, but were still in the desired direction (33.3% versus 23.1%).

Lesson: A behavioral health intervention that includes development of a written relapse prevention plan for the medical chart has an impact on physician-patient interactions concerning use of self-management and coping strategies.

9. Were primary care patients satisfied with the care they received in the intervention treatments?

Study 1: At the 4-month follow-up, significantly more intervention treatment patients with major depression rated quality of care as "good" to "excellent" compared to Usual Care patients (93.0% versus 75.0%). Intervention treatment patients with major depression also differed significantly from usual care patients with major depression in their frequency of rating medications as helping "somewhat" to "a great deal" at the 4-month follow-up (88.1% versus 63.3%). Minor depressives who received the intervention treatment were not significantly more likely than usual care patients to rate the quality of care they received for depression as "good" to "excellent" at the 4-month follow-up (94.4% versus 89.3%). Minor depressives in the intervention treatment were more likely to rate medications as helping "somewhat" to "a great deal" at the 4-month follow-up (81.8% versus 61.4%).

Study 2: At the 4-month follow-up, significantly more intervention patients with major depression rated the quality of care they received for depression as "good" to "excellent" compared to usual care patients (88.5% versus 56.0%). Among patients with major depression, intervention patients did not differ significantly from usual care patients in their frequency of rating medications as helping "somewhat" to "a great deal" at the 4-month follow-up. Minor depressives who received the integrated behavioral treatment were significantly more likely than usual care patients to rate the quality of care they received for depression as "good" to "excellent" (97% versus 71.4%) at the 4-month follow-up. Intervention and usual care patients with minor depression did not differ significantly at the 4-month follow-up in ratings about the helpfulness of antidepressant medications.

Lesson: *Depressed patients with major depression are more satisfied with both models of treatment than control patients are with the usual care they receive for depression. Minor depressives who receive a behavioral health intervention are more satisfied than usual care patients. In the ICP, we provide features of both interventions in an effort to effectively treat* and *satisfy patients with major and minor depression.*

10. Were interventions acceptable to primary care providers?

Study 1: At the end of the study, participating physicians were surveyed. Of twelve responding physicians, 10 indicated that participation in the study increased their satisfaction with treating depressed patients "a great deal" and two indicated that participation increased their satisfaction in treating depression "a little." Providers ranked the six components of the intervention in the following order, starting with the most essential and proceeding to the least essential:

1. The primary care physician having more time to treat the patient
2. Having on-site psychiatric consultation available
3. Patient education materials
4. Lunch time didactic and case conferences
5. Having a handbook on antidepressant therapy
6. Using structured interviews with patients

All six components received many more ratings of "definitely useful" or "essential" than ratings of "possibly useful" or "not useful." For example, **86% of the physicians perceived availability of patient education materials as "definitely useful."**

Study 2: Sixteen of 19 physicians responded to a post-study evaluation of the intervention in Study 2. The physicians rated all aspects of the program positively. **Most (88%) indicated that they were able to use intervention information placed in patient medical charts easily with patients. One hundred percent of the physicians reported that they preferred the intervention to usual treatment of depression, which included referral of patients for treatment in a staff model mental health service seven miles away.**

Lesson: *Primary care physicians prefer on-site mental health services for their patients. They would also like to have more time with depressed patients. Physicians welcome on-site behavioral treatment and assistance with developing relapse prevention plans. Concerning antidepressant therapy, they find medication risk assessments, as well as education and monitoring services useful. Physicians like consultants to provide same-day charting of mental health treatments and appreciate educational materials for themselves as well as their patients. The ICP incorporates most of the features of the evaluated interventions that were well received by primary care physicians.*

Summary and Helpful Hints

This chapter provides detailed information about the empirical basis of the ICP. Consider the following suggestions.

1. Use information from the studies reported in this chapter in a lunch-hour presentation in primary care.
2. Select a finding from this chapter to publish in your first issue of a primary care behavioral health newsletter.

3. Give a copy of the list of references titled "The Empirical Basis of the ICP" to your colleagues who have doubts about treating depression in primary care.

References

1. Costa, P.T., & McCrae, R. R. (1985). *The Neo Personality Inventory Manual.* Odessa, Florida, Psychological Assessment Resources.
2. Derogatis, L.R., Rickels, K., Uhlenhuth, E.H., & Covi, L. (1974). The Hopkins Symptom Checklist: A measure of primary symptom dimensions. In P. Pichot (Ed.), *Psychological Measurements in Psychopharmacology: Problems in Pharmacopsychiatry*. Switzerland: Kargerman, Basil.
3. Von Korff, M., Wagner, E.H., & Saunders, K. (1992). A chronic disease score from automated pharmacy data. *Journal of Clinical Epidemiology, 45,* 197-203.

The Empirical Basis of the ICP

1. Beck, A., & Beck, R.W. (1972). Screening depressed patients in family practice: A rapid technic. *Postgraduate Medicine, 52,* 81-85.
Provides information regarding the Beck Depression Inventory-Short Form.

2. Brown, R.A., & Lewinsohn, P.M. (1984). A psychoeducational approach to the treatment of depression: Comparison of group, individual, and minimal contact procedures. *Journal of Consulting and Clinical Psychology, 52*(5), 774-783.
Provides information on the effectiveness of psychoeducational treatment under group and individual conditions and the extent to which therapist contact is critical to treatment success.

3. Brown, C., & Schulberg, H.C. (1995). The efficacy of psychosocial treatments in primary care: A review of randomized clinical trials. *General Hospital Psychiatry, 17,* 414-424.
Reviews earlier clinical trials concerning psychosocial interventions in primary care.

4. Burns, D.D., & Nolen-Hoeksema, S. (1991). Coping styles, homework compliance, and the effectiveness of cognitive-behavioral therapy. *Journal of Consulting and Clinical Psychology, 59*(2), 305-311.
Provides information of the role of coping strategies in the treatment of depression.

5. Bush, T., Robinson, P., Katon, W., Von Korff, M., Lin, E., Walker, E., & Simon, G. (1996). Positivity of evaluation of patient education materials for depressed primary care patients and subsequent use of recommended coping strategies. In preparation for submission.
Summarizes the relationships between patient use of recommended strategies and evaluation of educational materials.

6. deShazer, S., Kim-Berg, I., Lipchik, E., Nunnally, E., Molnar, A., Gingrich, W., & Weiner-Davis, M. (1986). Brief therapy: Focused solution development. *Family Process, 25,* 207-221.
Provides ideas for structuring brief therapeutic interactions with patients.

7. Gath, D. *A Manual for Problem Solving Treatment in the General Medical Setting.* Unpublished.
Treatment manual that supported randomized trial in primary care.

8. Hayes, S.C. (1987). A contextual approach to therapeutic change. In N. Jacobson (Ed.), *Psychotherapists in clinical practice: Cognitive and behavioral perspectives* (pp. 327-387). New York: Guilford.
Provides information about use of psychological acceptance strategies in treatment of behavior disorders.

9. Hayes, S.C., Strosahl, K., & Wilson, K. G. (1999). *Acceptance and commitment therapy: An experiential approach to behavior change.* New York, NY: Guilford.
Provides information on application of psychological acceptance strategies with patients with behavior disorders.

10. Howard, K.I., Kopta, S. M., Krause, M.S., & Orlinsky, D.E. (1986). The dose-response relationship in psychotherapy. *American Psychologist, 41,* 159-164.
Provides information on length of treatment and outcome in psychotherapy.

11. Jacobowski, P., & Lange, A.J. (1978). *The assertive option: Your rights and responsibilities.* Champaign, IL: Research Press Company.
Provides practical information on helping patients become more assertive.

12. Jacobson, N. *A Conflict Resolution Manual for Couples.* Unpublished.

Provides guidelines for effective problem-solving in the context of an intimate relationship.

13. Kabat-Zinn, J. (1990). *Full catastrophe living: Using the wisdom of your body and mind to face stress, pain, and illness.* New York: Hyperion.
Provides practical information on helping patients use mind-body strategies.

14. Katon, W., Lin, E., Von Korff, M., Bush, T., Walker, E., Simon, G., & Robinson, P. (1994). The predictors of persistence of depression in primary care. *Journal of Affective Disorders, 31,* 81-90.
Provides information to help in identifying patients who respond less well to treatment.

15. Katon, W., Robinson, P. Von Korff, M., Lin, E., Bush, T., Ludman, E., Simon, G., & Walker, E. (1996). A multifaceted intervention to improve treatment of depression in primary care. *Archives of General Psychiatry.*
Describes details of a randomized clinical trial evaluating the integrated behavioral treatment of depression in the primary care setting.

16. Katon, W., Von Korff, M., Lin, E., Bush, T., Russo, J., Lipscomb, P., & Wagner, E. (1992). A randomized trial of psychiatric consultation with distressed high utilizers. *General Hospital Psychiatry, 14,* 86-98.
Describes an early primary care intervention involving evaluation of liaison psychiatry services in a randomized trial of high utilizers, many of whom were depressed.

17. Katon, W., Von Korff, M., Lin, E., Walker, E., Simon, G., Bush, T., Robinson, P., & Russo, J. (1994). Collaborative management to achieve treatment guidelines: Impact on depression in primary care. *Journal of the American Medical Association, 273,* 1026-1031.
Describes details of a randomized clinical trial evaluating a method of care for treatment of depression in the primary care setting.

18. Lazarus, A. (1992). The multimodal approach to the treatment of minor depression. *American Journal of Psychotherapy, XIV* (1), 50-57.
Provides practical information on use of multimodal therapy with patients who have minor depression.

19. Lazarus, A., & Faye, L. (1979). *I can if I want to.* New York: Quill, William Morrow.
A brief self-help book with good behavior change strategies.

20. Lin, E., Von Korff, M., Katon, W., Bush, T., Simon, G., Walker, E., & Robinson, P. (1995). *Achieving Guidelines for the Treatment of Depression in Primary Care: Training Model vs. Reorganization of Service Delivery.* Presented at the Eighth Annual NIMH International Research Conference on Mental Health Problems in the General Health Care Sector, McLean, Virginia, September 7-9, 1994.
Examines the stability of change in primary care provider prescribing behaviors.

21. Lin, E., Von Korff, M., Katon, W., Bush, T., Simon, G., Walker, E., & Robinson, P. (1995). The role of the primary care physician in patient's adherence to antidepressant therapy. *Medical Care, 33*(1), 67-74.
Provides information on primary care antidepressant treatment.

22. Lewinsohn, P.M., Antonuccio, D.O., Breckenridge, J.S., & Teri, L. (1984). *The coping with depression course: A psychoeducational intervention for unipolar depression.* Eugene, OR: Castalia Publishing Company.
Treatment manual for implementing a cognitive behavioral group treatment for depressed patients.

23. Miranda, J., & Munoz, R.F. (1994). Intervention for minor depression in primary care patients. *Psychosomatic Medicine, 56*, 136-141.
Provides information on treating minor depressives in primary care.

24. Mynors-Wallace, L., Gath, D.H., Lloyd-Thomas, A.R., & Tomlinson, D. (1995). Randomized controlled trial comparing problem solving treatment with amitriptyline and placebo for major depression in primary care. *British Medical Journal, 310*, 441-446.
Describes details of a randomized clinical trial comparing problem-solving and antidepressant treatment of depression in the primary care setting.

25. Public Health Service Agency for Health Care Policy and Research. (1993). *Depression in Primary Care: Volume 2. Treatment of Major Depression.* U.S. Department of Health and Human Services (AHCPR Publication No. 93-051). Rockville, MD.
Provides guidelines for treatment of depression in primary care, which are based upon research findings and expert opinion.

26. Robson, M.H., France, R., & Bland, M. (1984). Clinical psychologists in primary care: Controlled trial and economic evaluation. *British Medical Journal, 288*, 1805-1808.
Provides information on primary care roles for psychologists.

27. Robinson, P., Bush, T., Von Korff, M., Katon, W., Lin, E., Simon, G.E., & Walker, E. (1995). Primary care physician use of cognitive behavioral techniques with depressed patients. *Journal of Family Practice, 40*(4), 352-357.
Provides information on behavioral techniques used by primary care physicians in the course of starting patients in antidepressant therapy.

28. Robinson, P., Bush, T., Von Korff, M., Katon, W., Simon, G., Walker, E., & Lin, E. (1996). Educational materials for depressed primary care patients and subsequent use of suggested coping strategies. Submitted for publication.
Summarizes the relationship between reading/viewing educational materials and subsequent use of coping strategies suggested by the materials.

29. Robinson, P. Katon, W., Von Korff, M., Bush, T., Lin, E., Walker, E., & Simon, G. (1996). The education of depressed primary care patients: What do patients think of interactive booklets and a video? *Group Health Medical Staff Forum, Fall.*
Provides information on depressed patient evaluation of educational materials.

30. Robinson, P., Katon, W., Von Korff, M., Bush, T., Ludman, E., Simon, G., Lin, E., & Walker, E. (1996). *Use of coping strategies by depressed primary care patients: Results of a randomized controlled trial.* Submitted for publication.
Describes details of a randomized clinical trial evaluating a method of care for treatment of depression in the primary care setting.

31. Rush, A.J., Beck, A.T., Kovacs, M., & Hollon, S. (1977). Comparative efficacy of cognitive therapy and pharmacotherapy in the treatment of depressed outpatients. *Cognitive Therapy and Research, 1*(1), 17-37.
Describes details of a randomized clinical trial evaluating treatment of depression.

32. Scott, A.I., & Freeman, C.P.L. (1992). Edinburgh primary care depression study: Treatment outcome, patient satisfaction, and cost after 16 weeks. *British Medical Journal, 304*, 883-887.
Describes details of a study evaluating treatment of depression in the primary care setting.

33. Schulberg, H., McClelland, M., & Gooding, W. (1987). Six month outcome for medical patients with major depressive disorders. *Journal of General Internal Medicine, 2*, 312-317.
Addresses the response of depressed medical patients to treatments.

34. Schulberg, H.C., Coulehan, J.L., Block, M.R., Lave, J., Rodriquez, E., Scott, C.P., Madonia, J.S., Imber, S., & Perel, J. (1993). Clinical trials of primary care treatment for major depression: Issues in design, recruitment and treatment. International *Journal of Psychiatry and Medicine, 23*, 29-42.
Suggests methodological strategies for primary care research efforts.

35. Schulberg, H.C., Block, M.R., Madonia, M.J., Scott, C.P., Rodriguez, E., Imber, S.D., Perel J., Lave, J., Houchk, P.R., & Coulehan, J.L. (1996). Treating major depression in primary care practice: Eight-month clinical outcomes. Accepted by *Archives of General Psychiatry*.
Presents early results of a randomized trial investigating treatment of depression in primary care.

36. Schulberg, H.C. (1994). *A Randomized Clinical Trial Comparing Interpersonal Therapy, Nortriptyline, and Usual Care in the Treatment of Depressed Primary Care Patients.* A presentation at the NIMH Conference: Treatment of Mental Problems in General Medical Settings.
Presents early results of a randomized trial investigating treatment of depression in primary care.

37. Simon, A.D., Gordon, J.S., Monroe, S.M., & Thase, M.E. (1995). Toward an integration of psychologic, social and biologic factors in depression: Effects on outcome and course of cognitive therapy. *Journal of Consulting and Clinical Psychology, 63*, 369-377.
Describes details of a randomized clinical trial evaluating methods for treatment of depression.

38. Sherbourne, E.D., Hays, R.D., & Wells, K.B. (1995). Personal and psychosocial risk factors for physical and mental health outcomes and course of depression among depressed patients. *Journal of Consulting and Clinical Psychology, 63*, 369-377.
Provides data for understanding the relationship between risk factors and treatment outcomes with depressed patients.

39. Waxman, H.M., Carner, E.A., & Blum, A. (1983). Depressive symptoms and health service utilization among the community elderly. *Journal of the American Geriatric Society, 31*, 417-420.
Provides information on the impact of depression on utilization of medical services by older patients.

40. Wright, J.H. (1994). Combined therapy and pharmacotherapy of depression. In A. Freeman & F.M. Dattilio (Eds.), *Casebook of Cognitive Behavioral Therapy*. New York, NY: Plenum Publishing Corp.
Provides strategies for using cognitive techniques to help patients use medications and guidelines for "team treatment" of depression.

ICP Assessment Form

Level 1 ICP Assessment (Patient Completes)

Patient:	Provider(s):

Dear Patient: Please respond to the following questions. If you need help with any of the questions, ask your doctor or nurse.

Mark an "X" by any symptom that has troubled you *more days than not* during the past ☐ one or ☐ two (*check one*) week(s).	Today's Date	Return Visit Date
1. Anger or Irritability – often during the day	☐	☐
2. Sadness – often during the day	☐	☐
3. Sleep Problems: ☐ too much; ☐ slow to go to sleep; ☐ waking in middle of night; ☐ early morning waking	☐	☐
4. Interest Problems – a lack of interest in others and in activities you usually enjoy	☐	☐
5. Guilt, self critical thoughts, feeling inadequate or worthless	☐	☐
6. Energy Problems – tired most of the time	☐	☐
7. Concentration Problems	☐	☐
8. Appetite Changes: ☐ significantly greater; ☐ significantly less; ☐ weight gain; ☐ weight loss	☐	☐
9. Psychomotor Problems: ☐ very "slowed down" or ☐ very "speeded up"	☐	☐
10. Pain Problems – more aches and more pain	☐	☐
11. Suicidal Thoughts	☐	☐

How often have you used the following coping strategies in the past ☐ one or ☐ two (*check one*) week(s).

0 = Not at all; 1 = Once; 2 = Several times; 3 = Almost Daily; 4 = Daily

1. Participating in pleasurable activities	______	______
2. Participating in activities that boost your confidence	______	______
3. Simply being aware of an uncomfortable thought, feeling, or emotion without struggling with it.	______	______
4. Participating in activities that help you relax	______	______
5. Using problem-solving techniques for problems you're having in life such as problems with your job or relationships	______	______
6. Noticing negative thoughts and replacing them with more realistic thoughts	______	______
7. Participating in creative activities	______	______

Level 2 ICP Assessment – Page 1 (Patient Completes)

Patient:	Provider(s):

Dear Patient: Please respond to the following questions. If you need help with any of the questions, ask your doctor or nurse.

Mark an "X" by any symptom that has troubled you *more days than not* during the past ☐ one or ☐ two (*check one*) week(s).	Today's Date	Return Visit Date
1. Anger or Irritability – often during the day	☐	☐
2. Sadness – often during the day	☐	☐
3. Sleep Problems: ☐ too much; ☐ slow to go to sleep; ☐ waking in middle of night; ☐ early morning waking	☐	☐
4. Interest Problems – a lack of interest in others and in activities you usually enjoy	☐	☐
5. Guilt, self critical thoughts, feeling inadequate or worthless	☐	☐
6. Energy Problems – tired most of the time	☐	☐
7. Concentration Problems	☐	☐
8. Appetite Changes: ☐ significantly greater; ☐ significantly less; ☐ weight gain; ☐ weight loss	☐	☐
9. Psychomotor Problems: ☐ very "slowed down" or ☐ very "speeded up"	☐	☐
10. Pain Problems – more aches and more pain	☐	☐
11. Suicidal Thoughts	☐	☐

How often have you used the following coping strategies in the past ☐ one or ☐ two (*check one*) week(s).

0 = Not at all; 1 = Once; 2 = Several times; 3 = Almost Daily; 4 = Daily

1. Participating in pleasurable activities	______	______
2. Participating in activities that boost your confidence	______	______
3. Simply being aware of an uncomfortable thought, feeling, or emotion without struggling with it.	______	______
4. Participating in activities that help you relax	______	______
5. Using problem-solving techniques for problems you're having in life such as problems with your job or relationships	______	______
6. Noticing negative thoughts and replacing them with more realistic thoughts	______	______
7. Participating in creative activities	______	______

Level 2 ICP Assessment – Page 2 (Patient Completes)

Which of these emotions have you experienced on a daily basis during the past week and with how much intensity (1 = "not intense" to 10 = "very intense") and willingness (1= "I cannot tolerate this feeling" to 10 = "I accept this feeling completely")?

Today's Date:			Return Visit Date:		
	Intensity of Feeling	Willingness to Feel		Intensity of Feeling	Willingness to Feel
1. Sadness	1.	1.	1. Sadness	1.	1.
2. Anger	2.	2.	2. Anger	2.	2.
3. Fear	3.	3.	3. Fear	3.	3.

Please record a number beside each activity to indicate how much you "lived your values" in that area *during the past week.* Use this rating scale:

1 2 3 4 5 6 7 8 9 10

Did not live what I value — *Lived according to my values*

	Today's Date:	Return Visit Date:
1. Enjoying Things Alone	1.	1.
2. Accomplishing Things Alone	2.	2.
3. Talking with Others	3.	3.
4. Contentment with Work	4.	4.
5. Sensual Experience	5.	5.
6. Fun with Others	6.	6.
7. Images of a Better Future	7.	7.

For Health Care Provider's Use

If additional measurement used, indicate whether:

☐ *Beck Inventory – Short Form or* ☐ *Geriatric Scale*

☐ *Other:* ____________________

The Beck Inventory – Short Form has the following norms:

0 - 4 = None or minimal; 5 - 7 = Mild; 8 - 15 = Moderate; 16+ = Severe

Today's Date	Score	Return Visit Date	Score

Level 2 ICP Assessment – Page 3 (Provider Completes)

Note: After reviewing the patient's responses on pages 1 and 2, complete the following assessment to determine the impact of a patient's symptoms on her/his functioning. Interview the patient to clarify the extent of limitation. The format allows you to rate each area today and again at treatment completion. **Critical areas of functioning are in bold font** and need greater weighting in planning treatment intensity.

Today's Date	Return Visit Date	**Functional Limitations / Severity Ratings:** 0 = Absent/Nonpathological; 1 = Moderate; 2 = Debilitating; 3 = Incapacitating; 4 = Imminently dangerous*

***Severity Rating (0 - 4)**		***Family Limitations* (Check if limitation is present)**
1. ______	1. ______	1. ☐ Family dysfunction
2. ______	2. ______	2. ☐ Family dysfunction with substance abuse
3. ______	3. ______	3. ☐ Marital/relationship dysfunction
4. ______	4. ______	4. ☐ **Marital/relationship dysfunction with violent behavior**

***Severity Rating (0 - 4)**		***Work and Productivity Limitations* (Check if limitation is present**
1. ______	1. ______	1. ☐ Work dissatisfaction
2. ______	2. ______	2. ☐ Work performance problems
3. ______	3. ______	3. ☐ Educational performance deficits
4. ______	4. ______	4. ☐ **Inadequate survival skills**

***Severity Rating (0 - 4)**		***Social Limitations* (Check if limitation is present)**
1. ______	1. ______	1. ☐ **Assaultiveness**
2. ______	2. ______	2. ☐ Manipulativeness
3. ______	3. ______	3. ☐ Social withdrawal
4. ______	4. ______	4. ☐ Oppositionalism
5. ______	5. ______	5. ☐ Uncommunicativeness
6. ______	6. ______	6. ☐ Verbal aggressiveness

***Severity Rating (0 - 4)**		***Emotional Experiencing Limitations* (Check if limitation is present)**
1. ______	**1.** ______	**1.** ☐ **Self-mutilation**
2. ______	**2.** ______	**2.** ☐ **Substance abuse history**
3. ______	3. ______	3. ☐ Hopelessness
4. ______	**4.** ______	**4.** ☐ **Suicidal thoughts/behavior**

***Severity Rating (0 - 4)**		***Psychobiological Limitations* (Check if limitation is present)**
1. ______	1. ______	1. ☐ Altered sleep
2. ______	2. ______	2. ☐ Decreased concentration
3. ______	3. ______	3. ☐ Decreased frustration tolerance
4. ______	4. ______	4. ☐ Dysphoric mood
5. ______	**5.** ______	**5.** ☐ **Mood lability**
6. ______	**6.** ______	**6.** ☐ **Psychomotor agitation**
7. ______	**7.** ______	**7.** ☐ **Psychomotor retardation**
8. ______	**8.** ______	**8.** ☐ **Concomitant medical condition**
9. ______	9. ______	9. ☐ Medical treatment noncompliance
10. ______	**10.** ______	10. ☐ **Inadequate health care skills**

ICP Medication Assessment Questionnaire

ICP Medication Assessment Questionnaire – Page 1

Dear Patient: Your answers to the following questions will assist you and your primary care provider in developing an effective treatment plan.

Patient:	Provider(s):	Today's Date:

Have you used an antidepressant medication previously? ☐ Yes ☐ No

If Yes, what medication did you use? ____________

When? ____________

For how long? ____________

Did you have any side effects? ☐ Yes ☐ No

If Yes, what? ____________

How much did you benefit from the medication? Use a scale ranging from 0 to 100%, where 0 is "feeling very bad" and 100% is your "normal." How much *did* you improve when you used this medicine? ____________

Are you taking an antidepressant medication now? ☐ Yes ☐ No

If Yes, what medication are you taking? ____________

When did you start taking this medication? ____________

What symptoms have not yet improved? ____________

Are you having any troubling side effects with this medicine? ☐ Yes ☐ No

If Yes, what? ____________

How much have you benefited from the medication? Use a scale ranging from 0 to 100%, where 0 is "feeling very bad" and 100% is your "normal." How much improved are you now? ____________

Do you want to take an antidepressant medication? ☐ Yes ☐ No

If yes, what specific symptoms do you want the medication to address?

____

Sometimes we have beliefs about medications that make using medications successfully more difficult. Put an "X" by any of the following statements that you believe, even a little, concerning medications or drugs prescribed by doctors for treatment of anxiety and depression.

	X	Belief
1.	☐	These kinds of drugs are not the answer to problems in one's life.
2.	☐	These kinds of drugs are a crutch.
3.	☐	I would be the one to get severe side effects.
4.	☐	I should be able to get by without using these kinds of drugs.
5.	☐	I could get addicted.
6.	☐	My family would not want me to use these kinds of drugs.
7.	☐	I will not be able to work if I take these kinds of drugs.
8.	☐	These kinds of drugs are overused.
9.	☐	It is harmful to take too many different kinds of drugs.
10.	☐	These kinds of drugs should not be taken long-term.
11.	☐	Drugs that doctors prescribe for anxiety and depression are dangerous.

ICP Medication Assessment Questionnaire – Page 2

Antidepressant medications often have side effects. Following is a list of common side effects and strategies for coping effectively with the side effects. Side effects tend to lessen after several weeks of use of a medication. **Put an "X" by any side effect that you would have difficulties tolerating.**

	Side Effect	Coping Strategy
1. ☐	Dry Mouth	Drink plenty of water, chew sugarless gum, & use sugarless drops.
2. ☐	Constipation	Eat more fiber-rich foods or take a stool softener.
3. ☐	Drowsiness	Get fresh air and take frequent walks. Try taking your medicine earlier in the evening. If you are taking your medicine in the day ask you doctor if you can take it at night.
4. ☐	Wakefulness	Take medications early in the day. Learn more about insomnia. Take a warm bath and have a light snack before bed.
5. ☐	Blurred Vision	Remind yourself that this will be a temporary difficulty. Contact your doctor if it persists.
6. ☐	Dizziness	Get up more slowly; drink plenty of fluids. If you are worried, call your doctor.
7. ☐	Feeling Speeded Up	Tell yourself, "This will go away within three to five days." If not, call your doctor or nurse.
8. ☐	Sexual Problem	Talk with your doctor.
9. ☐	Nausea or Appetite Loss	Take the medicine with food. Eat small healthy meals.

The following information is important. Do you have any questions about any of these instructions?

(1) It will take 2 to 3 weeks for you to begin to experience beneficial effects from the medication.
(2) You will need to take the medicine every day.
(3) Stop the medicine only when you decide with your provider that it is time to stop.
(4) Call your doctor if you are concerned about an unpleasant sensation that you think might be related to your medication.

ICP Treatment Plan Form

Treatment Plan (Provider Completes)			
Mark an "X" by treatment(s) selected.	Today's Date:	Review Date	Completion Date
1. ☐ Clinical Management by Primary Care Team			
☐ Antidepressant Treatment by Primary Care Team Medication: Target Dose:			
2. ☐ Behavioral Health Treatment by Primary Care Mental Health Consultant ☐ Brief ☐ Behavioral			
3. ☐ Consultation with Medication Specialist			
Medication: Target Dose:			
4. ☐ Intensive Treatment Delivered Externally			

Relapse Prevention Support

We developed a relapse prevention plan with the patient on __________. The relapse prevention plan pertains to the following 6-month period: __________ to __________.

We will contact the patient by phone to evaluate the on-going helpfulness of this plan according to the following schedule.

Dates to Call Patient to Support Relapse Prevention Plan*	Results of Call
1.	1.
2.	2.
3.	3.
4.	4.

*2, 4, 12, and 24 weeks after active treatment

Indicate the patient's level of satisfaction with the initial treatment plan and satisfaction at the time of withdrawal or completion of treatment.

1 2 3 4 5 6 7 8 9 10

Not Satisfied *Very Satisfied*

Patient describes her/his satisfaction with our **initial** treatment plan as: __________________

Patient describes her/his satisfaction with this program of care at the time of :

☐ **withdrawal** as: ____

☐ **completion** as: ____

Instructions Concerning ICP Booklets

Both booklets are presented in two formats. The first format is designed to help you read the booklets easily in this book. The second format is designed to help you create booklets for patients. You will need to use a photocopy machine capable of converting 1-sided copies into 2-sided copies to make the booklets. Follow these step-by-step instructions to create the booklets. You may use a sheet of colored paper for the booklet covers.

Seven Ways to Cope

1. Photocopy the twelve pages.
2. Leave the pages facing the direction they face in the book (every other page faces in toward the spine of this book).
3. Place the 12 single sheets in the photocopy machine with the first page on top, last on bottom.
4. Select 'convert 1-sided to 2-sided copies.'
5. Select the number of booklets you want to make.
6. Copy.
7. Remove the twelve pages from output tray.
8. Fold the twelve pages in half to create a 24-page booklet.
9. Add two staples to the "spine" of the booklets if you like.

Using Medications Successfully

1. Photocopy the 8 pages.
2. Follow steps 2 through 7 and step 9 for Seven Ways to Cope (above).
3. Fold the eight pages in half to create a 12-page booklet.

Note: You may want to use the large print version of the booklets to create an 8½ x 11 inch booklet to use with visually challenged patients.

ICP Patient Education Booklets

Seven Ways to Cope

An ICP Booklet

Context Press
Reno, Nevada

What is Depression?

Depression is a response to problems in living. When we become exhausted in our efforts to cope with life, we begin to experience symptoms of depression. Following is a list of common symptoms of depression. Make a check in the box beside any symptom you have had almost daily for the past two weeks.

1. ☐ Anger or irritability
2. ☐ Sadness
3. ☐ Sleeping too much or too little
4. ☐ A lack of interest in others and in activities you usually enjoy
5. ☐ Guilt, self critical thoughts, feeling inadequate or worthless
6. ☐ Feeling tired most of the time
7. ☐ Concentration difficulties
8. ☐ Appetite change — eating significantly more or less
9. ☐ Feeling very "slowed down" or very "speeded up"
10. ☐ More aches and pain
11. ☐ Thoughts of suicide or death in general

Total Symptoms:_____

If you checked four or more symptoms, talk with your health care provider. Also, use this booklet to make a plan to address these symptoms.

This booklet describes seven coping strategies for addressing symptoms of depression, solving problems in living and creating the life you want.

The Cycle of Depression

People become depressed for many reasons. Most often, depression is related to stressful life circumstances, such as marital problems, death of a loved one, loss of a job, or a child leaving home. Depression may also be related to physical problems such as chronic pain or medical illness.

Depression Occurs In Three Ways

The Body Feels Depressed

When the body is depressed, a person sleeps poorly, eats differently, has less energy, struggles with concentration, and has more aches and pains.

Behavior Is Depressed

When behavior is depressed, a person does much less than usual. She/he talks less, produces less, and socializes less.

The Mind Is Depressed

When the mind is depressed, thinking changes. A depressed person experiences more intensely negative and painful thoughts about the past, the present and the future.

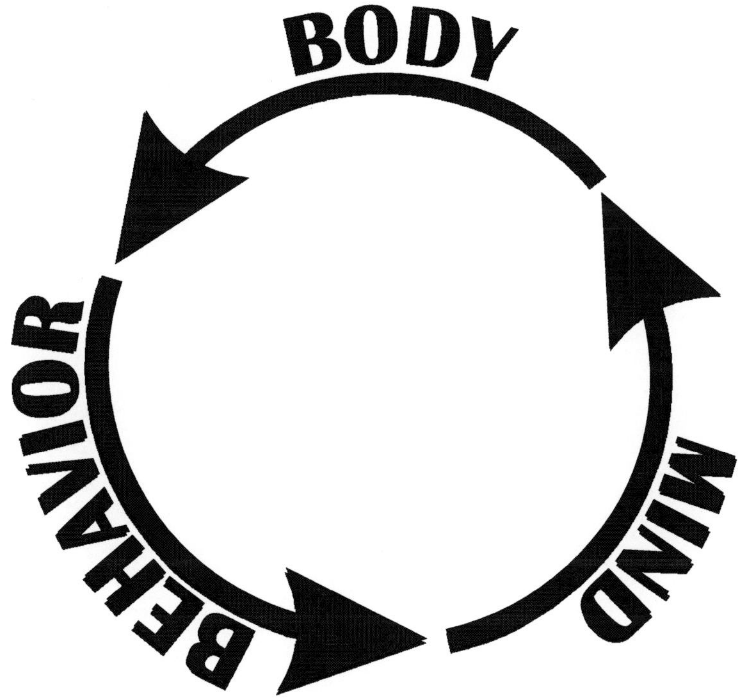

A person's body, behavior, and mind interact continuously. Once depression becomes a problem, this interaction may lead to a "downward spiral" in mood, hopefulness and energy. Two courses of action help reverse the downward direction and create a "positive spiral."

1. *Strategic Use of Coping Strategies*

Use of active coping strategies helps you reverse the downward spiral of depression. When you address life problems with effective strategies, you have more opportunities to create positive conditions in your life context. **This booklet suggests seven coping strategies for you to use to restore your body, behavior and mind *and* to effectively address life problems.** If you make a concerted effort to work with your health care provider in using these strategies, you can make significant and lasting changes to your lifestyle.

2. Use of Medications

Medications may also help you to feel better. Antidepressant medications help restore the presence of neurotransmitter substances that become depleted by stress. However, these medications work somewhat slowly. The impact of effective coping is more immediate. If you decide to use medications, use coping strategies as well. Coping strategies will complement the action of medications on the body's neurochemistry.

The First Strategy:

Hoping…Planning…Doing

Hope is the foundation of a healthy life. Without hope, most people avoid constructive activity. Another way of stating this is that hopefulness is a good predictor of action. In turn, action is a good predictor of mood improvement.

Try this exercise to help you increase your sense of hopefulness.

> *Sit in a quiet place for a few minutes and ask yourself about your explanation of your current troubles. Are you blaming yourself? If so, stop. You are well-intentioned and worthy of self-respect. Decide upon an explanation for your current difficulties that reflects a sense of respect for who you are. You may be stressed or overwhelmed or simply lacking skills you need to overcome challenging circumstances. Write down your* ***revised*** *explanation of your present situation here.*

____

____

____

____

____

Planning and doing are also important behavioral skills for coping with stress and depression. With a little hope, you can make a "behavioral health plan" to address needed changes in your daily life. Read and respond to each of the following seven steps to make a behavioral health plan for this week.

1. **Choose an area of life that you want to make better.** Possible areas include: enjoying things alone or with others, accomplishing difficult and unpleasant tasks, talking to or "making connections" with others, contentment with your work, sensual experiencing, or imagining a better future. Write down your choice here.

   ____

2. **Imagine yourself doing something different in the activity area you choose.** Write down what you imagine.

   ____

3. **Plan a specific time and place** to engage in an activity that represents making an improvement to the area of life you want to make more satisfying.

   Activity: ______________________________

   Time: ______________________________

   Place: ______________________________

4. During and after you conduct this "experiment in mood change," **watch what happens**, *inside* you (your thoughts, feelings and behaviors) and *outside* of you (what others say and do). Write down your observations here.

   Inside you: ______________________________

   Outside of you: ______________________________

5. **Think about your findings** or results.

6. **Talk with others** about your results and draw conclusions. Write down your conclusions here.

   ____

   ____

7. **Plan your next "behavioral health plan."**

   Activity: ______________________________

   Time: ______________________________

   Place: ______________________________

Try to make a behavioral health plan *weekly* for the next month. The positive impact of small changes in two or three areas of your life can become highly significant with three or four weeks of effort. Try to find a friend who will support your on-going use of this strategy.

The Second Strategy:

Building Acceptance and Making Value-Based Choices

We often respond to a difficult circumstance, whether it is internal or external, with an action that moves us away from the source of unwanted distress. While we may avoid some external stresses, we cannot avoid painful internal events. Internal events include thoughts and feelings — positive and negative. *Psychological acceptance* is a strategy that involves actively embracing unwanted, painful thoughts and feelings.

When we use psychological acceptance strategies, we are more free to make decisions about our behavior. We can make choices to behave in accordance with our values. Our daily activities take on greater meaning when they reflect our values rather than our attempts to control unwanted thoughts and feelings. Try these exercises to improve your skills in using strategies of psychological acceptance and value-based behavioral planning.

1. Write down feelings (for example, fear, sadness, anxiety, depression, panic, anger) that you have difficulty tolerating.

   ____

   ____

2. Decide on a psychological acceptance procedure or method for observing unwanted feelings and thoughts.

Options include visualizing the feeling or seeing or listening to the words associated with the feeling. You may use the phrase, "I am having the sensation of: ____________________" or "I am having the thought that: ____________________."

3. Follow this procedure during acceptance or self observation practice periods.

   - Take four deep breaths and move into "observation mode."

   - Start to use your method of observation to help you stay in the "observation mode" (i.e., visualize your thoughts or use a phrase to prompt acceptance).

4. Practice daily for 5 to 10 minutes for a week. Record the number of minutes you practice each day.

   Day 1: _____ Day 2: _____ Day 3: _____

   Day 4: _____ Day 5: _____ Day 6: _____

   Day 7: _____

When you are ready, begin using the psychological acceptance procedure in daily situations that provoke painful thoughts and feelings. Record situations where you used your breathing and observation method and made a behavior choice that reflected your values.

____

____

The Third Strategy:

Appreciating Your Mind and Body

Using this strategy will help you become more aware of your body and more able to create sensations of physical well-being in your body. Basic body listening skills strengthen your ability to cope with physical *and* psychological health problems. Experiment with the following exercises.

I.

Rest for a few minutes in a favorite "quiet" place. Take several deep breaths and recall *or* fantasize an image of a serene environment. Give yourself time to develop this image with many details, including sounds, smells, colors, etc. Practicing this image on a daily basis will help you learn to create the image and associated sensations of wellness efficiently during highly stressful moments of daily living.

II.

Cultivate playfulness, curiosity, and openness. These mental states are related to well-being. If you are overly serious, controlled, or "closed off," make behavioral health plans to help you play and explore. For example, you may want to attend a comedy show, rekindle an old hobby, or go for a treasure hunt in a park. A good way to get started with use of these strategies is to watch young children, as most demonstrate these qualities very nicely.

The Fourth Strategy:

Solving Problems

Self-efficacy is a reflection of your confidence in solving the problems you encounter in life. Mastery of problem-solving skills improves your confidence and, hence, your self-efficacy. The following steps are prerequisites for effective problem solving.

- Identifying that something is a problem
- Accepting the possibility that something can be done about it
- Expressing a desire to change
- Being willing to make an effort to change

Use the following problem-solving exercise to review the critical steps in strategic problem-solving and address a current problem in your life.

1. **Pinpoint a current problem**. Write the problem down here. Define the problem so that it is a problem with a solution.

   ____

   ____

   ____

   ____

2. **Brainstorm solutions**. Generate at least 3 possible solutions.

   ____

   ____

   ____

3. **Evaluate potential solutions**. Describe advantages and disadvantages of each solution.

   ____

   ____

   ____

4. **Identify the first step** you will take to implement the solution you choose.

   ____

5. **Anticipate and plan for obstacles** to your implementing the solution you choose.

   Anticipated obstacles: ______________________

   ____

   ____

Plan to address obstacles: ______________________

____

____

6. **DO IT**! Record here when you did it.

____

7. **Evaluate the results** and continue working toward the solution by simply determining and planning a next step or going through these seven steps again.

Results suggest that:

____

____

Next step: ____________________________________

____

____

Remember To Celebrate Your Efforts, As Well As Your Successes!

The Fifth Strategy:

Responding to Interpersonal Conflicts

Our patterns of responding to conflict may cost more than we want to pay. If we believe that we must avoid conflict, we may withhold information needed to have healthy relationships. We may passively punish a person who makes a hurtful statement by ceasing to talk to that person. We may sacrifice self-respect to maintain the status quo when we use these strategies to respond to interpersonal conflict.

Alternatively, we may seek power and control over others more directly. We may use verbal and non-verbal expressions to frighten others. When we approach conflict in these ways, we are likely to have few friends and we are vulnerable to a host of physical problems associated with excessive arousal or anger.

If you want to become more skillful in this area, try the following exercises:

1. Acknowledge yourself on a daily basis. You may simply say to yourself, “I allow myself to be,” or “I am okay as I am.”

2. Whenever you notice tension in your body, ask yourself, “How do I feel right now?”

3. Give yourself a choice about expressing or not expressing feelings and opinions. It is okay to keep your feelings private or share them.

The following exercises are useful if you are currently in a close relationship and want to become more skillful in responding to conflict in this close relationship.

- Try scheduling a "problem solving" meeting. Allow 30 minutes.
- Set the agenda for your meeting. Keep it simple and make it agreeable to both of you.
- Convene your meetings when you are both rested and free from distraction.
- Positively and specifically define the problem you plan to address.
- Use "I" statements (e.g., "I want to have 20 minutes alone everyday" or "I feel upset about being without a job"). These statements help you responsibly express your feelings and make requests without blaming.
- Discuss only one problem at a time.
- Focus on solutions. Avoid trying to be "right."
- Compromise. Select a solution that allows both of you to "win."
- Set a time to "reconvene" and evaluate how your solution is working.

The Sixth Strategy:

Expressing Yourself

There are two important skills involved in the strategy of "expressing yourself." The first is *personal assertion* and the second is *creative expression*. Both of these skills require "balancing." Personal assertion requires on-going balancing of respect for yourself with respect for others. Creative expression involves balancing who you are with what you have to work with right now.

Personal assertion skills form the basis of your ability to make direct and honest statements and to stand up for your rights. Development of effective assertion skills may help you improve your mood, your sense of hopefulness, and your energy for enjoying life.

Creative expression is engaging in any activity for the sole purpose of expressing yourself. The possibilities for creative expression are many and change over the course of a lifetime. The loss of an avenue for creative expression may actually provoke symptoms of depression and anxiety. Try the following exercises to strengthen your skills in strategic self-expression.

Personal Assertion Exercise

Do you believe that you have the following rights? Make a check in the first box of any right you claim for yourself.

Does your day-to-day life indicate that you give yourself these rights? Make a check in the second box of any right that you "live" in your day-to-day behavior.

1. ☐ ☐ The right to say no without feeling guilty.
2. ☐ ☐ The right to be treated with respect.
3. ☐ ☐ The right to experience your feelings.
4. ☐ ☐ The right to change your mind.
5. ☐ ☐ The right to do less than you are capable of doing.
6. ☐ ☐ The right to make mistakes.

These are only a few basic assertive rights. If your beliefs are weak in any of the above areas or if your day-to-day life does not reflect your beliefs, you may want to develop a program to strengthen your beliefs in your assertive rights and your *behavioral expression* of these rights. You may want to read more about personal assertion and join a personal assertion class. Classes may be available within your health care system or in your community. Make a behavioral health plan to help you start a program of strengthening skills in this critical area.

Creative Expression

List five creative expression activities that you enjoy and that are consistent with your values. Indicate how many hours you have spent in each of these activities in the past week.

Creative Expression Activity	# Hours in Past Week
1.	1.
2.	2.
3.	3.
4.	4.
5.	5.

If you had difficulty identifying activities, take time to evaluate your "gifts" or "interests" and available resources or materials in you life at the present moment. If you spent little time in identified activities, consider "scheduling" time for these important activities. Write down your findings here and make a behavioral health plan to engage in creative activities on a *daily* basis.

Gifts: ______________________________________

____

Interests: ______________________________________

____

Resources: ______________________________________

____

The Seventh Strategy:

Balancing Your Thinking

When life is going well, we tend to have two positive thoughts to every negative thought. When we become depressed, the balance changes to two negative thoughts to every positive thought. "Realistic" thinking probably lies somewhere in between.

Shifting the balance in the direction of more positive thoughts is difficult to do, especially without someone to help you. Friends can help when you give them an opportunity and ask for their opinion on something. Knowing how to change the balance of your thoughts is important because it can help you catch yourself when you start to become depressed.

Use the following steps and suggested exercises to help you balance your thoughts.

- Identify a favorite saying or thought that inspires courage or optimism for you in difficult times.
- Try changing your perspective on something of little importance to you from an exaggerated negative perspective to a realistic or slightly positive point of view.
- Identify someone who tends to be a "realist" or "optimist" and contact this person. They can help you balance your thoughts.

Exercises to Help Balance Thinking

Write down favorite sayings and thoughts that inspire courage or optimism.

What positive thoughts do you want to keep in mind right now?

Who helps you balance your thinking on different issues?

Getting Started

Which of the seven strategies discussed in this booklet, if any, do you think will work best for you at present? Place an "X" in the box to indicate the extent to which each of the strategies might help you now. Use a rating scale where:

1 = Not Helpful and 4 = Very Helpful

Strategy	*1*	*2*	*3*	*4*
Hoping…Planning…Doing				
Building Acceptance and Making Value-Based Choices				
Appreciating Your Mind and Body				
Solving Problems				
Responding to Interpersonal Conflicts				
Expressing Yourself				
Balancing Your Thinking				

Are you ready to start trying the strategies that you think will be most helpful to you?

My level of readiness is:

☐ *Not Ready* ☐ *Unsure* ☐ *Ready*

Can you identify friends, relatives or professionals who can help you make a plan to use one or more of the seven strategies suggested in this booklet *and* support you in staying with the plan over the next month? ☐ Yes ☐ No

Persons who will help and support:____________________

____

____

____

Take this booklet with you when you visit your health care provider. She or he will want to look at your responses.

If you want to read more on the use of strategies suggested in this booklet, read the book, ***Living Life Well: New Strategies for Hard Times*** by Patricia Robinson, Ph.D.

Notes:

Using Medications Successfully

An ICP Booklet

CONTEXT PRESS
Reno, Nevada

What is Depression?

Depression is a response to problems in living. When we become exhausted in our efforts to cope with life, we begin to experience symptoms of depression. Following is a list of common symptoms of depression. Make a check in the box beside any symptom you have had almost daily for the past two weeks.

1. ☐ Anger or irritability
2. ☐ Sadness
3. ☐ Sleeping too much or too little
4. ☐ A lack of interest in others and in activities you usually enjoy
5. ☐ Guilt, self critical thoughts, feeling inadequate or worthless
6. ☐ Feeling tired most of the time
7. ☐ Concentration difficulties
8. ☐ Appetite change — eating significantly more or less
9. ☐ Feeling very “slowed down” or very “speeded up”
10. ☐ More aches and pain
11. ☐ Thoughts of suicide or death in general

Total Symptoms:_____

The Cycle of Depression

People become depressed for many reasons. This booklet describes strategies for using medications successfully to alleviate symptoms of depression. Most often, depression is related to stressful life circumstances, such as marital problems, death of a loved one, loss of a job, or a child leaving home. Depression may also be related to physical problems such as chronic pain or medical illness.

Depression Occurs In Three Ways

The Body Feels Depressed

When the body is depressed, a person sleeps poorly, eats differently, has less energy, struggles with concentration, and has more aches and pains.

Behavior Is Depressed

When behavior is depressed, a person does much less than usual. She/he talks less, produces less, and socializes less.

The Mind Is Depressed

When the mind is depressed, thinking changes. A depressed person experiences more intensely negative and painful thoughts about the past, the present and the future.

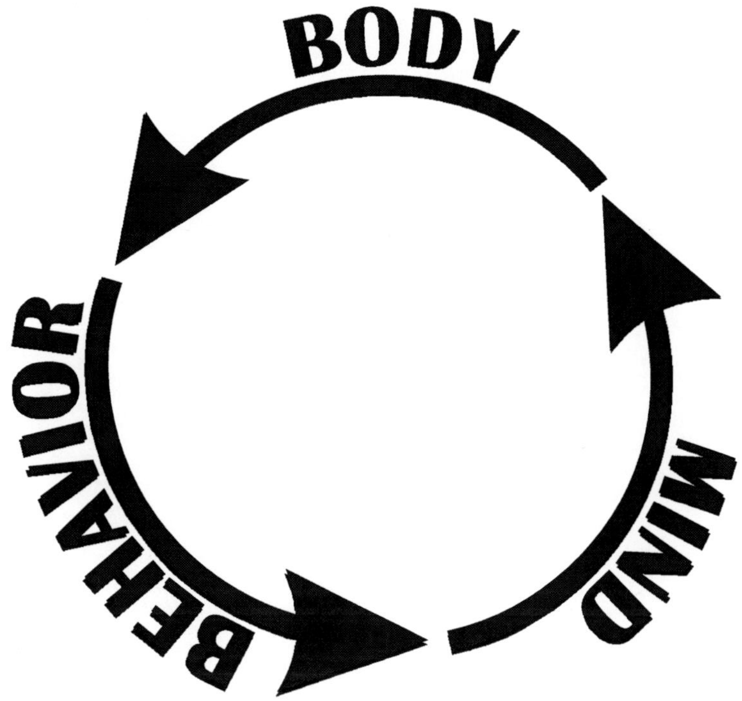

A person's body, behavior, and thoughts interact continuously. Once depression becomes a problem, this interaction may lead to a "downward spiral" in mood and hopefulness. Two courses of action help reverse the downward direction and create a "positive spiral."

1. *Use of Medications*

Medications may help you to feel better. Antidepressant medications restore the presence of neurotransmitter substances that become depleted by stress. Medications may work somewhat slowly. Therefore, it is best to use medications in combination with behavioral planning and use of coping strategies. **This booklet will help you use medications successfully.** Antidepressant therapy and behavioral health planning are complementary treatments for depression and anxiety.

2. Strategic Use of Coping Strategies

Use of active coping strategies helps you reverse the downward spiral of depression. When you address life problems with effective strategies, you have more opportunities to create positive conditions in your life context.

Make a concerted effort to work with your health care provider in planning medication treatment and skillful use of coping strategies. You will soon be feeling better.

Using Medications Successfully

There are four important areas to address in order to use medications successfully. They include:

1. Your Past Experiences with Medications
2. Your Beliefs about Medications
3. Your Knowledge about Medications
4. Your Ability to Anticipate and Plan for Problems in Using Medications

This booklet will help you assess and prepare for success in each of these key areas.

Your Past Experiences with Medications

Take a moment to recall your past experiences with use of medications for depression and anxiety.

1. Have you ever used a medicine to help alleviate symptoms of depression or anxiety? ☐ Yes ☐ No
2. Try to recall the medication name, dosage, and length of treatment.

Name	Dose	Length of Treatment

1. Also, recall any side effects you had with this medication. How much did they trouble you?

Side Effect	Bothered A Little	Bothered A Lot
1.	☐	☐
2.	☐	☐
3.	☐	☐

4. How much did you benefit from use of medication when you tried medication before?

☐	☐	☐	☐	☐
None	*A Little*	*Some*	*Quite A Lot*	*Very Much*

This information will be helpful to you and your provider in making a decision about medication use and selection of a specific medication.

If you did have a limited response to medication treatment or experienced bothersome side effects in the past, you may still be a candidate for medication treatment. Several new types of antidepressant medications have become available in recent years. New medications are equally effective and have fewer side effects.

Your Beliefs about Medications

Your beliefs have a significant impact on your success in using antidepressant medications. Take stock of your beliefs right now. Mark an "X" by any of the following statements that you believe.

- ☐ I'll be the one to get terrible side effects.
- ☐ My family would not want me to use medications for depression and anxiety.
- ☐ These types of medications are overused.
- ☐ I should be able to get over my problems without taking medicine.
- ☐ I'll get addicted.

If you believe any of these statements, discuss the belief with your health care provider. She/he may be able to provide you with additional information to help you re-evaluate beliefs which might make medication use more difficult for you.

Your Knowledge about Medications

You are much more likely to succeed in antidepressant treatment when you have accurate information about all aspects of medication use. Please review the following details and discuss any questions you have with your health care providers.

Starting medication . . .

Start your medicine as soon as it is prescribed. The sooner you start, the sooner you will experience the desired benefits.

Remembering to take medicine . . .

Take your medicine at a certain time of day every day. During the first several weeks, you may want to leave yourself several reminder notes. Some people use a behavioral hygiene task, such as teeth brushing, as a cue to take their medication. Also, some people may want to leave an extra bottle of medication in a desk drawer at work in the event that they forget to take the medicine at home.

Deciding how to take the medication . . .

Some medications are best taken in one dose, while others are best divided into several doses during the day. Some medications cause drowsiness, while others are more activating. Medications with a sedative effect are taken at night, and activating medications are taken in the morning.

Carrying on with other activities . . .

You may continue with your normal activities while taking antidepressant medications. If you do notice minor sedation or sleepiness in starting a medicine, avoid driving or carrying out hazardous activities. Sleepiness will usually diminish. If it does not, talk with your provider about a medication change.

Taking antidepressants with other medications . . .

You may take antidepressants with most other types of medications. However, do talk with your provider about the compatibility of antidepressant medications with other medications you are taking.

Taking antidepressant medications and consuming alcohol . . .

Do not drink alcohol while taking antidepressant medications.

Increasing medication dose . . .

Increase your medication dose according to the directions of your provider. In starting some antidepressant medications, you start with small doses initially and increase gradually. Do not worry that you are "taking too many pills." Your provider is prescribing a slow increase in dose in order to help you avoid side effects. After you reach your "therapeutic dose," your provider will probably prescribe tablets that are larger in dosage, which then allows you to take fewer tablets.

Continuing to take the medication . . .

Take the medicine until you and your provider decide that you are ready to stop the medicine. In most cases, your provider will ask you to take the medicine for at least four months after you reach a therapeutic dose. Do not stop taking the medicine because you feel better. Wait and plan *how and when* to stop with your provider.

Your Ability to Anticipate and Plan for Problems in Using Medications

Most antidepressant medications have mild side effects. The side effects are usually temporary and diminish or disappear during the first few weeks of treatment. **If you experience side effects that are more severe, call your doctor.** She/he will probably suggest one or more of the following strategies:

- Change the time that you take the medicine
- Change the dose of the medicine
- Use a remedy for the side effect
- Add a second medication
- Change to a different medication

The following table summarizes common side effects and possible remedies or strategies for coping with side effects. Most medications have only one or two of the side effects listed in this table.

Common Side Effects and Remedies	
Dry Mouth	Drink plenty of water. Chew sugarless gum. Use sugarless gum drops.
Constipation	Eat more fiber-rich foods. Take a stool softener.
Drowsiness	Get fresh air and take frequent walks. Try taking your medicine earlier in the evening, or if you're taking your medicine in the day ask your doctor if you can take it at night.
Wakefulness	Take medications early in the day. Learn more about insomnia. Take a warm bath and have a light snack before bed. Avoid exercising vigorously late in the evening.
Blurred Vision	Remind yourself that this will be a temporary difficulty. Talk with your doctor if it persists.
Dizziness	Stand up slowly. Drink plenty of fluids. If you are worried, call your doctor.
Feeling Speeded Up	Tell yourself, "This will go away within three to five days." If it does not, call your doctor or nurse.
Sexual Problem	Talk with your doctor. A change in medications or a medication holiday may help.
Nausea or Appetite Loss	Take the medicine with food. Prepare food so that it is appetizing and colorful. Eat small healthy meals.

Remember to Ask for Help

Starting antidepressant treatment is not easy. Remember to ask for the support of your health care team. Take this booklet with you to your next visit with your health care provider. She/he is prepared to skillfully address your concerns about use of medications and plan successful treatment with you.

If you want more information on using behavioral strategies to alleviate depression and anxiety consider reading *Living Life Well: New Strategies for Hard Times* by Patricia Robinson, Ph.D.

Notes:

Seven Ways to Cope

An ICP Booklet

CONTEXT PRESS
Reno, Nevada

What is Depression?

Depression is a response to problems in living. When we become exhausted in our efforts to cope with life, we begin to experience symptoms of depression. Following is a list of common symptoms of depression. Make a check in the box beside any symptom you have had almost daily for the past two weeks.

1. ☐ Anger or irritability
2. ☐ Sadness
3. ☐ Sleeping too much or too little
4. ☐ A lack of interest in others and in activities you usually enjoy
5. ☐ Guilt, self critical thoughts, feeling inadequate or worthless
6. ☐ Feeling tired most of the time
7. ☐ Concentration difficulties
8. ☐ Appetite change — eating significantly more or less
9. ☐ Feeling very "slowed down" or very "speeded up"
10. ☐ More aches and pain
11. ☐ Thoughts of suicide or death in general

Total Symptoms:_____

Are you ready to start trying the strategies that you think will be most helpful to you?

My level of readiness is:

☐ *Not Ready* ☐ *Unsure* ☐ *Ready*

Can you identify friends, relatives or professionals who can help you make a plan to use one or more of the seven strategies suggested in this booklet *and* support you in staying with the plan over the next month? ☐ Yes ☐ No

Persons who will help and support:________________

____

____

____

Take this booklet with you when you visit your health care provider. She or he will want to look at your responses.

If you want to read more on the use of strategies suggested in this booklet, read the book, ***Living Life Well: New Strategies for Hard Times*** by Patricia Robinson, Ph.D.

Getting Started

Which of the seven strategies discussed in this booklet, if any, do you think will work best for you at present? Place an "X" in the box to indicate the extent to which each of the strategies might help you now. Use a rating scale where:

1 = Not Helpful and 4 = Very Helpful

Strategy	*1*	*2*	*3*	*4*
Hoping...Planning...Doing				
Building Acceptance and Making Value-Based Choices				
Appreciating Your Mind and Body				
Solving Problems				
Responding to Interpersonal Conflicts				
Expressing Yourself				
Balancing Your Thinking				

If you checked four or more symptoms, talk with your health care provider. Also, use this booklet to make a plan to address these symptoms.

This booklet describes seven coping strategies for addressing symptoms of depression, solving problems in living and creating the life you want.

The Cycle of Depression

People become depressed for many reasons. Most often, depression is related to stressful life circumstances, such as marital problems, death of a loved one, loss of a job, or a child leaving home. Depression may also be related to physical problems such as chronic pain or medical illness.

Depression Occurs In Three Ways

The Body Feels Depressed

When the body is depressed, a person sleeps poorly, eats differently, has less energy, struggles with concentration, and has more aches and pains.

Behavior Is Depressed

When behavior is depressed, a person does much less than usual. She/he talks less, produces less, and socializes less.

The Mind Is Depressed

When the mind is depressed, thinking changes. A depressed person experiences more intensely negative and painful thoughts about the past, the present and the future.

A person's body, behavior, and mind interact continuously. Once depression becomes a problem, this interaction may lead to a "downward spiral" in mood, hopefulness and energy. Two courses of action help reverse the downward direction and create a "positive spiral."

Exercises to Help Balance Thinking

Write down favorite sayings and thoughts that inspire courage or optimism.

____

____

____

____

____

What positive thoughts do you want to keep in mind right now?

____

____

____

____

____

Who helps you balance your thinking on different issues?

____

____

____

The Seventh Strategy:

Balancing Your Thinking

When life is going well, we tend to have two positive thoughts to every negative thought. When we become depressed, the balance changes to two negative thoughts to every positive thought. "Realistic" thinking probably lies somewhere in between.

Shifting the balance in the direction of more positive thoughts is difficult to do, especially without someone to help you. Friends can help when you give them an opportunity and ask for their opinion on something. Knowing how to change the balance of your thoughts is important because it can help you catch yourself when you start to become depressed.

Use the following steps and suggested exercises to help you balance your thoughts.

- Identify a favorite saying or thought that inspires courage or optimism for you in difficult times.
- Try changing your perspective on something of little importance to you from an exaggerated negative perspective to a realistic or slightly positive point of view.
- Identify someone who tends to be a "realist" or "optimist" and contact this person. They can help you balance your thoughts.

1. ***Strategic Use of Coping Strategies***

Use of active coping strategies helps you reverse the downward spiral of depression. When you address life problems with effective strategies, you have more opportunities to create positive conditions in your life context. **This booklet suggests seven coping strategies for you to use to restore your body, behavior and mind *and* to effectively address life problems.** If you make a concerted effort to work with your health care provider in using these strategies, you can make significant and lasting changes to your lifestyle.

2. ***Use of Medications***

Medications may also help you to feel better. Antidepressant medications help restore the presence of neurotransmitter substances that become depleted by stress. However, these medications work somewhat slowly. The impact of effective coping is more immediate. If you decide to use medications, use coping strategies as well. Coping strategies will complement the action of medications on the body's neurochemistry.

The First Strategy:

Hoping...Planning...Doing

Hope is the foundation of a healthy life. Without hope, most people avoid constructive activity. Another way of stating this is that hopefulness is a good predictor of action. In turn, action is a good predictor of mood improvement.

Try this exercise to help you increase your sense of hopefulness.

Sit in a quiet place for a few minutes and ask yourself about your explanation of your current troubles. Are you blaming yourself? If so, stop. You are well-intentioned and worthy of self-respect. Decide upon an explanation for your current difficulties that reflects a sense of respect for who you are. You may be stressed or overwhelmed or simply lacking skills you need to overcome challenging circumstances. Write down your ***revised*** *explanation of your present situation here.*

____

____

____

____

____

Creative Expression

List five creative expression activities that you enjoy and that are consistent with your values. Indicate how many hours you have spent in each of these activities in the past week.

Creative Expression Activity	# Hours in Past Week
1.	1.
2.	2.
3.	3.
4.	4.
5.	5.

If you had difficulty identifying activities, take time to evaluate your "gifts" or "interests" and available resources or materials in you life at the present moment. If you spent little time in identified activities, consider "scheduling" time for these important activities. Write down your findings here and make a behavioral health plan to engage in creative activities on a *daily* basis.

Gifts: __________________________________

____

Interests: _______________________________

____

Resources: ______________________________

____

Personal Assertion Exercise

Do you believe that you have the following rights? Make a check in the first box of any right you claim for yourself.

Does your day-to-day life indicate that you give yourself these rights? Make a check in the second box of any right that you "live" in your day-to-day behavior.

1. ☐ ☐ The right to say no without feeling guilty.
2. ☐ ☐ The right to be treated with respect.
3. ☐ ☐ The right to experience your feelings.
4. ☐ ☐ The right to change your mind.
5. ☐ ☐ The right to do less than you are capable of doing.
6. ☐ ☐ The right to make mistakes.

These are only a few basic assertive rights. If your beliefs are weak in any of the above areas or if your day-to-day life does not reflect your beliefs, you may want to develop a program to strengthen your beliefs in your assertive rights and your *behavioral expression* of these rights. You may want to read more about personal assertion and join a personal assertion class. Classes may be available within your health care system or in your community. Make a behavioral health plan to help you start a program of strengthening skills in this critical area.

Planning and doing are also important behavioral skills for coping with stress and depression. With a little hope, you can make a "behavioral health plan" to address needed changes in your daily life. Read and respond to each of the following seven steps to make a behavioral health plan for this week.

1. **Choose an area of life that you want to make better.** Possible areas include: enjoying things alone or with others, accomplishing difficult and unpleasant tasks, talking to or "making connections" with others, contentment with your work, sensual experiencing, or imagining a better future. Write down your choice here.

   ____

2. **Imagine yourself doing something different in the activity area you choose.** Write down what you imagine.

   ____

3. **Plan a specific time and place** to engage in an activity that represents making an improvement to the area of life you want to make more satisfying.

   Activity: ______________________

   Time: ______________________

   Place: ______________________

4. During and after you conduct this "experiment in mood change," **watch what happens**, *inside* you (your thoughts, feelings and behaviors) and *outside* of you (what others say and do). Write down your observations here.

   Inside you: ______________________________

   Outside of you: ______________________________

5. **Think about your findings** or results.

6. **Talk with others** about your results and draw conclusions. Write down your conclusions here.

   ____

   ____

7. **Plan your next "behavioral health plan."**

   Activity: ______________________________

   Time: ______________________________

   Place: ______________________________

Try to make a behavioral health plan *weekly* for the next month. The positive impact of small changes in two or three areas of your life can become highly significant with three or four weeks of effort. Try to find a friend who will support your on-going use of this strategy.

The Sixth Strategy:

Expressing Yourself

There are two important skills involved in the strategy of "expressing yourself." The first is *personal assertion* and the second is *creative expression*. Both of these skills require "balancing." Personal assertion requires on-going balancing of respect for yourself with respect for others. Creative expression involves balancing who you are with what you have to work with right now.

Personal assertion skills form the basis of your ability to make direct and honest statements and to stand up for your rights. Development of effective assertion skills may help you improve your mood, your sense of hopefulness, and your energy for enjoying life.

Creative expression is engaging in any activity for the sole purpose of expressing yourself. The possibilities for creative expression are many and change over the course of a lifetime. The loss of an avenue for creative expression may actually provoke symptoms of depression and anxiety. Try the following exercises to strengthen your skills in strategic self-expression.

The following exercises are useful if you are currently in a close relationship and want to become more skillful in responding to conflict in this close relationship.

- Try scheduling a "problem solving" meeting. Allow 30 minutes.
- Set the agenda for your meeting. Keep it simple and make it agreeable to both of you.
- Convene your meetings when you are both rested and free from distraction.
- Positively and specifically define the problem you plan to address.
- Use "I" statements (e.g., "I want to have 20 minutes alone everyday" or "I feel upset about being without a job"). These statements help you responsibly express your feelings and make requests without blaming.
- Discuss only one problem at a time.
- Focus on solutions. Avoid trying to be "right."
- Compromise. Select a solution that allows both of you to "win."
- Set a time to "reconvene" and evaluate how your solution is working.

The Second Strategy:

Building Acceptance and Making Value-Based Choices

We often respond to a difficult circumstance, whether it is internal or external, with an action that moves us away from the source of unwanted distress. While we may avoid some external stresses, we cannot avoid painful internal events. Internal events include thoughts and feelings — positive and negative. *Psychological acceptance* is a strategy that involves actively embracing unwanted, painful thoughts and feelings.

When we use psychological acceptance strategies, we are more free to make decisions about our behavior. We can make choices to behave in accordance with our values. Our daily activities take on greater meaning when they reflect our values rather than our attempts to control unwanted thoughts and feelings. Try these exercises to improve your skills in using strategies of psychological acceptance and value-based behavioral planning.

1. Write down feelings (for example, fear, sadness, anxiety, depression, panic, anger) that you have difficulty tolerating.

   ____

   ____

2. Decide on a psychological acceptance procedure or method for observing unwanted feelings and thoughts.

Options include visualizing the feeling or seeing or listening to the words associated with the feeling. You may use the phrase, "I am having the sensation of: ____________________" or "I am having the thought that: ____________________."

3. Follow this procedure during acceptance or self observation practice periods.
    - Take four deep breaths and move into "observation mode."
    - Start to use your method of observation to help you stay in the "observation mode" (i.e., visualize your thoughts or use a phrase to prompt acceptance).

4. Practice daily for 5 to 10 minutes for a week. Record the number of minutes you practice each day.

    Day 1: _____ Day 2: _____ Day 3: _____

    Day 4: _____ Day 5: _____ Day 6: _____

    Day 7: _____

When you are ready, begin using the psychological acceptance procedure in daily situations that provoke painful thoughts and feelings. Record situations where you used your breathing and observation method and made a behavior choice that reflected your values.

____

____

The Fifth Strategy:

Responding to Interpersonal Conflicts

Our patterns of responding to conflict may cost more than we want to pay. If we believe that we must avoid conflict, we may withhold information needed to have healthy relationships. We may passively punish a person who makes a hurtful statement by ceasing to talk to that person. We may sacrifice self-respect to maintain the status quo when we use these strategies to respond to interpersonal conflict.

Alternatively, we may seek power and control over others more directly. We may use verbal and non-verbal expressions to frighten others. When we approach conflict in these ways, we are likely to have few friends and we are vulnerable to a host of physical problems associated with excessive arousal or anger.

If you want to become more skillful in this area, try the following exercises:

1. Acknowledge yourself on a daily basis. You may simply say to yourself, "I allow myself to be," or "I am okay as I am."
2. Whenever you notice tension in your body, ask yourself, "How do I feel right now?"
3. Give yourself a choice about expressing or not expressing feelings and opinions. It is okay to keep your feelings private or share them.

Plan to address obstacles: ____________________

____

____

6. **DO IT**! Record here when you did it.

____

7. **Evaluate the results** and continue working toward the solution by simply determining and planning a next step or going through these seven steps again.

Results suggest that:

____

____

Next step: ____________________________

____

____

Remember To Celebrate Your Efforts, As Well As Your Successes!

The Third Strategy:

Appreciating Your Mind and Body

Using this strategy will help you become more aware of your body and more able to create sensations of physical well-being in your body. Basic body listening skills strengthen your ability to cope with physical *and* psychological health problems. Experiment with the following exercises.

I.

Rest for a few minutes in a favorite "quiet" place. Take several deep breaths and recall *or* fantasize an image of a serene environment. Give yourself time to develop this image with many details, including sounds, smells, colors, etc. Practicing this image on a daily basis will help you learn to create the image and associated sensations of wellness efficiently during highly stressful moments of daily living.

II.

Cultivate playfulness, curiosity, and openness. These mental states are related to well-being. If you are overly serious, controlled, or "closed off," make behavioral health plans to help you play and explore. For example, you may want to attend a comedy show, rekindle an old hobby, or go for a treasure hunt in a park. A good way to get started with use of these strategies is to watch young children, as most demonstrate these qualities very nicely.

The Fourth Strategy:

Solving Problems

Self-efficacy is a reflection of your confidence in solving the problems you encounter in life. Mastery of problem-solving skills improves your confidence and, hence, your self-efficacy. The following steps are prerequisites for effective problem solving.

- Identifying that something is a problem
- Accepting the possibility that something can be done about it
- Expressing a desire to change
- Being willing to make an effort to change

Use the following problem-solving exercise to review the critical steps in strategic problem-solving and address a current problem in your life.

1. **Pinpoint a current problem**. Write the problem down here. Define the problem so that it is a problem with a solution.

2. **Brainstorm solutions**. Generate at least 3 possible solutions.

3. **Evaluate potential solutions**. Describe advantages and disadvantages of each solution.

4. **Identify the first step** you will take to implement the solution you choose.

5. **Anticipate and plan for obstacles** to your implementing the solution you choose.

   Anticipated obstacles: ____________________

Using Medications Successfully

An ICP Booklet

CONTEXT PRESS
Reno, Nevada

What is Depression?

Depression is a response to problems in living. When we become exhausted in our efforts to cope with life, we begin to experience symptoms of depression. Following is a list of common symptoms of depression. Make a check in the box beside any symptom you have had almost daily for the past two weeks.

1. ☐ Anger or irritability
2. ☐ Sadness
3. ☐ Sleeping too much or too little
4. ☐ A lack of interest in others and in activities you usually enjoy
5. ☐ Guilt, self critical thoughts, feeling inadequate or worthless
6. ☐ Feeling tired most of the time
7. ☐ Concentration difficulties
8. ☐ Appetite change — eating significantly more or less
9. ☐ Feeling very "slowed down" or very "speeded up"
10. ☐ More aches and pain
11. ☐ Thoughts of suicide or death in general

Total Symptoms:_____

The Cycle of Depression

People become depressed for many reasons. This booklet describes strategies for using medications successfully to alleviate symptoms of depression. Most often, depression is related to stressful life circumstances, such as marital problems, death of a loved one, loss of a job, or a child leaving home. Depression may also be related to physical problems such as chronic pain or medical illness.

Depression Occurs In Three Ways

The Body Feels Depressed

When the body is depressed, a person sleeps poorly, eats differently, has less energy, struggles with concentration, and has more aches and pains.

Behavior Is Depressed

When behavior is depressed, a person does much less than usual. She/he talks less, produces less, and socializes less.

The Mind Is Depressed

When the mind is depressed, thinking changes. A depressed person experiences more intensely negative and painful thoughts about the past, the present and the future.

A person's body, behavior, and thoughts interact continuously. Once depression becomes a problem, this interaction may lead to a "downward spiral" in mood and hopefulness. Two courses of action help reverse the downward direction and create a "positive spiral."

1. *Use of Medications*

Medications may help you to feel better. Antidepressant medications restore the presence of neurotransmitter substances that become depleted by stress. Medications may work somewhat slowly. Therefore, it is best to use medications in combination with behavioral planning and use of coping strategies. **This booklet will help you use medications successfully.** Antidepressant therapy and

Remember to Ask for Help

Starting antidepressant treatment is not easy. Remember to ask for the support of your health care team. Take this booklet with you to your next visit with your health care provider. She/he is prepared to skillfully address your concerns about use of medications and plan successful treatment with you.

If you want more information on using behavioral strategies to alleviate depression and anxiety consider reading *Living Life Well: New Strategies for Hard Times* by Patricia Robinson, Ph.D.

Common Side Effects and Remedies	
Dry Mouth	Drink plenty of water. Chew sugarless gum. Use sugarless gum drops.
Constipation	Eat more fiber-rich foods. Take a stool softener.
Drowsiness	Get fresh air and take frequent walks. Try taking your medicine earlier in the evening, or if you're taking your medicine in the day ask your doctor if you can take it at night.
Wakefulness	Take medications early in the day. Learn more about insomnia. Take a warm bath and have a light snack before bed. Avoid exercising vigorously late in the evening.
Blurred Vision	Remind yourself that this will be a temporary difficulty. Talk with your doctor if it persists.
Dizziness	Stand up slowly. Drink plenty of fluids. If you are worried, call your doctor.
Feeling Speeded Up	Tell yourself, "This will go away within three to five days." If it does not, call your doctor or nurse.
Sexual Problem	Talk with your doctor. A change in medications or a medication holiday may help.
Nausea or Appetite Loss	Take the medicine with food. Prepare food so that it is appetizing and colorful. Eat small healthy meals.

behavioral health planning are complementary treatments for depression and anxiety.

2. *Strategic Use of Coping Strategies*

Use of active coping strategies helps you reverse the downward spiral of depression. When you address life problems with effective strategies, you have more opportunities to create positive conditions in your life context.

Make a concerted effort to work with your health care provider in planning medication treatment and skillful use of coping strategies. You will soon be feeling better.

Using Medications Successfully

There are four important areas to address in order to use medications successfully. They include:

1. Your Past Experiences with Medications
2. Your Beliefs about Medications
3. Your Knowledge about Medications
4. Your Ability to Anticipate and Plan for Problems in Using Medications

This booklet will help you assess and prepare for success in each of these key areas.

Your Past Experiences with Medications

Take a moment to recall your past experiences with use of medications for depression and anxiety.

1. Have you ever used a medicine to help alleviate symptoms of depression or anxiety? ☐ Yes ☐ No
2. Try to recall the medication name, dosage, and length of treatment.

Name	Dose	Length of Treatment

Your Ability to Anticipate and Plan for Problems in Using Medications

Most antidepressant medications have mild side effects. The side effects are usually temporary and diminish or disappear during the first few weeks of treatment. **If you experience side effects that are more severe, call your doctor.** She/he will probably suggest one or more of the following strategies:

- Change the time that you take the medicine
- Change the dose of the medicine
- Use a remedy for the side effect
- Add a second medication
- Change to a different medication

The following table summarizes common side effects and possible remedies or strategies for coping with side effects. Most medications have only one or two of the side effects listed in this table.

Taking antidepressants with other medications . . .

You may take antidepressants with most other types of medications. However, do talk with your provider about the compatibility of antidepressant medications with other medications you are taking.

Taking antidepressant medications and consuming alcohol . . .

Do not drink alcohol while taking antidepressant medications.

Increasing medication dose . . .

Increase your medication dose according to the directions of your provider. In starting some antidepressant medications, you start with small doses initially and increase gradually. Do not worry that you are "taking too many pills." Your provider is prescribing a slow increase in dose in order to help you avoid side effects. After you reach your "therapeutic dose," your provider will probably prescribe tablets that are larger in dosage, which then allows you to take fewer tablets.

Continuing to take the medication . . .

Take the medicine until you and your provider decide that you are ready to stop the medicine. In most cases, your provider will ask you to take the medicine for at least four months after you reach a therapeutic dose. Do not stop taking the medicine because you feel better. Wait and plan *how and when* to stop with your provider.

1. Also, recall any side effects you had with this medication. How much did they trouble you?

Side Effect	Bothered A Little	Bothered A Lot
1.	☐	☐
2.	☐	☐
3.	☐	☐

4. How much did you benefit from use of medication when you tried medication before?

☐	☐	☐	☐	☐
None	*A Little*	*Some*	*Quite A Lot*	*Very Much*

This information will be helpful to you and your provider in making a decision about medication use and selection of a specific medication.

If you did have a limited response to medication treatment or experienced bothersome side effects in the past, you may still be a candidate for medication treatment. Several new types of antidepressant medications have become available in recent years. New medications are equally effective and have fewer side effects.

Your Beliefs about Medications

Your beliefs have a significant impact on your success in using antidepressant medications. Take stock of your beliefs right now. Mark an "X" by any of the following statements that you believe.

- ☐ I'll be the one to get terrible side effects.
- ☐ My family would not want me to use medications for depression and anxiety.
- ☐ These types of medications are overused.
- ☐ I should be able to get over my problems without taking medicine.
- ☐ I'll get addicted.

If you believe any of these statements, discuss the belief with your health care provider. She/he may be able to provide you with additional information to help you re-evaluate beliefs which might make medication use more difficult for you.

Your Knowledge about Medications

You are much more likely to succeed in antidepressant treatment when you have accurate information about all aspects of medication use. Please review the following details and discuss any questions you have with your health care providers.

Starting medication . . .

Start your medicine as soon as it is prescribed. The sooner you start, the sooner you will experience the desired benefits.

Remembering to take medicine . . .

Take your medicine at a certain time of day every day. During the first several weeks, you may want to leave yourself several reminder notes. Some people use a behavioral hygiene task, such as teeth brushing, as a cue to take their medication. Also, some people may want to leave an extra bottle of medication in a desk drawer at work in the event that they forget to take the medicine at home.

Deciding how to take the medication . . .

Some medications are best taken in one dose, while others are best divided into several doses during the day. Some medications cause drowsiness, while others are more activating. Medications with a sedative effect are taken at night, and activating medications are taken in the morning.

Carrying on with other activities . . .

You may continue with your normal activities while taking antidepressant medications. If you do notice minor sedation or sleepiness in starting a medicine, avoid driving or carrying out hazardous activities. Sleepiness will usually diminish. If it does not, talk with your provider about a medication change.

ICP Coping Plan

ICP Coping Plan – Page 1			
Name	**Number**	**Date of Birth**	**Date of Visit**
Dear Patient: Your answers to the following questions will assist you and your primary care provider in developing a helpful treatment plan.			

1. What is the major problem you would like help with?

2. What do you think is **causing** your problem? (Check all that apply.)
   ☐ Physical disorder or illness; ☐ Stress; ☐ Other
   Describe cause(s):

3. Which of the following do *you* think is or might be **helpful**? (Check all that apply.)
   ☐ Medications; ☐ Lifestyle adjustments; ☐ Other
   Describe:

4. If you have read the booklets, "*Seven Ways to Cope*" or "*Using Medications Successfully*," what questions do you have about them?

5. If you have ever had a period of depression before, **what helped** you start to feel better then?

6. List the activities or thoughts that have helped you feel even a little better in the past two weeks, no matter how brief the time that you felt better (for example, visiting a friend or going for a walk).

7. List the activities you'd be doing or the thoughts you'd be having if you started to feel even a little bit better in the coming week.

8. Who can help you start doing some things that help you feel better?

ICP Coping Plan – Page 2

Name	Number	Date of Birth	Date of Visit

Dear Patient: Your provider will complete this with you.

Medication Use

☐ None or:

☐ Imipramine	☐ 25 mg	☐ 50 mg	☐ Fluoxetine	☐ 10 mg	☐ 20 mg
☐ Desipramine	☐ 25 mg	☐ 50 mg	☐ Sertraline	☐ 25 mg	☐ 50 mg
☐ Nortriptyline	☐ 10 mg	☐ 25 mg	☐ Paroxetine	☐ 10 mg	☐ 20 mg
☐ Trazodone	☐ 25 mg	☐ 50 mg	☐ Other: ________		

☐ Dosage Plan:

Step One:	Take ________	every day for	________	days. Then, . . .
Step Two:	Take ________	every day for	________	days. Then, . . .
Step Three:	Take ________	every day for	________	days. Then, . . .
Continuation:	Take ________	every day for	________	months.

Most people find this medication works best when taken: ☐ In AM ☐ In PM

Most medications are started at a low dosage and increased slowly in order to give your body time to adapt. If you are having side effects, you can stay at a specific dosage for a longer period of time while you adjust and then increase the amount. Don't stop taking your medication. If you are having problems, call you doctor.

Lifestyle Goals and Activities

1. What will you do over the next few days to improve your mood?

2. What will you do to increase the time you spend with people who can help you feel better?

3. Who will support you in working toward these lifestyle changes?

Checkback Date	Time	Provider

ICP Coping Plan *Follow-Up* – Page 1

Name	Number	Date of Birth	Date of Visit

Dear Patient: Your answers to the following questions will help you and your primary care provider to evaluate your progress and plan further.

1. To what extent have you taken the medication prescribed in your last visit?

Name of Medication | Dose | Number of days taken

Any problems ☐ Yes ☐ No

Did it help? ☐ Yes ☐ No

If yes, how?

2. Mark an "X" beside any of the following difficulties you have had during the past week.

☐ Daytime sleepiness	☐ Dry mouth	☐ Constipation
☐ Blurred vision	☐ Hesitating on urination	☐ Weight gain
☐ Nausea	☐ Appetite Loss	☐ Sexual Problem
☐ Dizziness	☐ Trouble sleeping	☐ Feeling anxious/jumpy

3. To what extent have you completed the lifestyle changes we discussed in our last visit?

4. What do you think is helping you the most? (Check all that apply.)
   ☐ Medications; ☐ Lifestyle adjustments; ☐ Other
   Describe other:

5. List the activities or thoughts that have helped you feel even a little better in the last two weeks (for example, visiting a friend or going for a walk).

6. List the activities you'd be doing or the thoughts you'd be having if you started to feel a little bit better in the coming week.

7. Who can help you do more things that help you feel better?

8. What questions do you have about our treatment plan?

ICP Coping Plan *Follow-Up* – Page 2

Name	Number	Date of Birth	Date of Visit

Dear Patient: Your provider will complete this with you.

Medication Use

☐ None or:

☐ Imipramine	☐ 25 mg	☐ 50 mg	☐ Fluoxetine	☐ 10 mg	☐ 20 mg
☐ Desipramine	☐ 25 mg	☐ 50 mg	☐ Sertraline	☐ 25 mg	☐ 50 mg
☐ Nortriptyline	☐ 10 mg	☐ 25 mg	☐ Paroxetine	☐ 10 mg	☐ 20 mg
☐ Trazodone	☐ 25 mg	☐ 50 mg	☐ Other: ____________		

☐ Dosage Plan:

Step One:	Take	________	every day for	________	days. Then, . . .
Step Two:	Take	________	every day for	________	days. Then, . . .
Step Three:	Take	________	every day for	________	days. Then, . . .
Continuation:	Take	________	every day for	________	months.

Most people find this medication works best when taken: ☐ In AM ☐ In PM

Remember to use strategies suggested by your doctor for coping with side effects. You will be able to evaluate the full benefit of your medication after 4 to 6 weeks of use at your target dose. If you have any problems, call your doctor or nurse.

Lifestyle Goals and Activities

1. List activities you will do to create a healthy, satisfying lifestyle in the coming month.

2. When will you spend time with people who can help you feel better?

3. How will you reward yourself for making these lifestyle changes?

Checkback Date	Time	Provider

Living Life Well Behavioral Health Plan Formats

These planning formats are identical to the formats in the book, *Living Life Well: New Strategies for Hard Times*. You may want to have copies of these formats ready to use in concluding treatment sessions with patients who are using this book as a part of their treatment program.

Behavioral Health Plan

Building Hope And Planning To Improve Life

How do you explain your present difficulties?

Does this explanation assume that you are a creative person worthy of respect from yourself and others? ☐ Yes ☐ No

If needed, revise your explanation so it reflects the assumption that you are a person worthy of respect.

Does your revised explanation have a positive impact on your hopefulness? ☐ Yes ☐ No

The area of life I will target in my plan this week is:

- ☐ Enjoying Things Alone
- ☐ Accomplishing Things Alone
- ☐ Talking with Others
- ☐ Contentment with Work
- ☐ Sensual Experience
- ☐ Fun with Others
- ☐ Images of a Better Future

I plan to:

I will do this when:

I will do this where:

I will do this with whom:

Who will support my plan?

As a reward for following my Behavioral Health Plan, I will:

Am I 100% committed to this Plan? ☐ Yes ☐ No

Behavioral Health Plan

Acceptance Strategies

☐ I will make my lists of avoided psychological experiences and put them in a bowl on: (when).

To help me move into a perspective of observing my thoughts during psychological acceptance practices, I will (check 2 or more):

- ☐ Use 4 deep breathes, counting each inhale.
- ☐ Use this visual image: ______________________ .
- ☐ Use this verbal/auditory phrase: ______________________ .

☐ I will practice the BOSE ____________ (where) for ____________ .

minutes each day starting at ____________ (time), beginning on ________ (date).

Strategies For Expressing Values

The area of life I will target for expressing my values is:

- ☐ Enjoying Things Alone
- ☐ Accomplishing Things Alone
- ☐ Talking with Others
- ☐ Contentment with Work
- ☐ Sensual Experience
- ☐ Fun with Others
- ☐ Images of a Better Future

To improve my expression of values in this area, I will:

When:	Where:

With whom:

Who will support my plan?

As a reward for following my Behavioral Health Plan, I will:

Am I 100% committed to this Plan? ☐ Yes ☐ No

Behavioral Health Plan

Awareness And Body/Mind Integration Strategies

I will practice the following skills on a daily basis.

1. Awareness and Concentration Exercises:
   - ☐ Breathing Into the Body: ☐10 Areas or ☐ 6 Areas
   - ☐ Tensing and Relaxing
2. Exercises to Increase Body/Mind Integration:
   - ☐ Using A Cue
   - ☐ Using A Serenity Image
   - ☐ Aligning with Nature
   - ☐ Cultivating Neoteny through Planned Behavioral Activities, including:

Strategies For Expressing Values

The area of life I will target for expressing my values is:

☐ Enjoying Things Alone	☐ Sensual Experience
☐ Accomplishing Things Alone	☐ Fun with Others
☐ Talking with Others	☐ Images of a Better Future
☐ Contentment with Work	

To enhance my expression of values in this area, I will:

When:	Where:
With whom:	
Who will support my plan?	

As a reward for following my Behavioral Health Plan, I will:

Am I 100% committed to this Plan? ☐ Yes ☐ No

Behavioral Health Plan

Problem-Solving Strategies

I will focus on a new solution to the following problem this week:

I will complete a Problem-Solving Worksheet on: (date).

Who is a resource for me in solving this problem?

I will evaluate my results: (date).

Strategies For Expressing Values

The area of life I will target for expressing my values is:

- ☐ Enjoying Things Alone
- ☐ Accomplishing Things Alone
- ☐ Talking with Others
- ☐ Contentment with Work
- ☐ Sensual Experience
- ☐ Fun with Others
- ☐ Images of a Better Future

To improve my expression of values in this area, I will:

When: | Where:

With whom:

Who will support my plan?

As a reward for following my Behavioral Health Plan, I will:

Am I 100% committed to this Plan? ☐ Yes ☐ No

Behavioral Health Plan

Strategies For Responding to Interpersonal Conflict

This week I will use the following exercises:

- ☐ BEGINNING EXERCISES
  - ☐ Daily Caring Moment
  - ☐ Awareness of Personal Feelings
  - ☐ Respectful Expression of Feelings
- ☐ CONNECTING EXERCISES
  - ☐ Caring Days
  - ☐ Blending
- ☐ DANCING EXERCISES (actual formal practice of the guidelines)

Describe details concerning "where and when" you will apply the exercise(s) to solving an interpersonal conflict.

Strategies For Expressing Values

The area of life I will target for expressing my values is:

- ☐ Enjoying Things Alone
- ☐ Accomplishing Things Alone
- ☐ Talking with Others
- ☐ Contentment with Work
- ☐ Sensual Experience
- ☐ Fun with Others
- ☐ Images of a Better Future

To increase my expression of my values in this area, I will:

When:	Where:

With whom:

Who will support my plan?

As a reward for following my Behavioral Health Plan, I will:

Am I 100% committed to this Plan? ☐ Yes ☐ No

Behavioral Health Plan	
Strategies For Assertive Expression	
I will complete the Assertiveness Assessment Exercise on: (date).	
I will complete an Assertiveness Plan Worksheet on: (date).	
The person who supports me in becoming assertive is:	
I will ask her or him to give me an opportunity to practice assertive responses prior to implementing my plan. ☐ Yes ☐ No	
I will implement my Assertiveness Plan on (date) and evaluate it on (date).	
Strategies For Expressing Values	
The area of life I will target for expressing my values is: ☐ Enjoying Things Alone ☐ Sensual Experience ☐ Accomplishing Things Alone ☐ Fun with Others ☐ Talking with Others ☐ Images of a Better Future ☐ Contentment with Work	
To enhance my expression of values in this area, I will:	
When:	Where:
With whom:	
Who will support my plan?	
As a reward for following my Behavioral Health Plan, I will:	
Am I 100% committed to this Plan? ☐ Yes ☐ No	

Behavioral Health Plan	
Strategies For Creative Expression	
I will complete the Creativity Assessment on: (date).	
My Creativity Plan is:	
I will implement my Creativity Plan from to and evaluate it on (date).	
Strategies For Expressing Values	
The area of life I will target for expressing my values is: ☐ Enjoying Things Alone ☐ Sensual Experience ☐ Accomplishing Things Alone ☐ Fun with Others ☐ Talking with Others ☐ Images of a Better Future ☐ Contentment with Work	
To enhance my expression of values in this area, I will:	
When:	Where:
With whom:	
Who will support my plan?	
As a reward for following my Behavioral Health Plan, I will:	
Am I 100% committed to this Plan? ☐ Yes ☐ No	

Progress Plan

I. Monitoring Plan

To monitor my progress I will use:	☐ The Quality of Life Scale ☐ The Symptoms Checklist ☐ The Daily Wellness Check
I will monitor my progress:	☐ Weekly ☐ Every 2 weeks ☐ Monthly
I will monitor my progress on ______________ (day of the week).	

II. Specific Coping Strategies

I plan to use these coping strategies on a daily or weekly basis.

1.
2.
3.
4.

III. Lifestyle Goals

I plan to work toward the following lifestyle goals during the next 6 months.

1.
2.
3.
4.

IV. Emergency Plans

I define an emergency as low scores for 2 weeks on:	☐ The Quality of Life Scale ☐ The Symptoms Checklist ☐ The Daily Wellness Check ☐ Or:

My emergency plan is to:

1.
2.
3.
4.

The person that I am asking to support me in following this plan is:

ICP Provider Profile Forms

Behavioral Health Consultant	
Provider	Date
I started providing ICP Behavioral Health Consultation services on: ___________ During this time period, I have had _____ referrals. Of the _____ patients who started the ICP treatment involving the 4 to 7 session protocol, I have completed 4 or more sessions and participated in the development of a relapse prevention plan with _____ patients.	
Patients treated by me in this model reported mean satisfaction ratings of: _____ at the time of treatment planning, and _____ at the end of treatment. (The scale used in satisfaction ratings is 1 = not satisfied to 10 = very satisfied.)	

Medication Specialist	
Provider	Date
Behavioral Health Consultants and Primary Care Providers rated my work on each of the following 4 criteria on a scale ranging from 1 to 25. On this scale, **1 = the least positive evaluation and 25 = the most positive evaluation**. As of this report, ______ providers have contributed to the mean or average ratings below. I started providing ICP Medication Specialist services on ____________.	
Rating	**Performance Criteria**
1.	Medication specialist is easy to access.
2.	Medication specialist is thorough yet brief.
3.	Medication specialist provides education and training to me as part of the consultation.
4.	Patients are satisfied when they have a direct consultation with medication specialist.
	Total Score

*Formats for collecting provider profile data are presented in Chapter 7

ICP Provider Profile Formats*

External Mental Health Provider	
Provider	Date
Behavioral Health Consultants and Primary Care Providers rated my work on each of the following 4 criteria on a scale ranging from 1 to 25. On this scale, **1 = the least positive evaluation and 25 = the most positive evaluation.** As of this report, ______ providers have contributed to the mean or average ratings below. I started providing ICP External Mental Health Provider services on ___________.	
Rating	**Performance Criteria**
1.	External provider was easy to access.
2.	External provider used ICP materials.
3.	External provider provided efficacious treatment.
4.	External provider returned patient with a strong relapse prevention plan.
	Total Score